The SIOUX UPRISING IN MINNESOTA, 1862:

Jacob Nix's Eyewitness History

German/English Edition

Translated by
Gretchen Steinhauser, Don Heinrich Tolzmann & Eberhard Reichmann
and
Edited by
Don Heinrich Tolzmann

Max Kade German-American Center
Indiana University-Purdue University at Indianapolis
and
Indiana German Heritage Society, Inc.
Indianapolis

MAX KADE GERMAN-AMERICAN CENTER
INDIANA UNIVERSITY-PURDUE UNIVERSITY AT INDIANAPOLIS
and
INDIANA GERMAN HERITAGE SOCIETY, INC.

Deutsches Haus-Athenaeum, 401 East Michigan Street
Indianapolis, Indiana 46204

Eberhard Reichmann, Editor-in-Chief

Volume 5

Copyright © 1994 by Max Kade German–American Center
& Indiana German Heritage Society, Inc.
All Rights Reserved
ISBN 1-880788-02-0

Printed in the United States of America
by Indiana University Printing Services

Produced and distributed by NCSA Literatur
430 S. Kelp Grove Road, Nashville, Indiana 47448

Honor to Whom Honor is Due!
The German town of New Ulm
was defended and saved by Germans
on the 19th of August 1862,
and as long as New Ulm exists
this will be a memorable day in its history.

Captain Jacob Nix

~Table of Contents~

Foreword by Jacob Nix vii

Introduction by Don Heinrich Tolzmann ix

Part One—German Edition (1887) 1

Part Two—English Edition (1994) 73

Part Three—Illustrations 155

—Foreword—

In response to the requests of many friends that I provide an accurate account of the Sioux Uprising of August 1862, I would, therefore, like to present this history to the general public.

To be sure, there are already several publications dealing with this topic, but none of them provide a correct and reliable history of those days of horror; especially the English-language works are full of errors and distortions.

As I was an eyewitness during the entire time of these events, and moreover have been able to collect numerous details from the most reliable sources, the reader can rest assured that this work consists of history, rather than myth. So I present this small work to the public with the request that it be granted a kind reception.

Jacob Nix

–INTRODUCTION–

Der Ausbruch der Sioux-Indianer in Minnesota im August 1862 was written by a key player of the events that pitted the white man against the Native American in one of the darkest chapters of race relations on this continent. Having witnessed the vicious circle of maltreatment, hatred, violence and revenge, Capt. Jacob Nix, the first Commandant in the defense of New Ulm, embraced the prevailing anti-Indian bias of his time. Our bilingual edition wants to be understood not as pouring fuel into the embers of racial antagonism but as providing access to a colorful eyewitness account of a tragic American conflict.

The Author

Prior to his participation in the 1848 Revolution in Germany, we know rather little about Jacob Nix, other than that he was born in Bingen am Rhein on the 22nd of July 1822. According to reports, "when the revolutionary struggle broke out in 1848, his liberty-loving disposition prompted him to join with the revolutionists and he soon became the Captain of the Third Company of Zitz's Free Corps."[2] Franz Zitz became one of the leaders of the Revolution in Mainz, and had commanded a corps of six hundred troops in the Palatinate. Among them had been Jacob Nix, and it was here that he acquired his military experience and rank.[3]

The failure of the 1848 Revolution led to the arrest of numerous 48ers, as participants in this Revolution were called, including Nix, who, like many others was charged with high treason and sentenced to death. Nix then escaped to Antwerp, and from there to America, as did many of his 48er compatriots.[4]

After landing in New York, where he remained for a year, Nix then made his way to Cleveland, where he remained until 1858.[5] In 1852, he married Margaret Schneider, who was born in Ebersheim in Hessen, and had come to America with her parents as a child. Six children were born to this marriage, two of whom died in infancy.[6]

Like many 48ers, Nix became an active member of the German-American Turner societies, and participated in their national conventions.[7] In 1855, at the national meeting, held in Buffalo, New York, he and Wilhelm Pfaender, co-founder of the first Turner society in America, proposed the idea of a settlement, conceived of by the latter, which would consist of "workers and freethinkers in the Northwest where soil and lumber was abundant" and "where each family could have its garden plot." Also, there would be a society based on public ownership so that all would be "free from the evils of unemployment and want." The eastern Turner societies did not respond favorably to the proposal, but those in the west did, especially the Cincinnati Turngemeinde.[8] The Turners under Pfaender's leadership would eventually join forces with a Chicago German settlement society which had founded New Ulm on the Minnesota frontier in 1854.[9]

In 1858, the Nix family decided to join friends at the new German-American settlement in Minnesota. At the time of their arrival, the settlement had a population of 440, which had risen to 635 by 1860. At the time Brown County had a total population of 2,339.[10] Nix for the first few years was engaged in the mercantile business with a general store.

When news of the Uprising reached New Ulm, Nix was appointed Commandant of the town, which is not surprising given his military background and service in the 1848 Revolution. It was reported that "with the assistance of his brave neighbors and fellow citizens," the town "successfully withstood the first onslaught of the Indians upon the almost defenseless city." Later on he would join with reinforcements under the command of Col. Flandrau for the general defense of New Ulm, "but in the first battle he had sole charge of the defense. In that encounter he was wounded, but not sufficiently to prevent him from continuing in the fight."[11]

After the Uprising, Nix continued in military service on the frontier. From 1862 to 1864, Nix served in the U.S. Army. He was Captain of Company L of the First Regiment of Mounted Rangers and later served as Captain of Company G of the Second Regiment of Cavalry. While in service, he participated in the military expeditions under General Scully which pursued the Indians as far west as the Bad Lands in the Dakota Territory.

In 1864, he concluded his military service and returned home to New Ulm, where he again opened a business. His home at 528 Center Street "was one of the few buildings left standing in New Ulm after the outbreak, and the kitchen bore the imprints of a fire started by the Indians."[12] In 1858, it housed the Nix general store, and later his meat market.

In 1875, Nix decided to leave his business endeavors and enter the political arena. He was elected to the office of assessor, and in the following year he became the town clerk. He held that office for five successive terms until 1886, when he retired. Nix was an early member of the Turnverein of New Ulm, and also of the Hecker Post, G.A.R.

Aside from his community activities, Nix found time to write his eyewitness history dealing with the Sioux Uprising on the occasion of its twenty-fifth anniversary. This was printed by H.H. Zahn & Co., Milwaukee, Wisconsin. In 1891, when the Defenders Monument in New Ulm was dedicated, recognition of the role Nix had played in the First Battle of New Ulm was reflected by the inclusion of his name on the monument.

At the time of his death in 1897, Nix was widely respected in New Ulm, as well as elsewhere, especially amongst German-Americans. He was referred to as an "early New Ulm pioneer" who was "a man with a history," and one of New Ulm's most interesting characters. It was claimed that he was "a man of strong mind and firm determination. He exercised the greatest freedom of thought and was a ceaseless advocate of the principles in which he believed." Reports noted that "he gained the respect of neighbors and all who knew him." Moreover, "his public services, too, were of the nature that will cause his name to be long remembered."[13] His book was referred to as an "amazing saga" which "will be of interest to every local resident and should be preserved for future generations." [14]

At his funeral, held in the Turner Hall in New Ulm, the main address was delivered by Wilhelm Pfaender, a 48er who with Friedrich Hecker had co-founded the first American Turnverein in 1848 in Cincinnati.[15] Members of the New Ulm Turnverein, the Hecker Post and Company A attended the service, as did many New Ulmers.

Purpose of the Book

It is clear that Nix had several specific purposes in mind when he published his history of the Sioux Uprising. First, as he stated in the Foreword, he was doing so in response to the requests of many for "an accurate account," and he noted that there were already several works on the topic, "but none of them provides a correct and reliable history of those days of horror." In particular he notes that "the English-language works are full of errors and distortions."[16]

Here we see a common complaint from German-American historians—the monolingual Anglo-Americans have paid no attention to German-language source materials. This means that important primary and secondary sources have been overlooked and ignored. The kind of history thus presented is, hence, only a fragment of the story, but is often presented as if it were the whole story. In the case of Minnesota, where the German-American element is the single largest ethnic element, German-American sources are not only significant and important, they are absolutely essential to Minnesota history—without them, the history of Minnesota can simply not be told. Nix obviously realized this and pointed out the deficiency of English-language histories written by the Anglo-Americans, stressing that he "was an eyewitness during the entire time of these events." His work can thus not be ignored, as it is central to this history. His assertion that his work is "history and not myth" indicates his views on other works on the topic. The deficiency of such works is underscored by the fact that many of them do not mention Nix, and those that do, discuss him almost tangentially, if they treat the First Battle of New Ulm at all. This can be assigned to the fact that monolingual historians have not utilized Nix's history.[17]

A second point Nix wants to address is the question as to the cause of the Uprising. He places the cause solidly on the shoulders of the officials of the U.S. Government Indian agencies, as well as those of the traders there. He specifically points to their avarice, greed, corruption, and the generally unscrupulous treatment of the Sioux as the central cause of the Uprising. He soundly condemns this mistreatment. At the same time, he states that it provides no justification for the crimes which were committed.

Third, Nix addresses the question of crime and punishment by arguing for the execution of the Indians in Mankato. Against all those who were involved in the Uprising Nix conveys the deepest wrath. It should be remembered that of the nearly 2,000 Indians who surrendered, nearly 500 were given a military trial, of whom 306 were sentenced to death, and 18 to imprisonment. President Lincoln then commuted the death sentences of all but 38, maintaining that only those who could be proven guilty of murder and rape should be executed, while the others should be handled as prisoners of war. Nix clearly supported the execution of these murderers and rapists, but felt that this was inadequate in consideration of the more than 800 men, women, and children who had been murdered. Regardless of any and all injustices, in Nix's view there was no justification whatsoever for this butchery. He also condemns those who would attempt to "whitewash," or attempt to justify and rationalize such crimes. Such people Nix describes as "crazy, hypocritical puritans." Today, he would most likely describe them as the politically correct.

Fourth, Nix claims that he aims to ascribe "honor to whom honor is due." In this regard, he goes out of his way to record the names of those who played an important role in the various aspects of the Uprising. He states that it "never occurred to me to belittle the services rendered" by the various forces that came to the aid of New Ulm after the First Battle, "and especially so by brave Judge Flandrau." Apparently, Nix felt that his own role as New Ulm Commandant, as well as that of the New Ulm defenders had not been appropriately appraised. For example, the report of Flandrau, published in 1891, makes no reference to Captain Nix, or the fact that he had been Commandant in New Ulm. Flandrau, hence, does not actually belittle Nix and the New Ulmers, he totally ignores them by omission.[18] Since Nix claimed he never would have thought of belittling others, especially Flandrau, it is clear that he felt that he and the New Ulmers had been ignored.

Why would Flandrau exclude reference to the First Battle of New Ulm, as well as to Captain Nix? Nix presents the whole story, but Flandrau does not. Several factors can be considered here. First, by the time Flandrau had published his report, there existed already several editions of Alexander Berghold's work dealing with the Uprising, as well as the work by Nix. It is doubtful that Flandrau was unaware of the existence of these works, especially since Berghold's work had been a best-seller, and is still in print.[19] Also, in his report, Flandrau lists the various sources he had utilized, but nowhere does he list the German-American sources by Nix and Berghold. Again, this is strange, since the battles took place in New Ulm, and one would assume that such sources would be considered as primary in any treatment of the topic. A second factor is that Flandrau was not at all involved in the First Battle of New Ulm, only the Second. Perhaps he, therefore, focused his attention on that which he was knowledgeable of, namely, the Second Battle, and gave short shrift to the First? This might be plausible, but is certainly no justification for excluding reference altogether to the First Battle. He could have qualified his remarks by stating that the First Battle had taken place, and that New Ulm had been successfully defended etc., but he chose not to do so. His work is, hence, flawed and distorted.

Flandrau's total silence on the First Battle in general and on Nix in particular begs the question as to what he might have had to gain in a business and political sense by his version of the defense of New Ulm? Was it not in his own interest to emphasize his role and his alone?

Politically, Flandrau had much to gain, since he campaigned as a Democratic candidate after the Civil War as the so-called "Defender of New Ulm."[20] Even though this failed to win him election, it did provide the political basis for his reputation, and one which gained him statewide recognition. Nix could also have campaigned for state office, but did not. Flandrau, on the other hand, sought statewide recognition on this basis to seek office. This was also beneficial to him in terms of his own law practice.

In an article on the Minnesota Germans in the Civil War, Wolkerstorfer asks the question, which many Minnesota German-Americans asked, as to whether Flandrau's claims were made "to enhance his own image as leader and military strategist in saving the town."[21] In short, as a politician and as a practicing attorney-at-law, Flandrau had something to gain by his account, whereas Nix did not. In this one case, there is an ulterior motive. Politicians often "toot their own horn" and magnify their own accomplishments in their attempts to gain election to office. One may, hence, categorize Flandrau's account as a retrospective falsification, or distortion of history based on the personal ulterior motives of a political opportunist. This is not to deny that he played an important role in the Second Battle of New Ulm, but it is to say that he needs to definitely share the stage with the New Ulmers and Nix at the First Battle of New Ulm.

Related to this latter point, we may examine the public reception of Flandrau's and Nix's histories. Anglo-Americans tended to accept the former, while German-Americans held to the latter. Why? Of course, linguistically, Anglos would have been unable to read the works by Nix and Berghold, although Berghold's work also appeared in an English-language edition. Second, Flandrau, as noted, never cited these sources in his account, nor does he mention Nix, nor did he place any significance on the First Battle, but focused exclusively on himself and the Second Battle. One can see why the English-language reading public would accept the Flandrau version.

Another factor to consider why Nix's report would have been difficult for Anglo-Americans to accept can be found in the prevalence of the mid-nineteenth century Know-Nothing Movement, which found expression in anti-ethnic sentiments in general, and in anti-Germanism in particular.[22] New Ulm was not only a German town, it was one of those "infidel" German Turner towns. Anglo-oriented nativists would be loath to admit that the Minnesota frontier was saved and protected by German-American Turners. How much more comfortable and acceptable, how much more politically correct, to accept the line Flandrau was presenting. Folwell cites a contemporary report, which stated, for example, "Had they (the Germans of New Ulm) been Americans, familiar with the Indian nature, they could have rallied and held the enemy at bay."[23] Wolkerstorfer notes that nineteenth century accounts present the image of "cowardly German settlers relying largely on the defense measures of Anglo-Minnesotans," and indicates that this "does great injustice to the German settlers who fought bravely according to accounts written closer to the time of the events."[24] This anti-German attitude, rather than diminish, would, of course, become more pronounced in the early twentieth century with the advent of two world wars.[25] Only in the recent past, has there been a serious attempt nationally to re-examine American history with regard to its multicultural diversity so that the role played by various ethnic groups could be accorded its proper place.[26]

Clearly, Nix felt that the role German-Americans had played in the First Battle of New Ulm had not been emphasized properly, and he stresses that the main battle in the struggle of the Uprising was fought on the 19th of August, since this was the first place the Sioux were brought to a definite halt, and he states that this "bitterly fought" battle was waged by Germans. He states, "the German town was defended and saved by Germans on the 19th of August, and as long as New Ulm exists this will be a memorable day in its history." Nix is not only merely defending his role, but that of the New Ulm German defenders who organized with him the defense of the town. He points out that had the Sioux not been stopped there, they would have rolled right onward to Mankato. Could Mankato have stopped them, had they taken New Ulm? Had they taken New Ulm, then the Winnebagos would have attacked Mankato from the south, thus placing the latter in a pincer movement from north and south.

Finally, it can be seen that Nix aims to provide the reader with an appreciation, from his perspective, of life on the frontier—from its beauties to its dangers. The portrait he presents is a rugged one, which contrasts sharply with the television imagery of "Little House on the Prairie." His work reflects the frontier as experienced by one who lived there. Then, as today, the history by Nix gives pause for questions and discussion.

Among the many questions which could come to mind, are the following:

—Just as the Vietnam War Memorial lists thousands of names of the war dead, would it not also be appropriate to erect a monument to the approximately 800 men, women, and children who were slain during the Uprising—a monument which listed alphabetically in one place all of their names—lest we forget?

—How many really know what happened to those 800 victims?

—What happened to the children?

—What happened to the young girls and women?

—Did 38 individuals (those who were executed) kill 800 people, or were those only the ones for whom the proof could be found that they were involved in murder and rape?

—Although the memory of Flandrau has been monumentalized in a variety of ways, is there such a thing as a Nix Monument or a Nix Park, which identifies him as Commandant of New Ulm during the First Battle of New Ulm, indicating it was this Battle which saved New Ulm?

—Does a wrong committed against a people by a specific party entitle that people to commit wrongs indiscriminately against others, including rape, pillage, and murder?

Value of Nix's History

This history by Captain Nix is of value for several reasons. First, it represents an actual eyewitness account of the 1862 Uprising. The availability of such accounts sheds light on sometimes divergent perspectives by the various participants. Second, in its present bilingual edition it represents the first publication of the history in its entirety in the English language. Third, this history quite clearly demonstrates and establishes the importance of the First Battle of New Ulm, and the role played therein by the New Ulm Germans. Fourth, the history also illuminates a wide variety of aspects and dimensions of the Uprising, which may open new avenues for consideration, discussion, and further research. Finally, this history by Captain Nix demonstrates the importance of German-language source materials in the history of the state of Minnesota.

This Edition

In Part One, the original German edition will be found, which is followed in Part Two by the English-language edition. We decided to publish these consecutively in two parts, rather than the German and English interfacing each other. This was done since Nix's paragraphs often cover an entire page, which does not provide for a readable text. In the English-language edition many of these overly long paragraphs were broken down into several paragraphs, and entire sections were also provided with subtitles, as Nix did not break down his text into chapters, or into any subunits. In Part Three, relevant illustrations have been included.

As noted earlier, the German edition appeared in 1887 on the occasion of the twenty-fifth anniversary of the Uprising. In 1949, a granddaughter of Nix, Gretchen Steinhauser, undertook the project of translating his work "as a tribute to her grandfather and her part in the marking of the Minnesota Territorial Centennial." Her translation consisted of selections from the history, which were then published in the *New Ulm Review*.[27] The full text of the history was then translated by myself and Eberhard Reichmann, and the entire work reviewed and revised.

Acknowledgements

Among the acknowledgements which should be made are, first, to Eberhard Reichmann, Editor-in-Chief of Publications of the Max Kade German-American Center at Indianapolis, for bringing this work to my attention, and then in joining in the effort of translating this work. Also, a word of gratitude is due to Roberta Schilling, Eden Prairie, Minnesota, a great-granddaughter of Captain Jacob Nix, who had kept one of the few extant copies of the privately published German original. This volume became the basis for the translated edition project which Reichmann and I undertook together.

I would also like to express gratitude to the Brown County Historical Society in New Ulm, and especially to Darla Gebhard, Research Librarian, for the research assistance provided in the locating of archival materials and illustrations. The Brown County Historical Society's holdings represent a gold mine of German-Americana.

Family Acknowledgements

Finally, I would like to express gratitude to my father, Eckhart H. Tolzmann, Mankato, Minnesota, for taking the time with me in June 1992 to visit/re-visit the sites mentioned in this work. With many family connections in and around New Ulm, I took an immediate interest in working on this edition of the work of Nix. Although my family's farm was in Renville County, there was no doctor available in the area on the August night I was born, so my parents drove to Granite Falls in nearby Yellow Medicine County. I was born, not far from the site of the Upper Sioux Agency. My grandfather had grown up on the family farm near Redwood, the site of the Lower Sioux Agency. His family had moved there from a farm at German Lake in LeSueur County in 1869.

Their new farm had previously belonged to the Schwandt family, immigrants from Berlin, Germany, in 1858. In front of the family farm stands the Schwandt Monument. This monument was dedicated on the 18th of August 1915 in memory of the Schwandt family which had been massacred at the farm. The inscription reads "Erected by the State of Minnesota, 1915, In Memory of Martyrs of Civilization, Johan Schwandt, Christina Schwandt, and their Children, Frederick and Christina; John Walz, Karolina Schwandt Walz; John Frass; Murdered by Sioux Indians, August 18, 1862." At the dedication of the Monument in 1915, Dr. Warren Upham of the Minnesota Historical Society observed that the Monument told of "the awful tragedy of race hatred and massacre which befell a German family of pioneers. . . ." This German immigrant family, which had sought a better life in the New World in 1858, had been on the farm for only two months—so much for their dreams in the New World! All but two members of the Schwandt family had been brutally killed by the Sioux; surviving the attack were two children, August and his sister Mary.[28]

The story of the Schwandt family, and especially of Mary Emilia Schwandt, became well known in my family, as the Schwandt family had been the previous owners of the farm to which my great-grandfather, a German immigrant from Pomerania, had moved in 1869. His family was well aware of the Uprising. Indeed, in 1862, he had been released from military service at Fort Snelling to return home to his family at German Lake in LeSueur County to protect them.

After moving to the farm near Redwood, they soon learned that there were Indians in the area. According to my grandfather, they came to the home regularly asking for food, which they were always given. After being at the farm a short time, my grandfather was then kidnapped by them, and only released after his father paid a ransom of food.

Years after the massacre, Mary Schwandt came to her former home, and my grandfather met her. She told him that before the massacre the family had hidden gold coins underneath the stone slab which lay before the front door of her family's cabin, and asked if she could see if they were still there. My grandfather's family then helped her remove the stone, and they found the gold coins which were given to their rightful owner, Mary Schwandt.[29]

The story of what happened to the Schwandt family, of course became well known and almost symbolic of the many innocent victims of the Uprising. Indeed, Mary Schwandt's account of her victimization has recently been reprinted, and she continues to figure prominently in works dealing with the Uprising.[30]

In the 1970s, my parents retired to the beautiful little town of Lake Crystal, southeast of New Ulm and west of Mankato. Here I spent many an enjoyable afternoon at the park, where we held several family reunions. Little did I realize until reading the work by Nix that two unsuspecting Norwegian-Americans, a father and son, had been murdered there by the Sioux in the 1860s.

Hence, the history of the Uprising by Jacob Nix was something which was of great interest to me to work on, as it relates not only to the region from which I hail, but to my family as well.

Don Heinrich Tolzmann

Notes

1. There are numerous other works pertaining to the German heritage of Minnesota, which are in need of translation, but ultimately not all of them can be translated, only the significant ones. As Steven Rowan has noted, "in the last analysis what is most pressingly needed is not a bookshelf of translations but an increasing number of bilingual historians of America. The concentration of American historians on English to the exclusion of all other languages historically spoken and written in North America both destroys our usable past and impoverishes our present." See Steven Rowan, ed., *Germans for a Free Missouri: Translations from the St. Louis Radical Press, 1857-1862.* (Columbia: University of Missouri Pr., 1983), p. ix-x.
2. See "A Man with a History," *New Ulm Review.* (13 June 1897).
3. Regarding Zitz, see A.E. Zucker, *The Forty-Eighters: Political Refugees of the German Revolution of 1848.* (New York: Columbia University Pr., 1950), p. 357. For general information on the 48ers, see LaVern J. Rippley, *The German-Americans.* (Boston: Twayne, 1976).
4. For further information on the 48ers, see A.E. Zucker, cited above, and Carl F. Wittke, *Refugees of Revolution: The German Forty-Eighters in America.* (Philadelphia: University of Pennsylvania Pr., 1952). Also, see LaVern J. Rippley, "Status Versus Ethnicity: The Turners and the Bohemians of New Ulm," in: Charlotte L. Brancaforte, ed., *The German Forty-Eighters in the United States.* (New York: Peter Lang, 1989), pp. 257-78.
5. See "A Man with A History."
6. A son of the Nix family, Prof. Robert Nix, attained national prominence in educational and German-American circles by means of his service as Superintendent of the New Ulm Public Schools, Supervisor of German in the Public Schools of Indianapolis, and as National President of the North American Turnerbund. See "Prof. Nix is Dead," *New Ulm Review.* (19 Oct. 1910), and Eberhard Reichmann, ed., *George Theodore Probst's The Germans in Indianapolis, 1840-1918.* (Indianapolis: German-American Center & Indiana German Heritage Society, 1989), pp. 137, 139-40. Prof. Nix was an accomplished poet, and two of his poems dealt with the Sioux Uprising. One poem dealt with Little Crow and another with "Der Sturm auf New Ulm am 19. August 1862." See Robert Nix, *Poems.* (Spokane, Washington: Else Nix, 1930), Vol. 2, pp. 34-38.
7. For a history of the Turners, see Henry Metzner, *History of the American Turners.* 4th Revised Edition. (Louisville: National Council of the American Turners, 1989).
8. See A.E. Zucker, pp. 71-72.
9. For information on Pfaender, see Grace Lovell May and Wilhelmina Pfaender Leonholdt, *Memory's Trail.* (New Ulm: New Ulm Daily Journal, 1954).
10. See Fredric R. Steinhauser, *New Ulm Germans: Adults of German Birth Settled in New Ulm and Surrounding Areas 1860.* (Minneapolis: University of Minnesota, General College, 1986), p. 14. For further general information on the history of New Ulm, see Elroy E. Ubl, *A Chronology of New Ulm, Minnesota: 1853-1899.* (New Ulm: MMI Graphics, 1978), and LaVern J. Rippley, "Patterns and Marks of German Settlement in Minnesota," in: Clarence A. Glasrud and Diana M. Rankin, eds., *A Heritage Deferred: The German-Americans in Minnesota.* (Moorhead, Minnesota: Concordia College, 1981), pp. 49-66.
11. See "Captain Jacob Nix: Early New Ulm Pioneer," *New Ulm Review.* (4 Oct. 1947).
12. Ibid.
13. Ibid.
14. Ibid.
15. See A.E. Zucker, p. 326.
16. The contrast between the Anglo- and German-American histories is clearly seen in a review of the various histories in William Watts Folwell, "The First Battle of New Ulm," in Folwell's *A History of Minnesota.* (St. Paul: Minnesota Historical Society, 1924), Vol. 2, pp. 361-74. Folwell notes that New Ulmers "have been industrious in supporting the claim that

to the German townsmen alone should the credit wholly or in chief be given." This was strongly supported in a report by Charles Roos, Sheriff of Brown County at the time of the Uprising. A report by Roos in the form of an affidavit was published in *The New Ulm Post* (30 August 1912), which provides further documentary support for Nix's history. Hence, there is general agreement amongst New Ulmers that the history written by Nix is an accurate portrayal of the First Battle. This is further substantiated in the histories written by Alexander Berghold, which are also discussed by Folwell.

17. Ethnicity and the role ethnic groups have played in U.S. history has been a neglected dimension of American historical writing, as Rudolph Vecoli has pointed out. See Rudolph J. Vecoli, "Ethnicity: A Neglected Dimension of American History," in: Herbert J. Bass, ed., *The State of American History*. (Chicago: Quadrangle, 1970), pp. 70-88. One of the basic reasons why German-Americans began to write history was because of the exclusion of German-Americans from English-language histories. For a detailed discussion of this, see Don Heinrich Tolzmann, "German-American Studies, 1492-1992 and Beyond," in: Don Heinrich Tolzmann, ed., *Germany and America, 1450-1700: Julius Friedrich Sachse's History of the German Role in the Discovery, Exploration, and Settlement of the New World*. (Bowie, MD: Heritage Books, Inc., 1991), pp. 16-28. Here it is noted by Sachse that writers of American history have thus far failed to accord to German-Americans "the proper amount of credit" for the role they have played in American history. He observes that "instances are extremely rare where the average historian" has accorded such credit (pp. 33-34).

Henry Melchior Muhlenberg Richards observed that an examination of American historical writing indicates that the role German-Americans have played is unrecorded. He wrote, "As we turn, with expectant interest, to the pages of history, to learn somewhat of the character of these (German-American) deeds, we are astonished to find them unrecorded. To such an extent has this been the case that unthinking and unreasoning persons have been led to believe that the German element of this country has been practically a nonentity in its development." Richards felt that the main reason for this was linguistic, and that much had been written in the German language. He notes that "there have been various reasons for this historical silence. Our fathers, however, educated in other languages, spoke and wrote "in German" which others, too busy in recording and exploiting their own deeds and worth, had no interest in translating, and, therefore, their doings, to a certain extent, either became lost to the world, or were allowed to lie hidden until the children of this generation were permitted to bring them to light." See Don Heinrich Tolzmann, ed., *German-Americans in the American Revolution: Henry Melchior Richards' History*. (Bowie, MD: Heritage Books, Inc., 1992), pp. 1-2.

George Fenwick Jones writes in an essay on the role German-Americans played in the American Revolution that "although German-speaking people played a significant role in the military life of colonial Georgia, they have been largely ignored by most historians." He notes that the credit is usually assigned to Anglo-Americans. See George Fenwick Jones, "The 'Dutch' Participation in Georgia's Colonial Wars," *Georgia Historical Quarterly*. 75(1991): 771. What Jones has observed with regard to Georgia is symptomatic in general of Anglo-American historical writing and its treatment of the role German-Americans have played in American history.

18. Flandrau's report can be found in *Minnesota in the Civil and Indian Wars, 1861-1865*. (St. Paul: Pioneer Pr. Co., 1891), pp. 727-53.

19. See Alexander Berghold, *The Indians' Revenge; Or, Days of Horror: Some Appalling Events in the History of the Sioux*. (San Francisco: P.J. Thomas, 1891). For further information on the life and work of Berghold, see LaVern J. Rippley, "Alexander Berghold: Pioneer Priest and Prairie Poet," *The Report: A Journal of German-American History*. 37(1978): 43-56.

20. See Russell W. Fridley et al, eds., *Charles E. Flandrau and the Defense of New Ulm*. (New Ulm: Brown County Historical Society, 1962).

21. See Sister John Christine Wolkerstorfer, "Minnesota's Germans and the Civil War," in: Clarence A. Glasrud, ed., *A Heritage Fulfilled: German-Americans*. (Moorhead: Concordia College, 1984), p. 128.

22. Regarding the anti-German hysteria of World War One, see Carl H. Chrislock, *Watchdog of Loyalty: The Minnesota Commission of Public Safety During World War I*. (St. Paul: Minnesota Historical Society, 1991). Also, see LaVern J. Rippley, "Conflict in the Classroom: Anti-Germanism in Minnesota Schools, 1917-1919," *Minnesota History*. 47(1981): 170-83.

23. See Folwell, Vol. 2, p. 370.

24. Wolkerstorfer, p. 126.

25. For further information regarding the German-American experience during the world wars, see Don Heinrich Tolzmann, *German-Americana: A Bibliography*. (Metuchen, NJ: Scarecrow Pr., 1975), and also Don Heinrich Tolzmann, *Catalog of the German-Americana Collection, University of Cincinnati*. (München: K.G. Saur, 1990). For a survey of the role German-Americans have played in the military, see Don Heinrich Tolzmann, ed., *German-American Military Service: J.G. Rosengarten's History* (in preparation).

26. For a history of American ethnic groups, see Roger Daniels, *Coming to America: A History of Immigration and Ethnicity in American Life*. (New York: Harper-Collins, 1990).

27. See "Capt. Nix Tells Own Story of Indian Uprising of 1862," *New Ulm Review*. (1-22 Sept. 1949).

28. Regarding the Schwandt family, see Franklin Curtiss-Wedge, *The History of Renville County, Minnesota*. (Chicago: Hooper, 1916), Vol. 2, pp. 920-23, 1314, 1346, and 1348. Berghold describes what neighbors found when they came to the Schwandt farm: "Schwandt's son-in-law was lying on the door steps with three bullets in his body. His wife (Schwandt's daughter), who had been with child, was found dead, her womb cut open and the unborn child nailed to a tree. Her brother, a thirteen-year-old lad, whom the Indians thought they had killed, saw how the child was taken alive from the womb of his sister, and nailed to the tree, where it lived for a little while. This terrible deed was done in the forenoon of August the 18th. The mother was found in the field beheaded. Beside her lay the body of their hired man, Foss. Towards evening the boy regained a little strength and fled into the next settlement, a distance of three miles. He entered Bushe's house only to find some thirty corpses, and among them a three-year-old child, wounded, and sitting beside its dead mother. The boy took the child with him, carried it about four miles, and being unable to take it farther, left it at a house, promising to return the next morning. He did this in order to be able to save himself. He made good his escape to Fort Ridgely, traveling for four nights, and hiding the day. The child was afterwards found in captivity among the Indians, and was brought to Fort Ridgely, where it died from the effects of its wounds and exposure." See Berghold, pp. 164-65.

29. The brick home built by my great-grandfather, Carl Tolzmann, after he had moved to the Schwandt place, is still being used, as is the log barn he built.

30. Mary Schwandt's report on her captivity was reprinted in: *Captivities of Mrs. J. E. DeCamp Sweet, Nancy McClure and Mary Schwandt*. The Garland Library of Narratives of North American Indian Captivities, Vol. 99. (New York: Garland, 1977). The story of Mary Schwandt also figured prominently in Duane Schultz, *Over the Earth I Come: The Great Sioux Uprising of 1862*. (New York: St. Martin's Pr., 1992).

In her report, Mary Schwandt does not describe the details pertaining to the most horrific period of "the incidents of that dreadful night and the four following dreadful days" of her captivity, but does provide statements as to her conditions in captivity. Schwandt wrote, "While in Little Crow's village I saw some of my father's cattle and many of our household goods in the hands of the Indians. I now knew that my family had been plundered, and I believed murdered. I was very, very wretched, and cared not how soon I too was killed . . . my eyes were always red and swollen from constant weeping . . . But soon there came a time when I did not weep. I could not. The dreadful scenes I had witnessed, the suffering that I had undergone, the almost certainty that my family had all been killed, and that I was alone in the world, and the belief that I was destined to witness other things as horrible as those I had seen, and that my career of suffering and misery had only begun, all came to my comprehension, and when I realized my utterly wretched, helpless and hopeless situation, for I did not think I would ever be released, I became as one paralyzed and could hardly speak . . . and went about like a sleep-walker." See *Captivities*, p. 469.

Schwandt describes various experiences amongst her "savage and brutal" captors, including the following incident with Little Crow: "I shall always remember Little Crow from an incident that happened while I was in his village. One day I was sitting quietly and shrinkingly by a teepee when he came along dressed in full chief's costume and looking very grand. Suddenly he jerked his tomahawk from his belt and sprang toward me with the weapon uplifted as if he meant to cleave my head in two . . . he glared down upon me so savagely, that I thought he really would kill me; but I looked up at him, without any fear or care about my fate, and gazed quietly into his face without so much as winking my tear-swollen eyes. He brandished his tomahawk over me a few times, then laughed, put it back in his belt and walked away, still laughing and saying something in Indian, which, of course, I could not understand. Of course, he only meant to frighten me, but I do not think he was excusable for his conduct. He was a great chief and some people say he had many noble traits of character, but I have another opinion of any man, savage or civilized, who will take for a subject of sport a weak, defenseless, broken-hearted girl, a prisoner in his hands, who feels as if she could never smile again." In later life, Schwandt was able to report that she had seen Little Crow's scalp amongst the relics of the Minnesota Historical Society, and could not deny that she felt "satisfaction at the sight." See *Captivities*, p. 470.

For further information on the atrocities committed against the settlers, which Nix describes as "beyond words," see Berghold, pp. 80ff, pp. 92ff, pp. 106ff, pp. 152ff, pp. 162ff, and 177ff, and also Curtiss-Wedge, Vol. 1, pp. 139-245; Vol. 2, pp. 916-31.

According to J. Norman Heard, "within 40 days they (the Sioux) had massacred not less than 800 settlers." He cites C.M. Oehler, who noted that "It was the bloodiest Indian massacre the West has ever known, ten times deadlier as the Fetterman disaster, and with four times the fatalities of Custer's tragedy. Most of the victims were unarmed civilians." See J. Norman Heard, *Handbook of the American Frontier: Four Centuries of Indian-White Relationships: Volume III: The Great Plains.* (Metuchen, NJ: Scarecrow Pr., 1993), p. 166.

PART ONE—GERMAN EDITION (1887)

Der

Ausbruch der Sioux-Indianer

in Minnesota, im August 1862.

— Von —

Capitain Jacob Nix.

New Ulm, Minn.,
Verlag des Verfassers,
1887.

Entered according to act of Congress in the year 1887,

BY CAPT. JACOB NIX,

in the office of the Librarian of Congress, at Washington, D. C.

Den wackeren Vertheidigern
der
Stadt New Ulm,
— zur —
25jährigen Erinnerungsfeier,
Achtungsvoll gewidmet vom
Verfasser.

Vorrede.

Dem Wunsche vieler meiner Freunde entsprechend, eine wahrheitsgetreue Schilderung des Ausbruches der Sioux-Indianer im August des Jahres 1862 zu schreiben, erlaube ich mir, das nachfolgende Büchlein der Oeffentlichkeit zu übergeben.

Es sind allerdings schon mehrere Abhandlungen über diesen Gegenstand veröffentlicht worden, doch keine derselben liefert ein richtiges und zuverlässiges Bild jener Schreckensscenen; namentlich aber trotzen die in englischer Sprache erschienenen Aufzeichnungen von Unwahrheiten und Entstellungen.

Da ich mich nun während der ganzen Dauer jener Begebenheiten als Augenzeuge am Orte der Handlung befand, und außerdem in der Lage war, viele Einzelheiten aus den zuverläßigsten Quellen schöpfen zu können, so kann der freundliche Leser überzeugt sein, daß er nur Geschichte und keine Sage aus der Feder des Verfassers erhält.

Und so übergebe ich denn dies Büchlein der Oeffentlichkeit mit der Bitte, demselben eine gütige Aufnahme gewähren zu wollen.

Der Verfasser.

Die aufgehende Sonne des 18. August 1862 beschien mild und freundlich die Turnerstadt New Ulm und Umgegend im oberen Minnesota-Thale. Friedliche Ruhe lagerte über der herrlichen Landschaft, nur unterbrochen von dem Gezwitscher der gefiederten Sänger, die der eben am Firmament erscheinenden Aurora aus voller Brust entgegenjubelten.

Hier und dort begann es sich nun zu regen, doch keiner der vereinzelten Wanderer auf der Landstraße oder der sich nach ihren Feldern begebenden Landwirthe dachte daran, daß diese friedliche Ruhe so bald von dem Schmerzensgestöhn Verwundeter, dem Todesröcheln Sterbender, untermischt mit dem der Hölle entlehnten Schlachtgesang der Sioux-Indianer, in so schrecklicher Weise unterbrochen würde. Wohl wußten besser Unterrichtete, daß die Indianer auf ihren Auszahlungs-Plätzen in Folge von Zerwürfnissen mit den ihnen die Jahresgelder übermittelnden Agenten der Vereinigten Staaten-Regierung unzufrieden waren, und in Folge dessen sich sehr unruhig geberdeten; wohl wußten die meisten der auf den beiden Agenturen angestellten Beamten, daß die Wilden seit einigen Tagen finster und grollend einhergingen, und in ihren geheim abgehaltenen Versammlungen schreckliche Drohungen gegen die Bleichgesichter ausgestoßen hatten; wohl wußte man durch Aussagen und Warnungsrufe einiger dem weißen Manne wohlwollenden Indianer dies Alles—und doch legte man von Seiten der Regierungsbeamten kein großes Gewicht darauf, da dieselben in unverzeihlichem Leichtsinn sich mit dem Gedanken beruhigten, daß die auf den beiden Sammelplätzen der Indianer stationirte Handvoll Soldaten denselben mehr als nöthig überlegen sei. Es kam anders.

Die Beamten und Händler auf den beiden Agenturen sollten nur zu bald unter den Streichen des Tomahawk der Wilden ihre Vertrauensseligkeit zu bereuen haben. Doch wir wollen dem Laufe der nachfolgenden Begebenheiten nicht vorgreifen, und vorerst zu ermitteln suchen, was die sonst an ihren Auszahlungstagen sich so ziemlich ruhig verhaltenden Rothhäute jetzt in Bestien verwandelte, gegen die der Königstiger in den ostindischen Jungeln als ein noch Mitleidfühlendes Geschöpf betrachtet werden kann.

Der Vertrag zwischen der Regierung der Vereinigten Staaten einestheils und diesen Sioux-Indianern anderntheils enthielt die Klausel, daß die für die Abtretung eines großen Stück Landes an die erstere den Rothhäuten pro Kopf alljährlich baar zu zahlende Summe in gemünztem Golde der Vereinigten Staaten zu entrichten sei. Wer nun jemals mit den Indianern in geschäftlicher Beziehung gestanden, durch Aufkaufen von Fellen, Ahorn-Zucker u. s. w. Geld an sie auszuzahlen hatte (auf Tauschhandel läßt sich der rothe Mann nur in seltenen Fällen ein, er verkauft und kauft nur für baares Geld), der muß wissen, daß die Rothhaut von je her eine abergläubische, in den meisten Fällen aber gerechtfertigte Scheu vor allem Papiergelde der in damaliger Zeit wie Pilze aus der Erde wachsenden Banken in den Ver. Staaten und Canada hatte. Wir wollen nun gerade nicht behaupten, daß alle Spitzbuben und Betrüger Indianer-Agenten sind, daß aber ein großer Theil der letzteren auf den Ehrentitel „Gauner" Anspruch machen kann, wird mir kein vernünftiger Mensch, der mit den Indianern und ihren Agentur-Verhältnissen nur halbwegs vertraut ist, abzustreiten suchen. Wie viele Ausbrüche der Rothhäute mit ihrem Morden, Brennen und Sengen in den Ansiedelungen des weißen Mannes den Herrn Agenten in die Schuhe geschoben werden können, ist bis jetzt statistisch noch nicht festgestellt worden, doch ist ihre Anzahl eine ziemlich bedeutende, und jeder gefühlvolle Mensch wird und muß die feststehende Thatsache bedauern, daß dem Moloch des schnöden Gewinnes, der in der Form unerlaubter Bereicherung einzelner Schurken auftrat, schon Tausende und abermals Tausende von braven und fleißigen weißen Ansiedlern zum Opfer gefallen sind. Auch hier in Minnesota spielte die Begierde, Geld zu verdienen, bei den Gräuelscenen in der letzten Hälfte des August 1862 eine bedeutende Rolle, und es kann nicht bestritten werden, daß die Habgier eines damaligen Regierungs-Beamten viel, sehr viel zu dem schrecklichen Ausbruche der Sioux-Indianer im oberen Minnesota-Thale beigetragen, ja denselben, weil nur allein von dem Gedanken beseelt, so und so viel Dollars aus den Indianern herauszupressen, zum Verderben so vieler braver Ansiedler fast einzig und allein heraufbeschworen.

Ich werde mich nun bemühen klar und deutlich zu beweisen, daß mit der obigen Annahme der Nagel so ziemlich auf den Kopf getroffen ist, und daß alle andere Andeutungen über die Ursache des Ausbruchs der Sioux-Indianer in das Reich der Märchen gehören. Das vollständige Todtschweigen der darauf bezüglichen Thatsachen ist aber ein nicht hinweg zu läugnendes Verbrechen an der Geschichte; denn mit der Erklärung, daß man nicht ausfinden könne, was die Rothhäute bewogen, im August 1862 plötzlich den Kriegspfad gegen die Weißen zu betreten, und über 700 der letzteren abzuschlachten, kann sich doch kein vernünftiger Mensch abspeisen lassen, da es jedem einleuchten muß, daß irgend eine Ursache dazu vorhanden gewesen sein muß. Die weitere von gewisser Seite ausgesprochene Ansicht, daß der Geldpunkt bei dem furchtbaren Drama keine Rolle gespielt, sondern einige von der südlichen Rebellen=Regierung nach Minnesota gesandten Abgeordneten die Indianer aufgehetzt und ihnen die Hülfe des Südens versprochen, ist zwar fad und abgeschmackt, beweist aber dennoch, daß man unter dem Deckmantel, das Richtige gefunden zu haben, jede andere, wenn auch durch Thatsachen und Beweisen festgestellte Ursache zu vertuschen sucht.

Ich selbst war nie, und bin es heute nicht, ein Freund der südlichen Rebellen, aber dessen ungeachtet kann ich es nicht gelten lassen, daß sie es waren, welche den damaligen Indianer=Ausbruch verschuldeten.

Other Day, einer von den wenigen Indianer, welchen unter der rothen Haut ein menschliches und dankbares Herz schlug, Other Day, dessen Name sich in der Geschichte Minnesota's für alle Zeiten einen ehrenvollen Platz gesichert, weil der Träger desselben, in dankbarer Erinnerung an die stets offene Hand des weißen Mannes in Zeiten der Noth, seinen Stammesgenossen wiederholt abgerathen, den Kriegspfad gegen die Bleichgesichter zu betreten,—Other Day erklärte auf die spätere Anfrage ob irgend welche Abgeordneten der südlichen Rebellen=Regierung zur Zeit bei den Indianer erschienen, und dieselben unter irgend einer Vorspiegelung zum Kriege gegen die Weißen gereizt, daß dieses nicht der Fall, und wenn dennoch behauptet, er es für eine infame Lüge bezeichnen müßte. Und doch war es dieser brave Indianer, der allen geheimen Versammlungen seiner Stammesgenossen beiwohnte, in welchen er stets als Freund seiner weißen Brüder auftrat und zum Frieden mahnte, und so auch in der einen Tag vor dem Ausbruche gehaltenen letzten dieser Versammlungen hatte er gegen alle Gewaltthätigkeiten protestirt. Other Day, und wir können den Namen des braven Mannes nicht oft genug nennen, war es, der, als er überzeugt war, daß dem blutdürstigen Verlangen seiner entmenschten Stammesgenossen gegenüber alle versöhnenden Worte in den Wind gesprochen seien, sich mit dem Zurücklassen seines Rockes und Hutes aus dieser letzten und entscheidenden Berathung der Rothhäute flüchtete, weil Little Crow ihn während derselben wiederholt für einen Verräther seines Stammes und deshalb für vogelfrei erklärt hatte. Der brave Mann, jetzt wohlwissend, daß von dem Beschleunigen seiner Schritte, und dem kleinen Vorsprung, den er hatte, das Leben vieler weißen Menschen abhing, begab sich nun so schnell als er konnte nach der oberen Agentur, welche von jeder Zufluchtsstätte am entferntesten gelegen, und rettete 60 weiße Männern, Frauen und Kindern dadurch das Leben, daß er sie auf entlegenen Pfaden durch die Prairie nach einem sicheren Asyl brachte. Ehre seinem Andenken!

Der freundliche Leser wird mir nun gestatten direkt auf mein Ziel loszugehen, das heißt, den thatsächlichen Beweis zu liefern, daß die Habsucht, die Geldgier und Gewissenlosigkeit Einzelner als die Haupt=Ursache des Aufstandes der Sioux= Indianer zu betrachten ist.

Der Auszahlungstermin des Jahres 1862 war erschienen, und es hatten sich die betreffenden Indianer auf ihren beiden Agenturen, der sogenannten un= teren und oberen Agentur versammelt. Der Zahlmeister war gekommen, und es ward mit demjenigen Theile der Jahresauszahlung, welche in Munition, wollenen Decken u. s. w. bestand, begonnen. Alles verlief soweit gut. Doch jetzt kam das baare Geld an die Reihe. Der Beamte hatte Papiergeld, die Indianer wollten aber Gold haben, wozu sie kraft ihres Vertrages mit der Regierung berechtigt waren. Man suchte nun den Rothhäuten begreiflich zu machen, daß Papiergeld denselben Werth für sie habe, wie Gold. Doch sie glaubten es nicht und der Herr Zahlmeister entfernte sich von den Agenturen mit dem Versprechen, in kurzer Zeit wiederzukommen, um ihnen die Jahresgelder alsdann in klingender Münze auszubezahlen. Die Sioux waren vorläufig zufrieden, doch sie sollten sehr bald finden, daß man sie hinsichtlich des baldigen Zurückkommens des betreffenden Be= amten, um sie, wie es früher immer geschah, mit Gold auszubezahlen, getäuscht hatte. Tag auf Tag, Woche auf Woche verging, der Herr Zahlmeister kam nicht. Man wollte sie mürbe machen, diese wiederspenstigen Indianer, und dadurch zur Annahme des Papiergeldes zwingen. Gold hatte damals schon ein Agio von über 12 Prozent, und stieg von Tag zu Tag höher. Wer wollte den Gewinn bei diesem sauberen Geschäftchen in die Tasche stecken? Mittlerweile verweigerten die Kaufleute der Agenturen den Indianern den sonst so bereitwillig genehmigten Credit. Ja, einige der ersteren sollen ihnen bei dem Verlangen nach Lebensmittel auf Rechnung hohnlachend ins Gesicht gesagt haben: „Gras könnt ihr fressen!" In Folge dessen wuchs der Nothstand der Rothhäute entsetzlich, ja Augenzeugen versicherten später, daß viele kleine Kinder der Indianer buchstäblich verhungert seien. Die Farmer der Umgegend und die Bewohner der in der Nähe liegenden kleineren Städte thaten ihr Möglichstes dieses Elend zu lindern. Den bettelnden Indianern wurde jede nur mögliche Hülfe geleistet, und die Bewohner des oberen Minnesota=Thales überließen sich daher dem süßen Wahne, daß die ersteren mit denen sie bis jetzt auf dem freundschaftlichsten Fuße gestanden und denen sie bisher wiederholt Gutes er= zeigt, nicht daran denken würden, die Ansiedler in der Nähe der Agenturen für die nichts weniger als menschenwürdige Behandlung, welche den Rothhäuten auf den letzteren zu Theil wurde, verantwortlich zu machen. Doch wer mit Wilden jemals in Berührung gekommen, sei es in Afrika, Australien, Amerika oder auf einem anderen Stückchen Erde, wer mit ihnen näher verkehrt, und ihre Natur etwas genauer zum Gegenstande seiner Beobachtung gemacht, der weiß und muß es wissen, daß die Bestie in dem wilden Menschen nur schlummert, um, einmal geweckt, sich mit tigerartigem Blutdurst auf die nächsten besten Opfer zu stürzen. Das unselige Vertrauen der Bewohner des oberen Minnesota-Thales in die erhäuchelte Freundschaft und das dabei unterwürfige Wesen der Indianer denen sie oft in Zeiten der schweren Noth so bereitwillig beigestanden, in manchen Fällen sogar das Letzte mit ihnen getheilt, dieses blinde Vertrauen sollte einem großen Theil der Ansiedler zum Verderben gereichen. Umsonst waren alle Warnungsrufe zur Vorsicht, umsonst war es, daß einige noch etwas menschlich fühlende Indianer durch Gestikulationen die Schreckensscenen, welche bald ihr bluthrothes Erscheinen machen würden, beschrieben; alle und jede Warnung war in den Wind gesprochen. „Die Indianer sind unsre Freunde, wir haben ihnen so viel Gutes erwiesen und sie werden sich unter keinen Umständen an den Farmern der Umgegend und ihren Familien vergreifen." Doch in wie weit die rothen Bluthunde das in sie gesetzte Vertrauen ihrer weißen Freunde und Helfer in der Noth rechtfertigten, wie der Tomahawk des entmenschten Wilden die Hand des weißen Mannes und der weißen Frau mit einem einzigen Hiebe vom Körper trennte, dieselbe Hand, welche ihm und seinen hungernden Kinder noch einige Tage vorher mitleidig die labende Gabe gereicht, wie die bis dahin schlummernde Bestie in der Brust des rothen Teufels erwachte, wie die wilde Canaille den aufopferndsten Freund wie ihren erbittersten Feind behandelte, das muß uns zur Genüge beweisen, daß die einmal entfesselte Wuth des Indianers keinen Unterschied kennt zwischen Freund und Feind, und daß die Rothhaut, beherrscht von dieser diabolischen Gewalt, nur noch ihren blutdürstigen Begierden Rechnung tragen will. — Es liegt nun einmal in der Natur des Sohnes der Wildniß, die in seinem Inneren stets zum Sprunge bereite Bestie von Zeit zu Zeit auf die Menschen loszulassen, und wehe dann Denjenigen, welche sie sich zum Opfer auserkoren. Von Erbarmen ist dann keine Rede, der Wilde weiß davon ebenso wenig als der Tiger, denn dieser nimmt sich wenigstens nicht die Zeit, sein Opfer lange zu martern, sondern zermalmt es sofort zwischen seinen Zähnen. Und deswegen ist es ein doppeltes Verbrechen von Seiten der für die Indianer von der Regierung ernannten Beamten, wenn sie die verbissene aber zurückgedrängte Wuth der Rothhäute durch begangene Ungerechtigkeiten an denselben zum schrecklichen Durchbruch aufstacheln, die dann mit der Geschwindigkeit des Blitzes, und wie dieser Unheilbringend über den Häuptern argloser Ansiedler sich entladet. — Doch Hohngelächter der Hölle! Warum soll man den Indianern nicht von Zeit zu Zeit das Vergnügen gönnen, einige hundert Weiße zu massakriren, man überwältigt sie später ja doch wieder, zerschmettert sie, in den meisten Fällen allerdings erst nach einem langwierigen und sehr kostspieligen Kriege, und bringt dann die Gefangenen auf zu diesem Zweck neu errichtete Reservationen.

In diesen Versorgungsanstalten für überzählige Aemterjäger der sich am Ruder befindlichen Partei kann man einen Theil dieser politischen Maulwürfe durch Anstellungen befriedigen, denn in neu errichteten Indianerreservationen braucht man auch neue Beamten. Doch so lange als korrupte politische Parteien in dieser großen Republik bei den Wahlen sich gegenseitig in den Haaren liegen, so lange müssen auch nach dem Motto: „Dem Sieger gehört die Beute", die politischen Handlanger der siegreichen Partei versorgt werden, und zu einem Theil dieser Versorgung eignen sich die Indianer=Agenturen vortrefflich. Doch lassen wir nun die politischen Raubvögel vorläufig in ihren erbeuteten Nestern ausruhen und kehren wir im Geiste zurück nach dem stillen wunderschönen Morgen des 18. August 1862.

Am Tage vor dem verhängnißvollen Sommermorgen, also am 17. August, war in der Turnerstadt New Ulm ein reges Leben. Eine auf den beiden Agenturen für Onkel Sam angeworbene, zum Theil aus Halbindianern bestehende Compagnie Voluntäre erschien urplötzlich und wurde von der patriotischen Bevölkerung mit Jubel empfangen. Nur einige Wenige, denen die damaligen Zustände auf den Sammelplätzen der Indianer besser bekannt waren, wunderten sich, daß gerade jetzt einer der ersten Regierungs=Beamten mit dieser Compagnie von den Agenturen aufbrach, um sich mit derselben nach Fort Snelling, 100 Meilen von New Ulm, zu begeben. Wußte der Mann nicht, daß die hungernden Indianer seit einigen Tagen eine mehr als drohende Haltung annahmen, oder wollte er es nicht wissen? Es ist ein bis jetzt ungelöstes Räthsel. Einige behaupten zwar heute noch, der Herr wollte damals dem drohenden Unwetter aus dem Wege gehen, und seine Haut ins Trockene bringen, bevor die sich zu einem dunkeln Knäuel zusammenballenden Wolken sich entluden. Bemerkungen über das Vorhandensein einer Gefahr, über einen möglichen Angriff der Indianer auf die den beiden Agenturen zunächst gelegenen Farmen, wurden mit Entrüstung zurückgewiesen, denn, sagte man, wie würde dieser Beamte es gewagt haben, in einem solchen kritischen Augenblick seinen Posten zu verlassen. Man überließ sich denn auch in New Ulm sowohl, wie in der ganzen Umgegend in der Nacht vom 17. zum 18. August und an dem darauffolgenden Morgen einer Sorglosigkeit, welche von dem, sich um die beiden Agenturen zusammen ziehenden, Tod und Verderben in seinem Schooße bergenden, Gewittersturme keine Ahnung hatte. Da, wie der Blitz aus fast heiterem Himmel, ertönte der Schreckensruf: „Die Indianer sind ausgebrochen und ermorden alle Ansiedler, welche ihnen in die Hände fallen." —

Ein Schrei des Entsetzens, aber auch der Entrüstung, des gerechten Zornes über die Sorglosigkeit der Regierung, welche die beiden Agenturen, ja fast das ganze obere Minnesota=Thal schutzlos dem Tomahawk der rothen Bestien preisge=

geben hatte, drang gleichzeitig mit dieser Schauernachricht durch ganz Minnesota, denn man wußte nur zu gut, was die paar inhaltschweren Worte: „Die Indianer sind ausgebrochen", zu bedeuten hatten. Gleichzeitig mit vielen Flüchtlingen, unter denen sich einige Verwundete befanden, kam die Schreckenskunde zuerst nach Fort Ridgely, welches auf einem Plateau der Hügelkette gelegen, die sich auf der linken Seite des Minnesota Flußes hinzieht, und welches Fort 18 Meilen von New Ulm entfernt ist. Hier lag nur eine schwache Besatzung, bestehend aus einer Compagnie des 5ten Regiments Minnesotaer Volontäre, welche gerade stark genug war, eine Postenkette um diese Militär=Station zu ziehen. Unverzeihlicher Weise hatte man auch diesen Platz von Truppen entblößt, denn statt der hier in früherer Zeit stationirt gewesenen 4 Compagnien regulärer Truppen, unter denen sich noch obendrein eine Batterie mit 6 leichten Feldgeschützen befand, war jetzt nur eine Handvoll Freiwillige eines erst vor einigen Monaten in den Militär=Dienst einge= musterten Regiments als Besatzung hier. Aber der brave Commandant des Forts, Capitain Marsh, zögerte dennoch keinen Augenblick, den Bedrängten Hülfe zu bringen, und setzte sich sofort nach erhaltener Nachricht mit 50 Mann gegen die untere, 12 Meilen entfernte, Agentur in Bewegung.

Der pflichtgetreue Offizier und die meisten seiner braven Schaar sollten Fort Ridgely nicht wieder erblicken. Auf der Landstraße am linken Minnesota Ufer vordringend (die Agentur lag auf der rechten Seite), gelang es diesen wenigen Soldaten viele Flüchtlinge, meistens Frauen und Kinder, welche sämmtlich nach dem Fort sich zu retten suchten, von den herumstreifenden kleineren Banden der Rothhäute zu befreien, die letzteren zu zerstreuen und den armen Heimathlosen ihre Flucht so gut als möglich zu decken.

Nach einem mehrstündigen, gefahrvollen und mühseligen Marsche gelangte das kleine Commando in die Nähe des kleinen Fährtbootes, das nicht weit von der unteren Indianer=Agentur die Verbindung zwischen den beiden Ufern des Minne= sota=Flußes bewerkstelligte. Auf der rechten Seite des kleinen Stromes erschienen bei der Ankunft der Soldaten sofort einige Indianer, welche die ersteren aufforder= ten, herüber zu kommen, da sie, die Rothhäute, von der Mehrheit ihrer Stammes= genossen abgeschickt seien, um sich mit dem Militär freundschaftlichst zu verständi= gen. „Wir sind", riefen die rothen Hallunken, „immerwährend Freunde der Weißen gewesen, und sind es auch heute noch, ihr müßt uns daher nicht verant= wortlich dafür machen, was einige schlechte Subjekte unseres Stammes verbrochen haben." Capitain Marsh, den heimtückischen Charakter des Indianers nicht ge= nügend kennend, und gleichzeitig wohlwissend, daß er mit seinen geringen Streit= kräften der ganzen Bande gegenüber nichts ausrichten konnte, glaubte den heuch= lerischen rothen Spitzbuben, und gab, trotz der Warnung des ihn begleitenden

Dollmetschers, sofort den Befehl, auf das andere Ufer überzusetzen. Nichts ahnend verließ daher die kleine Schaar Soldaten die bis jetzt sie deckende Stellung, und begab sich in der Richtung nach dem Ferryboot zu nach dem Ufer des Flusses. Doch kaum waren sie hier angekommen, und ein großer Theil von ihnen hatte eben das Boot bestiegen, da krachten am jenseitigen Ufer des schmalen Flusses über hundert Schüsse, und tödtlich getroffen oder schwer verwundet lagen 37 brave Soldaten von verrätherischen Kugeln durchbohrt in ihrem Blute.

Die rothen Bestien hatten sich mehr als hundert an der Zahl, von dem Militär nicht bemerkt, hinter Gesträuchern und einigen Holzhaufen versteckt gehalten. Capitain Marsh, welcher einer der ersten war, die das Ferryboot bestiegen hatten, sprang, ob verwundet oder nicht konnte nicht festgestellt werden, in den Fluß, um sich durch Schwimmen zu retten; doch einige ihm nachgesandte Kugeln der indianischen Canaillen trafen und tödteten ihn sofort. Nur 13, also der vierte Theil, der am Morgen ausgezogenen braven Schaar konnten, unter mancherlei weiteren Gefahren, Fort Ridgely lebend wieder erreichen.

Unter den Erschossenen befand sich der Dollmetscher des Postens, Namens Quinn, ein geborener Irländer, welcher der Sioux=Sprache vollständig mächtig, eine Indianerin jenes Stammes zur Frau hatte und eine lange Reihe von Jahren mit und unter den Indianern gelebt. Daß die Wilden diesen Mann nicht schonten, sondern als einen der ersten niederschossen, bestätigt wiederholt die Thatsache, daß die Indianer im Allgemeinen, einige wenige ausgenommen, von dem Gefühl der Dankbarkeit keine Idee haben, und einmal am Morden, weder Freund noch Feind schonen. Quinn war der langjährige Freund ihres schurkischen Häuptlings Little Crow, und in Zeiten der höchsten Noth schlug das Herz dieses braven alten Mannes warm für die Stammesgenossen seiner Frau, denen er durch seine Fürsprache bei den Militär=Behörden in Fort Ridgely zum öfteren Lebensmittel aller Art verschaffte.

Doch überlassen wir Fort Ridgely mit seinen Kanonen und wenigen Soldaten vorläufig seinem Schicksale und wenden wir uns nach New Ulm, das den ersten Anprall der Indianer auszuhalten hatte.

Am Morgen des 18. August gegen 10 Uhr verließ eine Rekrutirungs=Parthie mit einer Musik=Kapelle im Gefolge auf mehreren Wagen die Stadt, und fuhr, um Rekruten für die Vereinigten Staaten anzuwerben, vorerst hinauf nach Milford, welches, an der Grenze der Indianer=Reservation gelegen, zu den am frühesten besiedelten und daher volkreichsten Towns in Brown County gehörte.

Der Kampf gegen die südliche Conföderation tobte ununterbrochen fort, und die neuerdings wieder aufgerufenen 500,000 Mann frischer Truppen bewiesen hinlänglich, daß es Onkel Sam bitterer Ernst sei, die Rebellen mit allen ihm zu

Gebot stehenden Mittel zu bekämpfen. Von Brown County und besonders aus der Hauptstadt desselben, der Stadt New Ulm, waren schon viele jüngere Männer dem Sternenbanner gefolgt, und wieder sollten zum Zwecke der Organisation einer Compagnie weitere Rekruten angeworben werden, um womöglich durch freiwilliges Aufbringen der letzteren dem so verhaßten Draften (Ausloosen) zuvor zu kommen. Darum der Auszug der oben erwähnten Rekrutirungs-Parthie am Morgen des 18. August 1862, welcher Auszug manchem der Betheiligten verhängnißvoll werden sollte.

Die Wirthschaft von Herrn Anton Henle, 8 Meilen von New Ulm, in genanntem Town Milford gelegen, war zum ersten Haltplatze bestimmt, und sollte hier mit dem Anwerben der nöthigen Mannschaften begonnen werden. Ungefähr eine halbe Meile von dem obigen Platze auf der Straße nach New Ulm zu kreuzt dieselbe eine kleine mit einer Brücke überspannte Schlucht. In jedem Frühjahr durch Wildwasser ausgewaschen, ist diese Schlucht hauptsächlich auf der rechten gegen den Minnesota-Fluß gelegene Seite der Brücke ziemlich tief und durch die an den Seiten angewachsenen Bäumen und Gesträucher so ziemlich verdeckt. Die Indianer sind nun, und das wird Jeder, der Indianerkriege mitgemacht, zugeben, wenn sie auch von der geregelten Kriegführung gar nichts verstehen, dennoch die besten Tirailleure der Welt. Jede kleine Bodenerhöhung, kaum fußhohes Gras, jedes wenn auch noch so kleine Gesträuch gewährt ihnen Deckung, und schlangenartig auf dem Bauche kriechend winden sie sich durch kleine Erdeinschnitte, und wehe Demjenigen, der ihnen im Kampfe gegenüber steht, und die so sehr nöthige Vorsicht einen Augenblick außer Acht läßt. In der nächsten Sekunde trifft den Unaufmerksamen der schwirrende Pfeil oder die pfeifende Kugel und das Skalpirmesser thut dann in der Regel seine abschließende, schreckliche Schuldigkeit. In offenem Kampfe ist die Rothhaut in der Regel eine feige Canaille und nur ausnahmsweise, wenn ein Häuptling oder eine beliebte Persönlichkeit ihrer näheren Blutsverwandten erschossen oder schwer verwundet wird, stürzt sich der Wilde in die Gefechtslinie, in den dichtesten Kugelregel und versucht mit heldenmüthiger Todesverachtung den Todten oder Verwundeten seinen Feinden zu entreißen.

Doch kehren wir nun nach der Abschweifung zurück zu unserer Rekrutirungs-Mannschaft. Die ersten Wagen hatten die verhängnißvolle kleine Brücke, welche über die Schlucht nahe Henle's Wirthschaft führte, kaum erreicht, da krachte eine Salve und zu Tode getroffen oder schwer verwundet fielen einige der Insassen dieser Fuhrwerke, die anderen hatten noch Zeit, sich durch eilige Flucht aus der Schußlinie zu retten. Die meuchelmörderischen Kugeln der wilden Bestien hatten, da die letzteren von dem Gesträuch der kleinen Schlucht gedeckt, den sich nähernden, keine Gefahr vermuthenden Weißen, sich in gesicherter Stellung gegenüber befanden, nur zu wohl ihr Ziel erreicht, denn drei der letzteren blieben auf dem Platze sofort liegen und einige andere, obgleich schwer verwundet konnten dennoch von den nachfolgenden Wagen aufgenommen und so gerettet werden. Diese Fuhrwerke traten nun ihren Rückzug so rasch als möglich nach New Ulm an, da an einen Widerstand gegen die Indianer darum nicht gedacht werden konnte, weil fast alle Theilnehmer an der Expedition unbewaffnet waren. Doch die drei auf dem Platze ermordeten New Ulmer Bürger, Fenske, Dietrich und Schneider, so wie überhaupt alle Theilnehmer an der Rekrutirungs=Parthie trugen sehr viel dazu bei, daß die Rothhäute in ihrer Mordlust nicht gleich weiter gingen, da sie wohl wußten, daß die Umgegend jetzt alarmirt war, und sie auf Widerstand stoßen würden, dem die feigen Canaillen, wo es immer angeht, gerne aus dem Wege gehen.

Mit Blitzesschnelle verbreitete sich nun die Schreckensnachricht von dem Ausbruch und den schon begangenem Greuelthaten der Indianer in der Umgegend, und von allen Seiten kamen die flüchtenden Landsleute mit ihren Familien auf Wagen, Pferden und zu Fuß nach dem schützenden New Ulm.

Sobald nun der damalige Sheriff von Brown County, Herr Charles Roos, ein braver und muthiger Mann, von der Sachlage unterrichtet war, begab er sich mit einer gut bewaffneten Sheriffsmannschaft nach dem Orte der That, da man immer noch der Ansicht war, daß nur einzelne kleine Banden der Rothhäute den Angriff auf die Rekrutirungs=Parthie und auf einzelne in der unmittelbaren Nähe der stattgefundenen Mordscenen wohnende Farmer unternommen hätten. Doch auch hier bestätigte sich wiederholt die Thatsache, daß der Wilde nur aus sicherem Hinterhalte, oder wenn die zehnfache Uebermacht auf seiner Seite ist, zu morden gewohnt ist; denn vor der kleinen bewaffneten Truppe des Sheriffs zogen sich die Indianer feige zurück, und der Sheriff hatte die Genugthuung, einige in den Kornfeldern versteckte Frauen und Kinder nebst einer Anzahl Verwundeter zu retten und nach New Ulm zu bringen.

Am späten Nachmittag desselben Tages wurde der Verfasser dieser Geschichte von dem Sheriff zum Platzkommandanten von New Ulm ernannt und als solcher in den Militärdienst des Staates Minnesota eingeschworen. Von nun an begann die eigentliche militärische Organisation, so gut diese in der Spanne Zeit, die noch bis zum vermuthlichen Angriffe der Indianer übrig blieb, bewerkstelligt werden konnte. Es befand sich allerdings sehr gutes Material unter den New Ulmer Bürgern und den in die Stadt geflüchteten Farmern zur Bildung von kleinen militärischen Körperschaften, aber dennoch muß jeder Vernünftige zugestehen, daß es keine geringe Aufgabe war, in dieses Durcheinander eine einigermaßen militärische Ordnung zu bringen, die es nur allein ermöglichen konnte, dem blutdürstigen, die Stadt vermuthlich bald angreifenden Feinde mit Nachdruck entgegen zu treten.

Wohlwissend, daß bei einem Massenangriffe der Indianer, welche über mehr als 900 wohlbewaffnete Krieger zu verfügen hatten, die geringen Streitkräfte der Stadt New Ulm und zudem die mangelhafte Bewaffnung der Vertheidiger selbst, nicht genügend seien, auf die Dauer den rothen Bluthunden einen energischen Widerstand entgegen zu setzen, und wohlwissend, daß mit der Zerstörung New Ulms das ganze untere Minnesota=Thal gefährdet würde und hauptsächlich die beiden tiefgelegenen Nachbarstädte Mankato und St. Peter zur Vertheidigung gegen die Wilden strategisch genommen keinen festen Anhaltspunkt boten, und daß daher dem Hülferufe New Ulms von dort her sofort freundnachbarlich entsprochen würde, sorgte der Commandant sogleich dafür, daß einige Ordonnanzen nach den beiden letztgenannten Städten entsandt wurden, welche die Bewohner derselben aufforderten, New Ulm sofort zu Hülfe zu eilen, da die Indianer ausgebrochen, und die Stadt sich in ernstlicher Gefahr befinde.

Prompt wurde dem Verlangen entsprochen und die Zusage gegeben, so bald als möglich mit allen disponibeln Kräften der bedrohten Stadt zu Hülfe zu eilen; doch konnten, worauf wir später zurückkommen werden, die ersten Hülfsmannschaf= ten erst gegen 7 Uhr Abends, am Dienstag, den 19. August, ihr Erscheinen hier machen.

Während dessen wurde mit der Eintheilung und Organisation der in der Stadt befindlichen und zum freiwilligen Dienste sich meldenden Männer und Jünglinge begonnen; ebenso wurde mit fieberhafter Hast der Bau von einigen Barikaden, zur besseren Vertheidigung, in Angriff genommen, und beim Licht der zu diesem Zwecke angezündeten Holzstöße während der Nacht bis zur nothdürftigen Vollendung fortgesetzt. Die mit den verschiedenartigsten Waffen versehenen Leute wurden in die folgenden Abtheilungen eingereiht, um mit ihnen wenigstens einiger= maßen militärisch operiren zu können:

I. Büchsen=Schützen, zum großen Theil frühere Cincinnatier Turner, unter Kommando von Louis Theobald, ungefähr 14 Mann.

II. Mit Doppelgewehren Bewaffnete, unter Kommando von E. F. Brunk, 18 Mann.

III. Mit einfachen, meistens schlechten Schrotflinten Bewaffnete, unter Kommando von J. Chaifowitz, 12 Mann.

Dazu kamen noch ungefähr 15 bis 18 Leute, die mit Schießgewehren der verschiedensten Gattung bewaffnet waren, aber sich keiner der obigen Abtheilungen anschließen wollten.

Das war also am Dienstag, den 19. August 1862, kurz vor dem Angriffe der Wilden, die mit Büchsen und Gewehren bewaffnete Macht der Stadt New Ulm, von welchen Waffen sich noch ein Theil als untauglich erwiesen. Dann kam allerdings eine Reserve, ausgerüstet mit Mist- und Heugabeln, Aexten jeder Art und einigen Revolvern, die aber nur dann zur Verwendung beordert werden konnte, wenn es den Indianern gelingen sollte, in die Stadt einzudringen. Wenn man nun bedenkt, daß sich zu der Zeit in New Ulm über 600 aus der Umgegend hereingeflüchtete und einheimische Frauen und Kinder befanden, daß viele Verwundete von auswärts hier Zuflucht gesucht, so kann man sich leicht vorstellen, daß es keine geringe Aufgabe war, so viele Hülflose vorläufig sicher unterzubringen. Frauen und Kinder waren denn auch in Backsteinhäusern und anderen gegen die Kugeln der Indianer gesicherten Gebäuden einquartiert, doch war ihnen der Raum daselbst sehr knapp zugemessen.

Während dieser Vorarbeiten und in dem Bewußtsein, daß der nächste Tag für New Ulm das Sein oder Nichtsein bestimmen würde, daß vielleicht schon am folgenden Abende die Stadt in einen Aschenhaufen verwandelt, und Hunderte von ihren Bewohnern unter demselben begraben sein würden, verbrachten der Platz-Kommandant und Sheriff sorgenvolle Stunden. Es war in der damaligen kleinen Sheriffs-Office an Minnesota-Straße wo die beiden Turner, Sheriff Roos und Platzkommandant Nix hinter einem kleinen Tische sitzend sich gegenseitig beriethen, um von Zeit zu Zeit die während der Nacht fortgesetzten Vertheidigungsarbeiten zu besichtigen.

Endlich, endlich brach der Morgen an. Ein schöner Morgen, wie der vorhergehende am 18. August, doch welcher Unterschied! Damals heiteres Lächeln und Vertrauen in die Zukunft und jetzt düstere Gedanken trotz aller Versicherungen und Ansprachen des Sheriffs und Kommandanten an die organisirten militärischen Abtheilungen, daß, wenn wir zusammen hielten, wir leicht Herr über das rothe Lumpengesindel werden könnten. Es war ein schöner aber trotz alledem ein trauriger Morgen, denn hatte nicht fast jeder der Vertheidiger eine Familie mit Frau und Kinder zu beschützen? Doch das letztere bezweckte, daß so Mancher, der vielleicht für den angestammten Fürsten in dem alten Vaterlande sich nicht halb so gut geschlagen, hier zum Helden wurde. Es galt ja, das treue Weib, die geliebten Kinder den Händen der rothen Bestien zu entreißen. Es galt hier nicht das angestammte Fürstenhaus, sondern die eigene theure Heimath zu beschützen; die Heimath, welche jetzt durch eine Handvoll braver Männer vertheidigt werden mußte, da die meisten jungen Leute sich schon in dem Dienste der Ver. Staaten-Regierung gegen die südliche Rebellion befanden. Es galt, mit wenigen Worten gesagt, Alles gegen Alles zu setzen, denn von Erbarmen, daß mußte man, konnte wenn siegend bei dem Indianer keine Sprache sein.

Der Verfasser dieses hat in seiner Jugend mit Vorliebe die Cooper'schen Romane gelesen. Hauptsächlich hat ihn „Der Letzte der Mohikaner" zur vollen

Begeisterung für die Rothhäute hingerissen; doch es ist von jeher das Unglück bei allen Romanen gewesen, daß die Phantasie die Hauptrolle gespielt und von Wahrheit auch keine Silbe daran war, denn hätte Cooper die wahre Natur der Indianer gekannt, er hätte sich vielleicht eher eine Kugel durch den Schädel gejagt, als so hirnverrücktes Zeug über die rothen Bluthunde zu schreiben. Ein schmutzigeres Gesindel, als die Indianer, mit welchen ich in Berührung gekommen, kann sich kein Mensch denken, und doch war es nicht der letzte der Mohikaner, den ich überhaupt niemals gesehen, sondern Stämme der rothen Bestien in Wisconsin, Minnesota, Dakota, Idaho, Montana und anderen nordwestlichen Gegenden, mit denen ich in nähere Berührung gekommen bin. Heimtückisch in seinem Charakter, dem Wohlthun und der aufrichtigsten Freundschaft von Seiten der Weißen ein kaltes, stolzes Benehmen gegenübersetzend, doch wenn hungernd, bettelnd und dann die verlangte Gabe unterwürfig empfangend, dabei mit einem Ho! Ho! dem Wohlthäter die Hand drückend, ihn aber, wo es angeht, bei der ersten, besten Gelegenheit feige zusammenschießen, das sind so ungefähr die Hauptkarakterzüge unsrer rothen Brüder.

Die Rothhäute im Allgemeinen hassen die Bleichgesichter, hassen sie glühend seit Jahrhunderten, seit jener Zeit wo die ersten Weißen auf diesem Continent erschienen sind, und man glaube ja nicht, daß die heutige Generation der Indianer vergessen habe, oder es nicht wisse, daß das ganze umfangreiche Gebiet der Vereinigten Staaten einst einzig und allein ihren Vorfahren gehörte, daß ihre Jagdgründe belebt und angefüllt mit dem verschiedenartigsten Wild gewesen; die Wilden wissen es ebenso gut, wie wir es wissen, und daher stammt ihr unversöhnlicher Haß gegen die Bleichgesichter, ein Haß, der nur auf Gelegenheit wartet, die letzteren zu vernichten. Man reize den Indianer nicht durch Ungerechtigkeiten, aber wenn er für die Schlechtigkeit Einzelner die Bewohner ganzer Länderstriche büßen läßt, mordend, brennend und sengend den friedlichen weißen Ansiedler überfällt, alles niedermacht, Männer und Weiber, Greise und Kinder, welche ihm vor Flinte, Bogen oder Tomahawk kommen, da rufe man jene fanatischen Pfaffen, welche sich sofort nach der Niederwerfung eines Indianer-Aufstandes der gefangenen rothen Mordbrenner salbungsvoll annehmen, da schleudere man den heuchlerischen, augenverdrehenden Dienern des Herrn aus ihrer Bibel die inhaltschweren Worte entgegen: Auge um Auge — Zahn um Zahn! Das heißt, man erschieße oder hänge jeden rothen Schurken, der sich an Gräuelscenen betheiligte, wie sie im Spätsommer 1862 in Minnesota stattgefunden, sofort nach seiner Gefangennahme ohne weiteres Federlesen. Doch vorwärts, nehmen wir den Faden unserer Geschichte wieder auf. Es war also nach einer ahnungsvoll verbrachten Nacht. Die aufgehende Sonne beschien abermals die schön gelegene Turnerstadt, doch wie ganz anders sah es hier aus, als vor 24 Stunden! Damals friedliche Ruhe, jetzt Waffengeräusch, Anrufen patrolirender Mannschaften, innere und äußere Vorpostenkette, Barikaden u. s. w., kurz die gestern noch so ruhige Stadt New Ulm war heute der Tummelplatz Bewaffneter, und wenn die letzteren auch nicht uniformirt, wenn auch nicht mit fliegenden Fahnen und klingendem Spiele auf= und abmarschiert wurde, so sah man doch den in bürgerlicher Kleidung bei dem Verlesen erscheinenden Männer an, daß sie wußten, weshalb sie die Rollen so schnell vertauscht, gestern noch ruhige Bürger und stille Landleute, und heute — Soldaten. Ja, man sah es den braven Vertheidigern der Stadt New Ulm auf den ersten Blick an, was ihnen heute die mörderischen Waffen in die Hand gedrückt. Es galt die Vertheidigung der Heimath und ihrer Lieben. Der Morgen verlief sonst ziemlich ruhig. Nur Gerüchtsweise verlautete es, daß sich eine Menge von Indianern oben in Milford gesammelt, und die Stadt sehr wahrscheinlich heute noch angegriffen würde. Alle Vorbereitungen für einen warmen Empfang der Rothhäute waren getroffen, die Barikaden gut besetzt, die inneren und äußeren Posten verdoppelt, und man sah so den Dingen, die da kommen würden, mit einem gewissen Selbstvertrauen entgegen.

Es war gegen 2 Uhr am Nachmittage, da kam die Nachricht in die Stadt, daß eine Parthie Farmer von Cottonwood, einem an New Ulm angrenzenden Town in Brown County, die sich in die Stadt zu flüchten beabsichtigten, mit ihren Familien ungefähr eine Meile von dem Centrum der letzteren, von Indianern eingeschlossen seien, und den letzteren in die Hände fallen würden, wenn sie nicht durch Hülfe aus der Stadt aus ihrer peinlichen Lage befreit würden. Bewaffnete Hülfe aus der Stadt, wie konnte man solche jetzt entbehren, da man nicht wußte, von welcher Seite und wann man von den Rothhäuten angegriffen würde! Der Commandant wies das Ansuchen zuerst energisch zurück, gab aber schließlich durch die Bitten so Vieler, den armen Leuten **zu** helfen, bewogen, seine Einwilligung und entsandte Louis Theobald mit seinen Schützen mit dem Rathe sich nicht allzulange da draußen aufzuhalten, das heißt wenn thunlich **die Leute zu** befreien, und dann so schnell als möglich mit ihnen nach der Stadt zu kommen.

Doch es verging mehr als eine halbe Stunde **und** weder die eingeschlossenen Cottonwooder noch die ihnen zur Hülfe gesandten Schützen kamen in Sicht. Weil nun das Ausbleiben der letzteren besorgen ließ, **daß** sie vielleicht selbst abgeschnitten seien, ward E. F. Brunk mit seiner **Mannschaft** beordert, im Laufschritt vorzugehen, Theobald helfend die Hand zu reichen, doch unter allen Umständen sollten alsdann beide Abtheilungen so schnell **wie möglich** nach New Ulm zurückkehren. Traurig aber wahr ist die Thatsache, daß **das Leben** so vieler braven Leute einem falschen Bericht, einer erbärmlichen Lüge **wegen auf** das Spiel gesetzt war, denn wie es sich später herausstellte, war von **den eingeschlossenen** Cottonwoodern nirgends eine Spur zu finden.

Jetzt war es nahezu 3 Uhr am Nachmittage, da wurden durch den Ingenieur Brockmann, der zu diesem Zwecke mit einem großen Fernrohre auf dem Plattdache eines hohen Backsteinhauses postirt war, die ersten Indianer gesehen. Sie ritten, von Milford kommend, die Anhöhe, welche sich oberhalb des städtischen Friedhofes gegen letzteres Town hinzieht, herab, theilten sich in der Nähe des Friedhofes in zwei Abtheilungen und schwenkten dann in weiten Bogen nach der Stadt.

Auf Eure Posten! Fertig zum Gefecht! ertönte das Kommando, und lange sollte man auf den Beginn des Gefechtes jetzt nicht mehr zu warten haben. Die Wilden welche hier auf den ersten Widerstand stießen, schäumten vor Wuth, näherten sich den Barikaden unter infernalischem Geschrei und schossen zuerst. Im nächsten Augenblicke tobte der erbitterte Kampf auf allen Seiten. Todte und Verwundete gab es sofort in den Reihen der Vertheidiger, wie auch auf Seiten der rothen Bluthunde. Hinter dem Commandanten, dem, nebenbei gesagt, eine der ersten feindlichen Kugeln den sogenannten Ring=Finger wegriß, und von ihm selbst nicht gesehen, trat ein dreizehnjähriges Mädchen, trotz dem vorhergegangenen strengen Befehle, daß alle, welche nicht direkt in das Gefecht eingreifen konnten, bis nach dem Verlaufe desselben die schützenden Häuser nicht verlassen sollten, aus einer der Hausthüren, und war eine halbe Minute später, von einer feindlichen Kugel in die Stirne getroffen, eine Leiche.

Mehr und mehr Indianer erschienen, alle gut bewaffnet, auf der Bildfläche, wüthender und wüthender wurden ihre Angriffe, und noch immer waren die bestbewaffneten der Vertheidiger draußen außerhalb der Gefechtslinie. Ob sie wohl das Schießen hören? Und sie hatten es gehört! Durch sein Fernrohr sah sie der Kommandirende deutlich.

Haltet aus Leute, wir sind bald Herr über das rothe Lumpengesindel, rief er, und sie hielten wacker aus, keinen Zoll lang hatten die wilden Bestien sich seit ihrem ersten Angriffe den Barikaden genähert. Ha! wie sie jetzt heranstürmten in einer langen gedehnten Linie, voran die Schützen Louis Theobald, John Spenner, John Hauenstein, Ernst Brandt, Charles Pfau und wie sie alle hießen, dann die mit Doppelt=Gewehren Bewaffneten unter Brunk, wie sie ihre Kugeln rechts und links in die Flanken der feige zurückfallenden Indianer entsendeten, nur von dem Gedanken beseelt, ihren bedrängten Kampfgenossen die so nöthige Hülfe zu bringen. Und sie war nöthig, diese Hülfe, denn immer mehr Indianer erschienen vor den Barikaden und anderen Vertheidigungswerken. Doch ihre oft wiederholten Angriffe, die, von bestialischem Geschrei begleitet, sich manchmal bis zur völligen Raserei steigerten, scheiterten an den wohlgezielten Schüssen, dem Muthe und der beharrlichen Ausdauer der Vertheidiger.

Immer wilder und wilder tobte jetzt der Kampf auf allen Seiten der ange=

griffenen Stadt. Die Indianer, meistens trefflich bewaffnet und hinreichend mit Munition versehen, hatten dieses den Belagerten voraus, denn die Munition hauptsächlich fing bei den letzteren bereits an knapp zu werden. Doch man wußte sich zu helfen, denn da Pulver selbst noch ziemlich vorhanden war, und es nur an Kugeln mangelte, so wurden alle Schrotsäcke mit ihrem Inhalte aus den Kaufläden geholt, und an geeigneten Plätzen wurden die kleinen, runden, bleiernen Kügelchen in vollwichtige Kugeln von jedem nöthigen Kaliber umgegossen. Mit furchtbarer Erbitterung wurde unterdessen weiter gekämpft. Auf der einen Seite die sich steigernde Wuth, daß bei allen ihren verzweifelten Angriffen kein weiterer Grund und Boden gewonnen werden konnte, auf der anderen Seite das Bewußtsein, daß, wenn es den rothen Mördern gelingen sollte in die Stadt einzudringen, dieselbe in einen Schutthaufen verwandelt, und das Loos der Ihrigen ein schreckliches, nicht zu beschreibendes sein würde.

Und doch Little Crow hatte es ja seinem Bruder Little Priest, dem Häuptling und Hauptspitzbuben der Winnebagos, versprochen, New Ulm mit dem vierten Theile seiner Krieger zu nehmen, und das gegenseitige Uebereinkommen dieser beiden Canaillen gipfelte in dem Endresultat, daß sobald New Ulm von den Sioux genommen, die Winnebagos sich der Stadt Mankato bemächtigen sollten, und daß alsdann die vereinten beiden Räuberbanden mordend, brennend und sengend das ganze Minnesota=Thal heimsuchen wollten.

Der Verfasser dieses, der im Frühjahr 1863 mit seiner Compagnie berittener „Rangers" in St. Peter, 30 Meilen unterhalb New Ulm am Minnesota=Fusse gelegen, stationirt war, bekam eines schönen Morgens von Oben herab den Befehl, den gewöhnlichen Landungsplatz der kleinen Dampfer, welche den Minnesota=Fluß befuhren, mit seiner Compagnie abzusperren, damit den von Mankato per Dampfer herabgebrachten Winnebago=Indianer, welche in andere Regionen versetzt werden sollten, kein Leid geschehe.

Ein harter Befehl allerdings, denn jeder seiner „Ranger" hätte lieber einem halben Dutzend der rothen Schufte den Hirnschädel gespalten, als ihnen Schutz gegen etwaige Angriffe der Bewohner von St. Peter und Umgegend gewährt. Bei dieser Gelegenheit lernte ich den Schuft Little Priest, der allerdings jetzt nicht gut auf seinen weiland Freund und Mordbruder Little Crow zu sprechen war, kennen und hörte aus seinem eigenen Munde die Bestätigung des oben Gesagten, das abgeschlossene Bündniß zwischen ihm und Little Crow. Der Kerl saß mit anderen Indianern seiner Bande Karten spielend auf dem Verdecke des kleinen Dampfers und erklärte auf Anfrage, daß es ihm, wenn Little Crow sein Wort gehalten, das heißt New Ulm am Dienstag den 19. August 1862 genommen, das größte Vergnügen bereitet hätte, so viele Skalps wie möglich in Mankato und anderen Plätzen des Minnesota-Thales zu nehmen. Man erlaube mir diese kleine Abschweifung, welche einfach die Thatsache unumstößlich feststellt, daß das tapfere Verhalten der Vertheidiger der Stadt New Ulm am 19. August 1862 dem Ausbruch der Winnebago's ein Halt zugerufen, und dadurch ein Unglück verhütet, das die Geschichte dieses schönen Landstriches bis jetzt noch nicht zu verzeichnen gehabt und hoffentlich auch nie zu verzeichnen bekommen wird. Und nun zurück zu unseren braven Vertheidigern der Stadt New Ulm.

Hier tobte der Kampf ununterbrochen fort. Wüthende oft wiederholte Angriffe der rothen Bestien folgten einer dem anderen, aber jedesmal, wenn die Indianer durch die Wirkung ihres schnell aufeinander folgenden Gewehrfeuer eben einen kleinen Vortheil über die Belagerten errungen hatten, so wurden sie doch innerhalb einer kurzen Spanne Zeit durch die letzteren aus ihren vorgerückten Stellungen wieder hinausgeworfen.

Die äußerste Grenze der Wuth bemächtigte sich nun der Wilden, ihr furchtbares Geschrei, das man selbst gehört haben muß, um darüber ein Urtheil zu fällen, entsetzte selbst Männer, die man sonst nicht zu Feiglingen stempeln konnte, und die auch während des Kampfes sich brav und tüchtig gehalten. Am hartnäckigsten wurde um den Besitz der Barrikade gekämpft, welche gegen den südlichen Theil der Stadt hin errichtet war. Mehrere Male versuchten die Indianer dieses Vertheidigungswerk der Belagerten im heftigen Ansturm zu nehmen, wurden jedoch jedesmal von den letzteren mit blutigen Köpfen zurückgetrieben. Auch von der nordwestlichen Seite her stürmten die Wilden mit toller Wuth, doch scheiterten ihre von dieser Seite her unternommenen Angriffe an dem kaltblütigen Muthe der dort aufgestellten Mannschaft und dem gut unterhaltenen Gewehrfeuer derselben. Hier war es, wo die rothen Hallunken drei außerhalb der Vertheidigungslinie gelegene Häuser in Brand steckten, doch waren diese drei Gebäude die einzigen, welche am 19. August 1862 bei dem Angriffe der Sioux-Indianer auf die Turnerstadt New Ulm in Flammen aufgingen.

Die Behauptung, daß bei dem ersten Angriff der Rothhäute dieselben die Stadt genommen, zum großen Theil abgebrannt, viele ihrer Einwohner ermordet, und die Ueberlebenden nur durch rechtzeitig eingetroffene Hülfe von auswärts gerettet worden seien, ist gelinde gesagt ein kolossaler Irrthum. Wäre an jenem verhängnißvollen Augusttage New Ulm genommen worden, hätte die Tapferkeit seiner braven Vertheidiger die Wilden dazumal nicht mit blutigen Köpfen heimgeschickt, dann wäre sicher und gewiß jenes Programm, das der Räuberhauptmann der Sioux, Little Crow, mit dem Räuberhauptmann der Winnebago's, Little Priest, aufgestellt, ausgeführt worden, und die früher erwähnte Katastrophe, der ein großer Theil der Bewohner des Minnesota-Thales zum Opfer gefallen wäre, hätte nicht lange auf sich warten lassen.

Der 19. August des Jahres 1862 wird daher in der Geschichte New Ulms für immer ein ebenso denkwürdiger Tag sein, eine ebenso hervorragende Stellung einnehmen, wie der 23. August desselben Jahres.

Die Indianer, auf der nordwestlichen Seite der Stadt zurückgetrieben, versuchten nun ihr Heil auf der nordöstlichen Seite. Aber auch hier stießen sie, nachdem sie sich, gedeckt durch das hohe Gras des German Park und einiger in demselben angepflanzter Kornfelder, herangeschlichen, auf den heftigsten Widerstand und mußten sich, einige ihrer Todten und Verwundeten, ihrem Gebrauche gemäß, mit sich nehmend, zurückziehen.

Von jetzt an, und nachdem sie wahrscheinlich weitere Verstärkung erhalten, änderten die rothen Bluthunde ihren Angriffsplan, und drangen mit ihrem furchtbaren Geschrei von allen Seiten gleichzeitig gegen die Stadt vor. Ein mörderischer Kampf entspann sich nun, denn es galt ja bei den Angegriffenen Alles gegen Alles zu setzen, und wacker hielten sie Stand. Da, es war gegen 4½ Uhr Nachmittags, kam ein Bundesgenosse den Belagerten zu Hülfe an den vorher Niemand gedacht hatte: die Natur selbst erklärte sich zu ihren Gunsten. Ein Gewitter zog, erst langsam und kaum hörbar, von Südosten herauf, entwickelte sich mehr und mehr je näher es der hart bedrängten Stadt kam, und entlud sich über dem Haupte derselben mit der furchtbaren Gewalt, wie sie diesen Naturerscheinungen im Minnesota-Thale gewöhnlich eigen ist. Furchtbarer Donner und strömender Regen, untermischt mit dem Heulen des begleitenden Sturmes unterbrachen den Kampf; die entfesselten Elemente hatten durch ihr Eingreifen den Angreifern Ruhe geboten. Seltener und seltener hörte man das Schießen der Indianer bis es zuletzt, etwas nach 5 Uhr, ganz aufhörte.

Der Kampf war für heute vorüber, die Belagerten athmeten auf, und das Selbstvertrauen des Siegers, das höhere Bewußtsein, einen übermächtigen, blutdürstigen Feind, besser bewaffnet als sie selbst, von ihrer Stadt zurückgetrieben zu haben, dieses Bewußtsein stählte ihre Nerven mit eiserner Kraft. Bei den Rothhäuten war das Entgegengesetzte der Fall. Sie, die seit ihrem gestrigen Ausbruch nirgends auf Widerstand gestoßen, nach Herzenslust morden, brennen und alle möglichen Gräuelthaten begehen konnten, sie wurden, und das wußten sie genau, heute von einer Handvoll tapferer Männer, mit blutigen Köpfen gerade von demjenigen Platze zurückgetrieben, den sie am 19. August ihren Verbündeten, den Winnebagos gegenüber, gewissermaßen contractlich gebunden, mit stürmender Hand zu nehmen versprochen hatten.

Die Ansichten, in wie weit der rollende Donner und der strömende Regen vereint mit der Tapferkeit der Belagerten zu dem endgültigen Siege derselben beigetragen, sind sehr verschieden. Die Einen behaupten, daß den Indianern das Pulver naß geworden und sie, dem Unwetter vollständig preisgegeben, in Folge dessen den Kampf einzustellen gezwungen waren. Die Anderen (und mit ihnen der Verfasser) beurtheilen das Aufgeben des Kampfes von Seiten der Rothhäute von einem anderen Standpunkte.

Der Aberglaube spielte von jeher bei allen wilden Völkern, welchem Welttheile sie auch angehören, eine Hauptrolle. Gewöhnliche Naturereignisse, wie Sonnen- und Mondfinsternisse, Erdbeben, der Blitz und Donner eines Gewitters, ja, selbst das Anbrechen der Nacht erschüttern mehr oder weniger das Nervensystem uncivilisirter Völker. „Manitou zürnt und überläßt uns der Gewalt des bösen Geistes," sagt der Indianer in der Regel bei einem sehr starken Gewitter, und viele Stämme der Rothhäute stellen, wenn auch zur Zeit im bewußten Vortheile, den Kampf ein und lassen ihre Waffen ruhen sobald die Nacht hereingebrochen, und die ersten Sterne am Firmamente erschienen sind. Der schaurige Kultus seiner Religion, seine medizinische „Wissenschaft" und Anderes mehr ruhen bei dem Indianer auf dem Fundamente des Aberglaubens. Man glaube ja nicht, daß der zum Christenthum übergetretene Indianer davon eine Ausnahme macht, im Gegentheil, er wird durch seinen Uebertritt nur noch mehr in der Meinung bestärkt, daß alle Vorgänge in der ungeheuren Unendlichkeit von unsichtbaren Geistern geleitet werden, und zu seinem indianischen kommt noch der christliche Gott, zu seinen ewigen Jagdgründen gesellt sich der Himmel und die Hölle und da er das Alte nicht lassen kann und das Neue auch glauben soll, so sind seine Sinne durch diese doppelten Eindrücke erst recht verwirrt und der zum Christenthum bekehrte wilde Natursohn ist abergläubischer als er es je vorher gewesen.

Die Vorgänge auf den beiden obengenannten Agenturen, wo sich viele zum Christenthum bekehrte Indianer befanden, welche sich gerade so gut wie die unbekehrten an der Abschlachtung der Weißen betheiligten, keinen Unterschied machend ob es ihr eigener christlicher Pfarrer und Doctor oder ein anderes christliches weißes Mitglied der Gesellschaft war, beweisen hinlänglich, daß der neubekehrte Indianer ein ebenso schlechtes, ja in gewissen Fällen noch viel schlechteres Subject ist, als die wildeste aller wilden Rothhäute. Nur durch gute, vernünftig geleitete Schulen, die hauptsächlich sich der Aufgabe unterziehen, auf die indianische Jugend belehrend einzuwirken, wird es möglich sein, später eine bessere Generation der Rothhäute heranzubilden; doch der sogenannte bekehrte alte Indianer ist, was er früher gewesen, ein Indianer, bei dem eben so gut, wie bei dem unbekehrten, bei der ersten besten Gelegenheit die in seinem Inneren hausende Bestie zum Durchbruche kommt.

Um nun den thatsächlichen Beweis zu liefern, daß die Rothhäute im Allgemeinen bei Naturereignissen, wie schweren Gewittern u. s. w. oder bei dem Anbrechen der Nacht, den Kampfplatz verlassen, selbst wenn sie im entschiedenen Vortheile sind, will der Verfasser eine kleine Episode aus seinem eigenen Leben erzählen.

Es war im August des Jahres 1864, an der Grenze von Dakota und Montana, als ich eines späten Nachmittags den Befehl erhielt mit 15 bis 20 meiner Leute abzusitzen, die Pferde der Betreffenden mit dem anderen Theil der Compagnie zurück zu lassen und mit Carabiner und Revolver bewaffnet zu Fuß eine gewisse mir näher bezeichnete Gegend nach einer ausgesandten und bis jetzt nicht zurückgekehrten Patrouille abzusuchen. Das Terrain war ein zerrissenes und zerklüftetes, wie es in den Lavabetten draußen in den Plains nicht anders angetroffen wird. Vorsichtig, Schritt auf Schritt genauen Auslug haltend, näherten wir uns eben einem kleinen Lavahügel, von dem wir wußten, daß die erwähnte Patrouille ihn passirt haben mußte; doch in demselben Augenblicke als wir uns eben an den Hügel anlehnten, um eine einigermaßen gedeckte Stellung zu ermöglichen, im Falle wir angegriffen würden, sahen wir aus allen Schluchten und hinter Felsen auf uns lauernde Indianer heran kommen, die uns im Augenblick den Rückzug abgeschnitten und dann vollständig umzingelt hatten. Wer nun die rothe Bestie kennt, wer da weiß mit welcher Wollust sie die in ihre Hände gerathenen Gefangenen langsam zu Tode martert, der wird es begreiflich finden, daß von einer Uebergabe an die zwanzigfache Uebermacht keine Rede sein konnte. Also Kampf auf Leben und Tod, und wenn nicht anders die letzte Kugel des Carabiners oder Revolvers für den eigenen Hirnschädel aufbewahrt.

Mittlerweile schlossen die Indianer ihren uns einschließenden Ring immer enger und enger, doch gedeckt durch Steinblöcke, ausgerüstet mit den besten Waffen, Sharp's Carabinern, Colt's Navy Revolvern (die Säbel waren, weil hindernd für den abgesessenen Cavalleristen beim Marschiren, bei der Compagnie zurückgeblieben) und hinreichend mit Munition versehen, konnten und mußten wir, da uns zudem nichts anderes übrig blieb, den Angriffen der Indianer ruhig entgegen sehen, da wir außerdem wußten, daß die mit dem gewohnten höllischen Geschrei sich nähernde große Zahl der Wilden aus ebenso vielen Feiglingen bestand, deren größte Masse noch obendrein nur mit Pfeil und Bogen und ein verschwindend kleiner Theil mit alten Schrotflinten bewaffnet war. Der Pfeil des Indianers, welcher im Besitze eines guten Bogens ist, und denselben, was ihnen übrigens von Kindheit an schon eingeprägt wird, gut zu handhaben versteht, verfehlt auf 70 bis 80 Schritte höchst selten sein Ziel, doch schon auf eine Entfernung von 120 bis 130 Schritte sinkt er in der Regel ermattet zu Boden.

Die uns nun angreifenden Rothhäute, meistens dem Stamme der Blackfeet angehörend, näherten sich mit der Schlauheit ihrer Race. Schlangen gleich kroch ein Theil derselben durch das sie deckende Steingerölle, während andere auf der freieren Seite unsrer Position unter fürchterlichem Geschrei in größerer Anzahl auf uns eindrangen, und, ob die Tragkraft unserer Waffen nicht genau kennend, oder aus welcher anderer Ursache sie sich diesmal, ganz gegen ihre sonstige Gewohnheit, zu nahe heran wagten, sie kamen in die Schußlinie, und auf das leise abgegebene Kommando: Aim! Fire! krachten achtzehn Carabiner und 10 bis 12 Indianer wälzten sich, einige sammt ihren Ponies zu Tode getroffen in ihrem Blute. Doch da ein Häuptling unter den Gefallenen war erneuerten sie, von allen Seiten anf uns eindringend, ihre Angriffe mit einem Wuthgeschrei das mir, wenn ich heute daran denke, noch in den Ohren klingt. Enger und enger ward aber jetzt der uns einschließende Kreis; Schuß auf Schuß krachte ohne indeß den sich jetzt hinter Steinen deckenden Rothhäuten weiteren großen Schaden zuzufügen. Unsere Situation war eine verzweifelte, denn das ununterbrochene Schießen hielt uns die rothen Teufel wohl vom Leibe, aber unsre Munition ging dadurch von Minute zu Minute mehr auf die Neige. Da zog vom Osten her ein Gewitter auf, es wurde früher dunkel als gewöhnlich, und ehe Hülfe zu unsrer Rettung herbei kam, gaben die Indianer den Kampf auf, obgleich sie sehr gut wußten, daß unsere Munition nahezu verbraucht war. Wie mir später von unsren Scouts, Halb= Indianern, denen ich die Einzelheiten dieses Gefechts erzählt, mitgetheilt wurde, fürchtet die Rothaut einen Kampf in der Nacht, ist aber noch ein aufziehendes Ge= witter mit derselben im Bündnisse, dann läßt der Indianer seine Waffen ruhen, und zieht sich von dem Kampfplatze unter jeder Bedingung zurück. Es ist der Aberglaube, daß der große Geist gegen ihn ist und ihn den bösen Geistern von jetzt ab preisgibt. Dies zur Erläuterung meiner Ansicht, daß das Gewitter, welches den braven Vertheidigern New Ulms am Nachmittage des 19. August 1862 zu Hülfe kam, die abergläubischen Indianer mehr zum Aufgeben des Kampfes be= wog, als das naßgewordene Pulver. Doch sei dem wie es wolle, nachdem die In= bianer an dem oben genannten Tage etwas nach 5 Uhr Nachmittags nach verzwei= feltem Kampfe zurückgetrieben waren, und ihnen dadurch die Ueberzeugung beige= bracht wurde, daß es, so wie Little Crow seinem Bundesgenossen Little Priest versprochen, keine so leichte Aufgabe war die Turnerstadt New Ulm mir nichts dir nichts einzunehmen und zu zerstören, da erst, nachdem der Kampf fast eine Stunde vorbei war, kam die erste Hülfe für New Ulm. Es war dieses die Bordman'sche Cavallerie, oder besser gesagt ungefähr 25 berittene Bürger von St. Peter und Umgegend. Es läßt sich nicht abläugnen, daß diese schnell der anderen vorausge= sandte Hülfe unsrer Nachbarstadt St. Peter freudig begrüßt wurde, um so mehr, da uns gleichzeitig die Kunde wurde, daß im Laufe der nächsten Nacht noch einige hundert Mann von St. Peter und Umgegend hier eintreffen würden. Es ist uns nie eingefallen, das Verdienst der auf unsren ersten Aufruf so bereitwillig herbei geeilte Hülfe unsrer Nachbarstädte St. Peter und Mankato und insbesondere des braven Judge Flandreau irgendwie schmälern zu wollen, aber dagegen müssen und werden wir jeder Zeit protestiren, weil es eine Unwahrheit ist, daß die Bordman'sche Cavallerie den Kampf in New Ulm am 19. August durch ihr Eingreifen in das Gefecht erst zur Entscheidung gebracht habe. Der Kampf war bei dem Erscheinen der 25 Berittenen faktisch vorüber, und die letzteren wurden gleich nach ihrer Ankunft in den beiden Gasthöfen Dakota= und Minnesota=House sammt ihren Pferden fürs erste einquartirt. Von Bürgern von St. Peter, welche während des ersten Kampfes vom Beginne desselben bis zu seinem Ende in der Stadt waren, möchte ich den späteren Gouverneur von Minnesota, Herrn Swift, anführen, der mit seinem langen Kentucky Rifle treffliche Dienste gethan; möglicher Weise war noch einer oder der andere von dort ebenfalls hier, doch sicher behaupten kann ich es nicht. Gerechtigkeit einem Jeden, aber auch Ehre wem Ehre gebührt. Der Hauptkampf zum Schutze der weißen Ansiedler im Minnesota=Thal ward am 19. August 1862 in New Ulm ausgekämpft; und dieser Kampf, der den blutdürstigen Rothhäuten ein: Bis hierher und nicht weiter! zugerufen, er ward mit verschwindend wenig Ausnahme nur von deutschen Männern ausgefochten. Die deutsche Stadt ward am 19. August 1862 durch Deutsche vertheidigt und gerettet, und wird dieser Tag so lange New Ulm steht ein ewig denkwürdiger in seiner Geschichte sein. Einige Englisch=Amerikaner, welche sich am Montag nach New Ulm geflüchtet, 13 bis 15 an der Zahl, bildeten für sich eine eigene Organisation, und verließen, trotz der Einsprache des Commandanten, am Morgen des entscheidenden Kampftages, alle trefflich bewaffnet, die Stadt, und kamen gegen das Ende des Gefechts, von den Indianern hart verfolgt, vier oder fünf Todte und mehrere Verwundete draußen lassend, zum zweiten Male Hülfe suchend nach New Ulm, welche ihnen auch bereitwilligst gewährt wurde.—Es ist die Pflicht des Geschichtschreibers, Namen vor die Oeffentlichkeit zu bringen, deren Träger sich durch geleistete Dienste der Wohlthätigkeit ein Anrecht darauf erworben. Keinem etwas zu lieb und keinem etwas zu leid; aber was Dr. Alfred Müller während des Kampfes der Rothhäute für Fort Ridgely gewesen, das war Dr. Carl Weschcke für New Ulm. Es war am späten Abend des in der Geschichte New Ulms mit rother Dinte verzeichneten Tages, als der Verfasser dieses in die Office des jungen Arztes trat, um sich die Wunde, welche er gleich bei dem Angriff der Indianer erhalten, untersuchen zu lassen. Der Anblick, welcher sich mir hier bot, wird meinem Gedächtnisse niemals entschwinden. Ringsherum an den Wänden lagen auf Betten und Matratzen Schwer= und Leichtverwundete; einer der ersteren bewußtlos mit dem Tode ringend, der ihn auch in derselben Nacht noch erlöste; und mitten unter ihnen auf einer Matratze lag der pflichtgetreue Arzt, auf den Tod ermüdet von der traurigen Arbeit des vergangenen Tages. Langsam, wie ich gekommen, verließ ich die Office, fest entschlossen, die Behandlung meiner Wunde selbst unkundigeren Händen anzuvertrauen, als dem braven jungen Mann die für ihn so nöthige Ruhe auch nur auf Augenblicke zu rauben. Der Namen Dr. Carl Weschcke, dessen Träger gegenwärtig Mayor der Stadt ist, wird in der Geschichte New Ulm's für immer einen hervorragenden Platz einnehmen, denn Ehre, wem Ehre gebührt!

Zum Theil noch in der Nacht und in der Frühe des folgenden Morgens traten die Indianer ihren Rückzug an, doch nur, um sich in der Gegend von Fort Ridgely mit anderen dort noch raubenden und mordenden Banden ihrer Sippschaft zu vereinigen und dann gemeinschaftlich das genannte Fort anzugreifen.

Lassen wir nun New Ulm sich von dem stattgefundenen Kampfe etwas erholen und folgen wir den rothen Teufeln nach dem Schauplatz ihrer nächsten mörderischen Thätigkeit, nach dem Fort selbst, um auszufinden, wie sie dort empfangen und bedient wurden.

Nach dem Abmarsche des braven Capitain Marsh und seiner 50 Mann, von denen, wie oben angegeben, nur 13 das Fort lebend wieder erreichten, übernahm der erste Lieutenant der Compagnie das Kommando über den Platz, doch faktisch war der, der regulären Armee angehörende, und dort stationirte Ordonnanz-Sergeant Jones (später Capitain der dritten Minnesotaer Batterie) der Kommandant. Die ganze dort nach dem Abzug der fünfzig Mann befindliche Besatzung an gesunden und waffenfähigen Soldaten mochte die Zahl zwanzig nicht übersteigen. Dazu kam allerdings eine große Anzahl hereingeflüchteter Farmer und Anderer, welche sich insgesammt zum Militärdienst bequemen mußten, und thaten einige derselben, früher gediente Soldaten, darunter Herr Werner Bösch, seit Jahren in New Ulm wohnhaft, treffliche Dienste. Fünfzig Mann unter Lieutenant Sheenah, welche von Fort Ripley, am oberen Mississippi in Minnesota gelegen, nach den beiden Agenturen verlegt waren, und am Tage vor dem Ausbruch der Indianer ihren Rückmarsch nach dem genannten Platze angetreten, waren durch eine Staffette zurück nach Fort Ridgely beordert, woselbst sie wohlbehalten noch zur rechten Zeit eintrafen. Weitere Hülfe erschien und konnten jetzt die Vertheidiger, außerdem gestützt auf ihre Kanonen und die treffliche Bedienung derselben, dem Angriff der Rothhäute mit Selbstvertrauen entgegen sehen. Vor den Kanonen hat der Indianer einen großen Respect, und dem letzteren war es auch wohl anzurechnen, daß einige Tage vor dem Ausbrechen der rothen Hallunken eine Bande derselben die Geschütze des Forts bei Nachtzeit mit Lumpen verstopfte, so, daß als sie abgefeuert werden sollten, sie natürlich versagten, und, als man die desfallsige

Urſache entdeckte, ſelbſtverſtändlich erſt von ihrem regelwibrigen Inhalte befreit werden mußten. Wie die Kerle ſich aber bis zu den Kanonen heranſchleichen konnten war und iſt heute noch ein ungelöſtes Räthſel. Wir wollen und können natürlich nicht die Einzelheiten des nun folgenden ſchrecklichen Kampfes der Reihe nach hier verzeichnen, vielmehr werden wir uns darauf beſchränken, zu erklären, daß die oft wiederholten, bis zur Raſerei ſich ſteigernden Angriffe der Indianer in dem blutigen zweitägigen Ringen um den Beſitz des Forts an dem kalten Muthe und dem wohlunterhaltenen Artillerie-Feuer der Vertheidiger ſtets ſcheiterten.

Hauptſächlich war es dem braven Sergeanten Jones, ſeinen Kanonen und der trefflichen Bedienungsmannſchaft derſelben zu verdanken, daß die Rothhäute auch hier mit blutigen Köpfen zurückgetrieben wurden. In den Reihen der weißen Vertheidiger dieſes Militär-Poſtens befanden ſich einige Halbindianer, welche gute Dienſte leiſteten.

Wiederholt wurden dieſe Halbwilden von den ſie angreifenden Indianern aufgefordert, zu ihnen überzutreten, weil von dem Blute des rothen Mannes in ihren Adern fließe; doch die jedesmalige Aufforderung ward mit Schüſſen beantwortet, welche ſelten ihr Ziel verfehlten. Zu guter Letzt kam der Haupthallunke, Little Crow, perſönlich herbei um die braven "Halfbreeds" zum Deſſertiren zu bewegen, aber einige um ſeinen Kopf pfeifende Kugeln belehrten ihn, daß der Platz ſich hier nicht gut dazu eigne, um ſein indianiſches Redner-Talent glänzen zu laſſen. Die braven Halbindianer konnten nicht bewogen werden, die Reihen ihrer weißen Freunde zu verlaſſen, und kämpften bis zum Ausgange des Kampfes mit heroiſchem Muthe für die Erhaltung des Forts und die Sache ihrer weißen Bundesgenoſſen. Es ſoll jedoch hiermit nicht geſagt ſein, daß ſämmtliche "Halfbreeds" der Sioux damals auf der Seite der Weißen waren, im Gegentheil kämpfte ein großer Theil derſelben in den Reihen der Rothhäute, und waren einige dieſer Halbwilden ebenſo grauſame Hallunken als die Indianer ſelbſt. Bemerkenswerth iſt die Thatſache, daß diejenigen Halbindianer, welche in der Zeit der höchſten Noth treu und ergeben an der Seite ihrer weißen Freunde kämpften, faſt alle von halbfranzöſiſcher Abkunft waren, was ihre Namen ſchon bekundeten, während viele derjenigen, welche als Verbündete Schulter an Schulter mit den Indianer mordeten, brannten und ſengten, Träger engliſcher Namen waren.

Man erlaube mir zur näheren Erklärung der Urſache des eben Geſagten eine abermalige kleine Abſchweifung, welche ein Licht auf viele unſaubere Vorgänge auf den Indianer-Agenturen und die Entſittlichung eines Theiles der daſelbſt mit den Rothhäuten verkehrenden Weißen, zu werfen beſtimmt iſt. Der im Weſten und Nordweſten der Vereinigten Staaten befindliche Franzoſe und hauptſächlich der franzöſiſche Canabier iſt in der Regel mit einer Indianerin verheirathet. Wenn nun auch nach den Begriffen von Staat und Kirche eine solche Ehe gewöhnlich keine legitime ist, so ist dieses eheliche Zusammenleben in den meisten Fällen doch ein für das Leben dauerndes. Die Kinder, welche einer solchen Ehe entsprossen, hängen, da sie unter den Augen eines weißen Vaters erzogen, sich stets im innigen Zusammenleben und unter der Aufsicht des letzteren befinden, mehr an der weißen als an der rothen Race. Die Mutter hat einen verschwindend kleinen Antheil bei der Erziehung ihrer Nachkommenschaft und hauptsächlich stehen die Söhne direkt unter der Controlle des Vaters. Anders verhält es sich bei jenen "Halfbreeds", welche väterlicherseits von nicht französischen Weißen abstammen. Ein guter Theil dieser Mischlinge kennt in der Regel den eigenen Vater nicht, und wenn auch, so kümmert sich der letztere in den meisten Fällen um seine in wilder Ehe erzeugte Nachkommenschaft blutwenig oder gar nicht und dieselben werden dann stets von den rothen Stammesgenossen erzogen. Solche vaterlose Halbindianer sind denn auch begreiflicher Weise ebenso erbitterte und sehr oft noch viel erbittertere Gegner der weißen Race, als der Indianer selbst. Der stets bittere Gedanken, von ihren schurkischen weißen Erzeuger hilf- und namenlos in die Arme ihrer rothen Stammesgenossen getrieben zu sein, kann nicht verfehlen, daß diese Art von Mischlingen im Falle eines Kampfes mit den Bleichgesichtern sehr oft grausamer mit den letzteren verfahren, als der Vollblut-Indianer. Und abermals wird hier die Thatsache bestätigt, daß für die begangenen Ungerechtigkeiten einiger Hallunken der kaukasischen Race zum öfteren der friedliche weiße Ansiedler büßen muß.

Ehrend soll hier noch erwähnt werden, mit welch' edler Selbstverleugnung Dr. Alfred Müller und seine Gattin Frau Elisa Müller sich der Verwundeten und Kranken annahmen, und wie besonders die brave Dame als der schützende Engel des Forts betrachtet werden kann.

Man sollte nun meinen, daß die Indianer nach den beiden Schlappen, welche sie in New Ulm und Fort Ridgely erhalten, ernstlich an das Aufgeben des Kampfes gedacht hätten; man sollte meinen, daß sie das Vergebliche der Fortsetzung des letzteren eingesehen; doch man täuscht sich mit dieser Annahme, denn die rothen Bestien hatten Blut gerochen, und waren wie der Tiger, wenn er solches gekostet, blutdürstiger als je zuvor. Zudem hatten sie New Ulm vorher nur mit einem Theil ihrer Krieger angegriffen, und wenn sie jetzt, nachdem sie vereinigt, den Angriff wiederholten, dann werden sie die Stadt sicher in ihre Hände bekommen, und o welche Wollust schon in dem Gedanken daran, dann kann man dem Morden, Brennen, Plündern und allen anderen Gräuelthaten sich hingeben. Das letztere war so ungefähr der Sinn der Worte, welche Little Crow nach dem Abzuge von Fort Ridgely an seine Krieger richtete, und darum fort ohne weiteren Aufenthalt nach New Ulm.

Kehren auch wir nun im Geiste nach der deutschen Stadt zurück bis zu der Zeit wo die zurückgeworfenen Rothhäute ihren Rückzug nach Fort Ridgely antraten. Es war Nachts ungefähr 12 Uhr, die Nacht nach dem verzweifelten Kampfe am Dienstag den 19. August 1862, da hörten die ausgestellten Wachen auf der Straße nach St. Peter und Mankato hin den regelmäßigen Tritt heranmarschirender Mannschaften. Dies können keine Indianer sein, aber dennoch wurden sie angerufen, und o Wonne! es war die ersehnte von der Bordman'schen Cavallerie schon angemeldete Hülfe von St. Peter und anderen Plätzen, voran der schon oft erprobte Freund der New Ulmer, der brave Judge Flandreau aus St. Peter. Ein Jubelruf, wie er zu einem Willkommen nicht herzlicher gedacht werden kann, begrüßte die braven Männer; denn man wußte in New Ulm nur zu wohl, daß nur ein Theil der Krieger Little Crow's am Tage vorher die Stadt angegriffen, und daß die rothen Bluthunde mehr als doppelt so stark in kurzer Zeit ihren Angriff erneuern würden. Am nächsten Tage kam denn auch noch Hülfe von allen Seiten. Von einigermaßen gut organisirten Compagnien, welche New Ulm zur Zeit der höchsten Noth zu Hülfe eilten, möchte ich besonders folgende erwähnen: St. Peter Compagnie unter Capitain Flandreau; Mankato Compagnie unter Capitain Bierbauer; Le Sueur Compagnie unter Capitain Saunders. Ueberdies waren viele Farmer aus der Umgegend in der Stadt, welche ihre Organisation ebenfalls so gut wie möglich bewerkstelligten; Milforder unter Capitain F. Meile, Cottonwooder unter Capitain Wm. Winkelmann, und die New Ulmer selbst unter Capitain J. Bellm. Weitere Organisationen welche nebst den genannten noch bestanden, kann ich nicht anführen, da fast die sämmtlichen Musterrollen abhanden gekommen sind.

Man kann selbstverständlich von dem Geschichtsschreiber nicht verlangen, daß er die Namen aller Derjenigen verzeichne, welche sich bei einem Kampfe, wie der, welcher am 23. August 1862 in New Ulm stattfand, mehr oder weniger ausgezeichnet, da die trotz aller gegebenen Mühe noch immerhin fehlerhafte, weil in einer kurzen Spanne Zeit bewerkstelligte, Organisation ein derartiges Verzeichniß nicht zuläßt, nur so viel können wir, selbst auf die Gefahr hin dem Laufe der nachfolgenden Begebenheiten vorzugreifen, versichern, daß die Vertheidiger New Ulm's bei dem zweiten Angriffe der Indianer sich ebenso brav und tapfer geschlagen, wie diejenigen, welche den ersten Angriff der Rothhäute am 19. August zurückschlugen. Irrthümer können bei der Beschreibung aufregender Ereignisse, über die keine richtige Controlle geführt werden kann, wie bei der zweimaligen Belagerung New Ulm's durch die Indianer, immerhin vorkommen, so auch der Irrthum, daß, wie schon erwähnt, New Ulm am 19. August von den Indianern zum größten Theil abgebrannt worden sei, obwohl an dem damaligen Gefechtstage nur drei Häuser in

Flammen aufgingen, während am 23. August bei dem zweiten Angriff der Roth=
häute, um den letzteren jeden Anhaltspunkt, jede Stütze, welche ihnen Deckung
gewähren konnte, zu entziehen, viele Gebäulichkeiten zerstört werden mußten.
Dazu kamen noch die beiden großen Dampfmühlen, Subilia's Destillerie, die
Turnhalle, eine Kirche und eine Anzahl zerstreut liegender Wohnhäuser, welche von
den rothen Mordbrennern eingeäschert wurden, ohne daß die braven Vertheidiger
der Stadt etwas zur Verhinderung dieser Zerstörung zu thun vermochten. New
Ulm liegt heute noch, und damals im Verhältniß zu der Größe der Stadt mehr,
auf einem Terrain, das zu vertheidigen, würde man alle die vom Centrum der
theilweise eine Meile und wohl noch weiter sich erstreckenden Gebäude bei einem
Angriffe in die Vertheidigungslinie einrahmen, eine kleine Armee von einigen
tausend Mann gut geschulter Soldaten erfordern würde. Doch darüber später
noch mehreres, und kehren wir nun zurück zu dem Morgen nach der Ankunft der
von auswärts erwarteten Hülfe.

Am Mittwoch, den 20. August, ward denn auch den Verhältnissen entsprechend,
die durch die Ankunft der Hülfsmannschaften von auswärts ganz andere waren,
als bei dem ersten Angriffe der Indianer, das Vertheidigungssystem ein weit aus=
gedehnteres, indem die schon vorhandenen Barikaden und sonstige Vertheidigungs=
werke bedeutend vorgeschoben wurden. Judge Flandreau, welcher früher Indianer=
Agent gewesen, und als solcher mit den Sitten, Gebräuchen und der Kriegführung
der Rothhäute vertraut geworden, ward zum Oberkommandanten ernannt, und
überhaupt alles sonst Mögliche gethan, was zum Schutze der Stadt für nothwendig
gehalten wurde.

Am Donnerstag Morgen wurde eine Recognoscirungs=Mannschaft ausge=
schickt, die den Auftrag hatte, die von der Stadt abgeschnittenen und in einer hilflo=
sen Lage befindlichen Farmer mit ihren Familien nach New Ulm zu bringen, und
gleichzeitig auszufinden, wo und welche Stellung die Indianer genommen. Daß
trotz der eingetroffenen Hülfe die Aufregung in der Stadt selbst eine große war,
läßt sich leicht denken, und daß sich auch ängstliche Gemüther in der letzteren befan=
den, war den Verhältnissen entsprechend nicht anders zu erwarten. Es ist halt
nicht Jeder zum Soldaten geeignet, und die Gräuelthaten, welche die rothen Blut=
hunde in den letzten Tagen verübt, waren auch nicht dazu angethan, beruhigend
auf Alle einzuwirken. Aber trotz alledem sah der größte Theil der Vertheidiger
dem kommenden Kampfe mit einer muthigen Begeisterung entgegen, die alten
schlachtgewohnten Soldaten Ehre gemacht hätte. Der dumpfe Schall abgefeuerter
Kanonen da oben in Fort Ridgely, der hier deutlich gehört wurde, ließ an der
Thatsache keinen Zweifel aufkommen, daß dorten ein heißer Kampf entbrannt sei.
Wie, hörte man oft die Befürchtung aussprechen, wenn es den Indianern gelingt

das Fort zu nehmen, und sie später mit den erbeuteten Kanonen die Stadt New Ulm beschießen—was dann? Die letztere hatte über kein einziges Geschütz zu verfügen. Doch es sollte so weit nicht kommen, die Rothhäute wurden, wie schon angegeben, von den braven Vertheidigern mit blutigen Köpfen von Fort Ridgely zurückgetrieben.

So unter Vorbereitung zum Kampfe auf Leben und Tod brach endlich Samstag, der 23. August 1862 an, jener denkwürdige Tag, der wieder blutig roth in der Geschichte New Ulm's verzeichnet ist. Wieder beschien die aufgehende Sonne anmuthig und freundlich die Turnerstadt, doch anders, noch viel kriegerischer sah das vor einer Woche noch so friedliche Städtchen mit seiner idyllisch gelegenen näheren Umgebung jetzt aus, als selbst an jenem denkwürdigen Morgen des 19. desselben Monats, denn die Spuren des am verflossenen Dienstag stattgefundenen Kampfes waren noch nicht verwischt, und schon wieder mußte man sich darauf vorbereiten, innerhalb weniger Stunden zum zweiten Male dem Angriffe eines grausamen, blutdürstigen Feindes wirksam entgegentreten zu können, da die ausgesandten und eben zurückgekehrten Scouts (Späher) berichteten, daß die Indianer von Fort Ridgely her auf beiden Seiten des Minnesota-Flusses gegen die Stadt heranrückten.

Die Vertheidigungsarbeiten, die vielen Bewaffneten auf den Straßen sagten ebenfalls deutlich und klar, daß man sich hier im Kriegszustande befinde, und in nächster Bälde Ereignissen von weittragender Bedeutung entgegen sehe. Die Sonne stieg höher und höher, da, es war gegen 10 Uhr Morgens, verkündeten rings um die Stadt aufsteigende Rauchsäulen, daß die rothen Bestien sengend und brennend sich New Ulm näherten. Nicht lange darauf krachten die ersten Schüsse, und der Kampf war alsbald auf mehreren Seiten, von dem bestialischen Geschrei der Rothhäute begleitet, entbrannt.

Die Indianer, wüthend über die schweren Verluste, welche sie in den letzten Tagen bei ihren Angriffen auf New Ulm und Fort Ridgely erlitten, und durch die feurige Ansprache ihres Häuptlings Little Crow noch mehr gereizt, machten dieses Mal die verzweifeltste Anstrengung, die Stadt in ihre Gewalt zu bekommen. Zuerst trieben sie einige vorgeschobene Posten gegen die Hauptaufstellung der Vertheidiger zurück und waren nahe daran, die Stellung der letzteren, welche sich auf offener Prairie, mit dem Rücken sich an die Stadt lehnend, befand, zu durchbrechen, aber ihr ungestümes Vorwärtsdrängen scheiterte an der zähen Ausdauer und dem höheren Muthe des weißen Mannes. Doch jetzt änderten die Wilden ihren Angriffsplan und suchten mit der ihrer Race eigenen Schlauheit Deckung hinter und in verlassenen-Gebäuden, von wo aus sie ein wirksameres Feuer auf die Vertheidiger unterhalten konnten. Wie bereits mitgetheilt, konnten die außerhalb der Verthei=

digungslinie zerstreut liegenden Wohnhäuser und sonstige Gebäude wegen Mangels an der dazu nöthigen Mannschaft nicht besetzt werden, und so war es dem wilden Feinde ein Leichtes, sich in den bestgelegenen festzusetzen, und andere, welche er eben nicht besetzen wollte, in Brand zu stecken, und war es daher bei dem zweiten Kampfe am 23. August und nicht, wie von vielen Seiten irrthümlich berichtet wurde, am 19., wo die Stadt New Ulm ernstlich in Gefahr war, in Flammen aufzugehen. Während nun die rothen Bestien die Brandfackel in die Wohnungen friedlicher Menschen, welche ihnen niemals etwas zu Leide gethan, schleuderten, tobte der Kampf mit gleicher Erbitterung fort.

Die Indianer hatten sich gleich im Anfange des Gefechts durch einen Flanken=Angriff der Turnhalle bemächtigt, und sich darin festgesetzt, doch kaum 400 bis 500 Fuß von der letzteren entfernt lag auf demselben Hügel mit ihr eine große Wind=mühle, in welcher sich ein Theil unserer Leute von der LeSueur und Mankato Compagnie verschanzt hatten, und diese hielten durch ihr gut unterhaltenes Gewehrfeuer die Wilden auf dieser Seite in respectvoller Entfernung. Der westliche Theil der Stadt war überdies noch durch ein Backstein=Gebäude gedeckt, das damalige Postamt, welches von tüchtigen Leuten besetzt war, die dem Feinde hier jedes Vordringen zur Unmöglichkeit machten. Auch die Nordseite hatte ein gutes Bollwerk, ein wohlbesetztes Backstein=Haus, und nur die Süd= und Südostseite, die schwächsten Punkte der Vertheidigung, boten den Rothhäuten die Möglichkeit von hier aus in das Centrum der belagerten Stadt einzudringen. Das wußte der schlaue Indianer=Häuptling sehr wohl, denn gerade hier hatte er seine besten Krieger zusammengezogen, während auf den anderen Punkten die weniger zuverlässigen die Aufgabe hatten, die Vertheidiger New Ulm's durch fortwährende Angriffe zu beschäftigen, um ihre Aufmerksamkeit von den schwächsten Stellen der Vertheidigung abzulenken. Der im Südosten der Stadt gelegene Theil des „German Park" war in damaliger Zeit mit hohen Grase bewachsen, durch welches gleich Schlangen durchzukriechen die Aufgabe der Indianer war. Und dieser Aufgabe waren sie vollständig gewachsen; denn wie schon erwähnt, sind die Kerle die besten Tirailleure der Welt. Gedeckt durch hohes Gras, von Südost mehr gegen Süden heranschleichend, gelang es den Rothhäuten, die Minnesota=Straße zu erreichen und sich hier in den von den Bewohnern verlassenen Häusern festzusetzen. Von hier aus war ihr Vormarsch immer mehr und mehr nach Norden, dem Mittelpunkt der Stadt, gerichtet.

Es war gegen 12 Uhr Mittags, als Capitain Dodd von St. Peter von einem einzigen Manne Namens Krieger von Milford begleitet, trotz wohlgemeinter Warnungen seiner Freunde, zum Auskundschaften die Minnesota=Straße in südlicher Richtung entlang sprengte. Doch kaum 150 Schritte von der nach dieser Richtung hin errichteten Barikade stürzte der Capitain durch mehrere Schüsse, abgefeuert aus von den Indianern besetzten Häusern, tödtlich verwundet zur Seite seines im selben Augenblick erschossenen Pferdes. Der Schwerverwundete wurde mit heldenmüthiger Todesverachtung von einigen unserer Leute hinweggetragen, (einer der letzteren, Herr Jakob Häberle, von Milford, ein allgemein geachteter, braver Mann holte sich bei dieser Gelegenheit seine Todeswunde) doch gab er schon nach einigen Stunden, trotz der sorgsamsten Pflege, seinen Geist auf. Der den Capitain auf dem Todesritt begleitende Milforder, ein alter deutscher Soldat, ward ebenfalls gefährlich verwundet, aber es gelang ihm, mit seinem Pferde die Stadt zu erreichen, doch nur um einige Monate später an den erhaltenen Wunden im Hospital daselbst zu sterben. Mittlerweile drängte der blutdürstige Feind Schritt um Schritt vor. Die Vertheidiger New Ulms hatten schon 6 Todte und über 20 Verwundete zu verzeichnen. Was aber sollte aus den von 800 bis 1000 zählenden Frauen und Kindern werden, wenn es den Indianern gelang, in die Stadt einzudringen? Sie waren vorläufig in sichere Häuser untergebracht, doch welches Loos hätte sie getroffen, wenn sie in die Gefangenschaft der Rothhäute gerathen wären! Nie und nimmer! Es darf nicht sein! Schutt und Leiche, Kampf bis zum letzten Blutstropfen, Sieg oder Tod! Das war die Loosung, die ausgegeben, und wehe dem Feigling, der vor dem anstürmenden Feinde sich geflüchtet hätte. Es war jetzt Nachmittags 3 Uhr, die Wilden hatten einige Häuser auf der Südseite der Minnesota-Straße besetzt, von welchen aus sie schon die nicht weit von Centre-Straße (Grenze zwischen Nord und Süd der Stadt) errichtete Barikade, ohne weitere Gefahr für sich selbst, bestreichen konnten. Immer näher und näher rückte die Stunde der Entscheidung. Ununterbrochen mit der größten Erbitterung wurde jetzt auf allen Seiten gekämpft. Wer wird Sieger bleiben? Es ist gegen die vierte Nachmittagsstunde noch nicht mit Gewißheit zu unterscheiden; doch es muß sein! Sie sollen und müssen zurückgeworfen werden. Mehr und mehr Indianer erschienen jetzt auf der Südseite der Minnesota-Straße. Sie kamen, gedeckt durch ihre eigenen Leute und das hohe Gras, vom German Park herauf. An der Südostecke von Minnesota- und Centre-Straße stand ein großes Blockhaus. Der vordere Theil dieses Gebäudes ward als Schmiede-Werkstätte benutzt, der hintere Theil als Wohnhaus des Schmiedes, Herrn August Kiesling.

Dieses starke Bollwerk lag außerhalb der Barikade, war aber von unsren Leuten besetzt. Da, es war gegen 5 Uhr am Nachmittag, drangen die Indianer fürchterlich schreiend mit Uebermacht vor, und nahmen das Blockhaus, die stärkste Position auf der Südost-Seite der Stadt. Jetzt war der Zeitpunkt gekommen, wo es sich um Sein oder Nichtsein der Stadt New Ulm handelte. Konnten die rothen Bestien innerhalb einer Viertelstunde aus der ihnen eben so günstigen wie für die

Vertheidigung gefährlichen Stellung nicht vertrieben werden, dann war Alles verloren; denn das Centrum der Stadt zwischen den beiden Hauptbarikaden an der Nordseite der Minnesota=Straße war von jetzt ab den Kugeln der Indianer preisgegeben, und zögerten die letzteren auch keine Minute, ihren errungenen Vortheil auf die bestmögliche Weise auszubeuten.

In diesem kritischen Augenblick, wo Alles auf dem Spiele stand, galt kein Zaudern, hier mußte gehandelt werden, und das sofort. Richter Flandreau und der Verfasser dieses sammelten dann auch mit Blitzesschnelle eine Schaar von 60 bis 70 beherzten Männern, sprangen an der Spitze dieser Tapferen über die Barikade und griffen mit einem Hurrah=Geschrei, das selbst den wildesten Indianer Ehre gemacht hätte, das genannte Blockhaus an. Hier entspann sich nun ein furchtbarer Kampf, ein blutiges Ringen auf Leben und Tod. Hier mußte jetzt innerhalb weniger Minuten das Schicksal der Turnerstadt New Ulm entschieden werden. Und es ward entschieden; denn die Indianer wurden, obgleich die vierfache Uebermacht auf ihrer Seite war, aus dem Blockhaus und mehreren in der Nähe desselben liegenden Gebäuden, welche sie während des Nachmittags besetzt hatten, mit großem Verlust hinausgetrieben, und die Stadt war gerettet. Aber mit welchen Opfern! Die Vertheidiger hatten hier während der kurzen Zeit, die dieser Kampf dauerte, aus ihren Reihen 5 Tode und 15 bis 18 Verwundete zu verzeichnen; doch das stolze Bewußtsein, daß der an dieser Stelle mit ihrem Blut getränkte Boden künftigen Generationen noch verkünden kann, wie hier eine kleine Schaar tapferer Männer den viermal überlegenen Feind auf das Haupt geschlagen, und durch den entscheidenden Sieg über eine Horde indianischer Bestien nahe an tausend Frauen und Kinder vor einem schrecklichen Schicksal bewahrt, dies schöne Bewußtsein stärkte das Vertrauen der Ueberlebenden auf die eigene Kraft und ließ selbst die Verwundeten die brennenden Schmerzen ihrer Wunden vergessen. Um nun den Indianern das abermalige Vordringen auf der Südost= und Südseite der Stadt und die wiederholte Besetzung der dort stehenden Gebäude, welche die Vertheidiger mit ihren geringen Streitkräften auf die Dauer nicht halten konnten, vollständig zu verleiden, um ferner ein für allemal einem nochmaligen Kampf auf dieser Seite vorzubeugen, wurden eine Anzahl leerstehender Wohnungen dem Untergang geweiht, und sofort zerstört. Mit einer Zähigkeit, die einer besseren Sache würdig gewesen wäre, setzten die Rothhäute trotz dem Verluste ihrer starken Position an Minnesota=Straße den Kampf fort, doch Eines konnte dem aufmerksamen Beobachter nicht entgehen: ihre Kraft war seit jener Schlappe an genannter Straße so ziemlich gebrochen. Nur von der Turnhalle aus sandten sie ihre Kugeln hageldicht und ununterbrochen gegen die oben erwähnte Windmühle, aber die Besatzung derselben war mit Munition reichlich versehen, hatte gute Deckung hinter gefüllten

Mehlsäcken u. s. w., und blieb daher den Wilden die Antwort auf ihre Schüsse nicht schuldig. Allein durch das Ausharren des Feindes an dieser Seite gereizt, und durch den eben an Minnesota=Straße erfochtenen Sieg über die rothen Bestien für einen weiteren Kampf begeistert, sammelte sich abermals eine Schaar braver Männer, welche fest entschlossen war, die Turnhalle im stürmenden Vormarsch zu nehmen. Da aber ein derartiges gewagtes Unternehmen während der Tageszeit wiederholt große Opfer gekostet, und eine größere Gefahr für die Stadt von dieser Seite aus nicht zu befürchten war, so verständigte man sich endgültig dahin, mit dem Erstürmen der besagten Halle zu warten bis zum Abend, wenn es dunkel geworden, wo man alsdann den rothen Mördern dort oben einen Besuch abstatten wollte.

Doch es kam nicht dazu, denn die Indianer, wohlwissend, daß sie sich in dem Gebäude auf die Dauer der Nacht nicht halten konnten, setzten dasselbe gleich bei dem Dunkelwerden in Brand, und innerhalb einer Stunde war die schöne Turnhalle in einen Aschenhaufen verwandelt. Ein ungelöstes Räthsel ist es bis jetzt noch, wer die Verüber gewesen, denn fast in derselben Zeit, als die erwähnte Halle schon lichterloh brannte, schlugen die Flammen an allen Ecken und Enden aus der bis jetzt so gut vertheidigten Windmühle. Auch dieses Gebäude, das bis jetzt zum Schutze der Stadt so viel beigetragen, war in kurzer Zeit eine ausgebrannte Ruine. Vermuthungen soll und darf der Geschichtsschreiber nicht aussprechen, doch immerhin kann ich hier nicht fest und sicher behaupten, daß es Indianer gewesen, welche dieses Bollwerk der Vertheidiger dem Feuergott geopfert. Unter fortwährendem Schießen, das aber von Seiten der Indianer immer schwächer und schwächer wurde, kam der Abend heran, und das Schießen hörte dann von Seiten der letzteren endlich ganz auf. —

Der Kampf der rothen Race gegen die weiße, der Kampf indianischer Mordbrenner gegen friedliche Menschen, welche den rothen Bestien nie etwas zu Leide gethan, war für heute eingestellt; die Waffen ruhten, nicht aber das entfesselte Element, der Feuerteufel. Hoch auf gegen das Firmament wirbelten die Flammensäulen, weithin Tageshelle verbreitend. Ein furchtbar grausiges Schauspiel, das, mit der Feder zu beschreiben, eine Unmöglichkeit ist, welches aber dem überlebenden Augenzeugen in schrecklicher Erinnerung für das ganze Leben hindurch ein tief eingeprägtes, unvergeßliches ist. Selbstverständlich können damit nur die Betheiligten der weißen Race gemeint sein; denn von den rothen Hallunken werden die heute noch lebenden mit ganz anderer Empfindung auf ihr furchtbares Zerstörungswerk von damals zurückblicken. Mit welchem diabolischen Entzücken die wilden Mordbrenner an jenem schauerlichen Abend des 23. August von den benachbarten Hügeln aus, auf die sie sich zurückgezogen hatten, auf die brennende Stadt herab=

gesehen, läßt sich leicht denken, und jetzt noch werden diejenigen der Sioux, welche sich an den Gräuelscenen in Minnesota im August 1862 betheiligt hatten, zu der Zeit den Kugeln des weißen Mannes und dem hundertfach verdienten Galgen entronnen, und sich heute noch unter den Lebenden befinden, jetzt noch werden sich diese Teufel in Menschengestalt darüber freuen, die Brandfackel in die von ihnen so gehaßte Stadt New Ulm geschleudert zu haben, in die Stadt von der sie zweimal mit blutigen Köpfen zurückgetrieben wurden.

Doch wie am Nachmittage über die Indianer, so wurden die braven Vertheidiger am Abend des verhängnißvollen Tages Herr über das Feuer und schon vor Mitternacht hatten sie das letztere vollständig unter ihrer Controle, und war das Centrum der Stadt, wo sich, wie schon angedeutet, so viele Frauen und Kinder befanden, wo die Verwundeten untergebracht waren, vor jeder Feuersgefahr sicher gestellt. Gegen Morgen sah man denn auch mit Genugthuung, daß da, wo am Abende vorher aus dem Gebäuden die Flammen lichterloh emporschlugen, nur noch in sich selbst zusammengestürzte glimmende Ruinen waren. Jetzt erst hatte man Muße, darüber nachzudenken, welche Fehler von den Belagerten im Laufe des verflossenen Tages begangen wurden, und man kam schließlich zu der Ueberzeugung, daß es keiner der geringsten gewesen, daß man am verhängnißvollen Samstag Morgen den 23. August eine Compagnie, über hundert Mann stark und wohl bewaffnet, über den Minnesota=Fluß beordert, welche, nachdem sie vollständig von einem übermächtigen Feinde von der Stadt abgeschnitten, und ihren Capitain nebst einigen ihrer Leute in dem ungleichen Kampfe gegen die Indianer verloren, auf ihre eigene Rettung bedacht sein mußte, und unter diesen Umständen für die Vertheidigung der Turner=Stadt New Ulm nichts, gar nichts zu thun im Stande waren.

Im Eilmarsche begaben sich die meisten der erwähnten Mannschaften nach St. Peter, wo sie mit noch anderen dahin kommenden Flüchtlingen die Nachricht verbreiteten, daß New Ulm niedergebrannt sei, also schon zum zweiten Male in einer Woche. So entstehen die irrigen Aufzeichnungen, und derartige Phantasie=Gemälde nennt man nachher wieder irrthümlich Geschichte.

Wer allerdings am Abend des 23. August 1862 aus der Ferne die hochaufschlagenden Flammensäulen in New Ulm gesehen, der konnte getäuscht werden, denn die Stadt war zur Zeit wirklich in großer Gefahr, von dem Feuer vernichtet zu werden; wer sich aber am Abend des 19. August dieser Stadt näherte, konnte höchstens einige kleine Wachtfeuer der Belagerten erblicken; denn die drei von den Indianern an dem letzteren Tage angezündeten Gebäude lagen an dem betreffenden Abende sammt und sonders in kaum noch glimmenden Ruinen.

Am Abende beschränkte sich denn auch das Gewehrfeuer der Belagerten auf einzelne Schüsse, welche entweder zufällig losgingen, oder auf irgend einen Gegen=

stand, den man in der Dunkelheit für einen Indianer hielt, abgefeuert wurden. Einem solchen Schuß fiel der Brodbäcker der Belagerten, während er am kühlen aber dunkeln Abend, mit einem Büffel-Rock bekleidet, sich nach seiner am Broadway gelegenen Bäckerei begeben wollte, zum Opfer. Der Name des pflichtgetreuen, während der Belagerung unermüdlichen Mannes, der auf eine so traurige Weise sein Leben verlor, war Jakob Castor. — Was das Schicksal derjenigen Mannschaften gewesen, welche beordert waren, die weit ausgedehnten in keinem Verhältnisse zu der Vertheidigung stehenden sogenannten Schützengräber zu besetzen, welche gefährliche Ehre hauptsächlich den New Ulmern zu Theil werden sollte, darüber nachzudenken hatte man jetzt Muße, und man kam bei dem endgültigen Nachdenken zu dem Schlusse, daß ohne das energische Entgegentreten seitens des Verfassers dieser Zeilen gegen jene Schützengraben-Besetzung die Stadt wenigstens 50 ihrer bravsten Bürger bei dem Kampfe mehr verloren hätte; denn die Indianer scheerten sich, wie man zu sagen pflegt, den Kukuk um diese noch obendrein in keinerlei Verbindung mit der Stadt stehenden ausgegrabenen Löcher, sondern sprengten, und wenn dieselben auch besetzt gewesen, mit ihren Ponies dazwischen durch, schnitten sie von der belagerten Stadt ab, und hätten die Insassen dieser Deckungslöcher auf jeden Fall lebendig oder todt in ihre Hände bekommen.

Zur weiteren Erläuterung von Schützengraben sei hier noch bemerkt, daß dieselben bei einer belagerten, wenn auch nur verschanzten Stadt, oder bei einer eingeschlossenen Festung stets nur von Seiten der Belagerer angelegt werden. Diese von Zeit zu Zeit vorgeschobenen Todtenlöcher (so genannt weil ihre Insassen sie selten lebend wieder verlassen) werden stets in dunkler Nacht ausgegraben, durch die ausgeworfene Erde und anderes Material in der Front noch mehr geschützt, in der Regel durch sehr gute Schützen besetzt, und haben den Zweck, den fortschreitenden Belagerungsarbeiten zum Schutze zu dienen. So lange sich diese Schützengraben außerhalb des Granatfeuers der Belagerten befinden, sind sie nicht so gefährlicher Natur, weil ihre Insassen blos vor etwaigen Ausfällen der Belagerten auf ihrer Hut sein müssen, sobald sie aber von den Sprenggeschossen der letzteren erreicht werden können, dann werden von vornherein die meisten ihrer Insassen auf die Todtenliste gesetzt, denn in den wenigsten Fällen verlassen sie lebend ihre sich selbst gegrabenen Gräber.

Bei der Belagerung von Sebastopol, im Krimkriege, spielten diese Schützengraben eine Hauptrolle, denn unter dem Schutze derselben wurden die Belagerungsarbeiten gegen die belagerte Festung stets vorgeschoben, aber wie viele Opfer an Menschenleben sie gekostet, das wußten die englischen und hauptsächlich die französi chen Verlustlisten genau zu erzählen. Als zu guter Letzt General Pelissier den Malakoff erstürmte, und nach der Erstürmung über 10,000 Franzosenleichen um dieses furchtbar starke Bollwerk lagen, da konnte er trotz alledem nach Paris berichten: „Besser auf einmal, als nach und nach." Es braucht daher keiner den Vanban gelesen und studirt zu haben, um zu wissen, daß Schützengraben bei Belagerungen nur von den Belagerern angelegt und noch obendrein durch Batterien in der Regel gedeckt werden. So viel von Schützengraben im Allgemeinen.

Im Besonderen von den am 23. August 1862 bei New Ulm angelegten sei noch gesagt, daß sie, ohne Verbindung mit der belagerten Stadt und ohne etwelche Deckung, da die Belagerten über keine einzige Kanone zu verfügen hatten, schon von vornherein als verlorene Posten zu verzeichnen waren. Der Rest der Nacht verlief ruhig, doch daß bei den meisten der Vertheidiger an Schlaf nicht gedacht werden konnte, kann man sich bei der Aufregung des stattgehabten Kampfes mit dem Feinde sowohl, als auch mit der Ueberwältigung des Feuers leicht denken. Während des verflossenen Nachmittags und fast die ganze Nacht hindurch sorgte ein guter Stab von Aerzten unermüdlich in treuer Pflichterfüllung für die Verwundeten, und der Verfasser dieses hält es für seine Pflicht, die Namen dieser braven Männer an dieser Stelle zu veröffentlichen. Es waren Dr. McMahan von Mankato, Dr. Mayo und Dr. Ayer von Le Sueur, Dr. Daniels von St. Peter und Dr. Weschcke von New Ulm. Alle diese genannten edelen Männer waren aufopfernd in Erfüllung ihrer traurigen Pflichten und leisteten den Verwundeten den bestmöglichen Beistand. Ehre den braven Männern!

Endlich nach einer, wie schon erwähnt, ruhelos verbrachten Nacht brach der ersehnte Morgen an. Es war ein schöner Sonntag Morgen; doch wie ganz anders sah es hier aus, als an dem letzten Sonntag! Eine Woche nur, und doch diese furchtbare Veränderung. Damals heitere Stimmung, munteres Lachen und sorgenloses, frohes Blicken in die Zukunft; und heute düsterer Ernst auf allen Gesichtern, Zerstörung an allen Ecken und Enden, rauchende Trümmer wo noch vor einer Woche die schönsten Wohn= und Geschäftshäuser glücklicher Menschen gestanden, und der verzweifelnde Blick in die nächste Zukunft. Das Einbringen von weitern Ermordeten am Morgen war gewiß nicht geeignet dazu, diese trübe Stimmung zu verscheuchen. Doch man hatte nicht viel Zeit übrig, sich mit düsteren Gedanken zu beschäftigen; denn auf allen Seiten zeigten sich schon seit Tagesanbruch Indianer, und jeden Augenblick konnte der Kampf aufs Neue beginnen. Doch die Rothhäute, durch die am Tage vorher erhaltenen Verluste so ziemlich entmuthigt, und durch das Niederbrennen der außerhalb der Vertheidigungslinie liegenden Häuser jedwelcher Deckung beraubt, sammelten sich zwar abermals um die Stadt herum in kleinen Banden, und hatte es den Anschein, als wollten sie ihre ungestümen Angriffe wiederholen; aber der aufmerksame Beobachter konnte alsbald bemerken, daß das Mißgeschick von gestern die Kraft und Energie der Wilden gebrochen hatte.

Immerhin mußten die Vertheidiger auf ihrer Hut und darauf vorbereitet sein, einen erneuerten Angriff der Indianer durch kraftvolles, muthiges Entgegentreten zurück schlagen zu können. Man kannte ja den erbitterten, und durch die gestern erhaltene Schlappe noch mehr gesteigerten Haß der rothen Hallunken gegen die Bleichgesichter zu gut, als daß man annehmen konnte, die Wilden würden, ohne einen weiteren Versuch zur Ueberwältigung derselben, der Stadt New Ulm den Rücken zeigen, und ruhig abziehen. Und man hatte sich nicht geirrt, denn einen Augenblick schien es wirklich, als ob sie ihre Angriffe zu wiederholen entschlossen seien. Da, als schon die ersten weiteres Unheil verkündenden Schüsse krachten, verfielen die Belagerten auf eine ebenso glückliche wie originelle Idee, welche, alsbald in Scene gesetzt, viel dazu beitrug, daß die Indianer von jedem ferneren Versuch, die Stadt in ihre Gewalt zu bekommen abstanden, und ihren Rückzug so schnell als möglich antraten. Kanonendonner ist, wie schon erwähnt, für die Rothhaut keine liebliche Musik, und Kanonendonner, wenn auch sehr unschuldiger Natur, wie wir gleich erfahren werden, war es, der den abziehenden rothen Mördern ans Ohr schlug.

Zwei Schmiede-Amboße wurden so aufeinander gelegt, daß die in denselben befindlichen Löcher genau aufeinander paßten. Die Höhlungen derselben waren mit Pulver ausgefüllt, das durch eine Zündschnur, welche an der Wand des einen Amboßes herunter hing, leicht und ohne Gefahr entzündet werden konnte. In der Front dieses etwas kurios aussehenden Geschützes wurde auf einen Hinterwagen ein Ofenrohr so angebracht, daß es von fern einem Kanonenrohr sehr ähnlich sah. Dieses improvisirte Geschütz ward gegen Süden gerichtet, und in dem Augenblicke abgefeuert, als sich einige Indianer nach dieser Richtung hin zeigten. Was nun den Donner selbst anbelangt, so konnte sich diese Amboß-Kanone ganz gut mit dem Krachen eines Sechs-Pfünders messen, und war die Wirkung auf die auf der Südseite versammelten Rothhäute eine gewaltige, denn die letzteren verschwanden sofort von der Bildfläche ohne auch nur einen einzigen Schuß abzufeuern. Natürlich wurde mit dem Abfeuern der Amboß-Ofenrohr-Kanone jetzt nicht mehr gezögert. Schuß folgte auf Schuß und so lange ward das Schießen fortgesetzt, bis zu guter Letzt keine Indianer mehr zu sehen waren. Wie einige der rothen Hallunken, von den über 300 Gefangenen, welche später in Mankato internirt waren, dem Verfasser mittheilten, hatten sie vor dem Amboß-Ofenrohr-Geschütz deswegen einen so gewaltigen Respect, weil sie dasselbe für eine wirkliche Kanone hielten, welche entweder von Fort Snelling oder von Fort Ridgely den New Ulmern zur wirksameren Vertheidigung hergesandt worden sei. Etwas nach 12 Uhr Mittags, ungefähr eine Stunde nach dem Abzuge der Indianer, kam eine am Tage vorher von St. Peter abmarschirte Compagnie unter Commando von Capitain Cox zur weiteren Hülfe nach der Stadt. Der Kampf war vor deren Eintreffen factisch beendet. Was den

Kommandirenden dieser Compagnie bewogen hatte, statt im scharfen Vormarsche während der verflossenen Nacht der bedrängten Stadt so rasch als möglich zu Hilfe zu kommen, mit seinen Leuten nahe Nicollet, 15 engl. Meilen von New Ulm, liegen zu bleiben, und erst spät am anderen Morgen aufzubrechen, ist und bleibt wieder ein Räthsel, dessen Auflösung bis jetzt noch auf sich warten läßt. Daß aber das Eintreffen dieser letzten Hülfsmannschaften viel, sehr viel mit dem eben so gefährlichen als schmählichen Abzuge von New Ulm, dem vollständigen Aufgeben der Stadt zu thun hatte, ist leider bittere Wahrheit. Der Abzug von New Ulm, am Dienstag den 26. August 1862, das nach zweimaligem Siege über die Indianer erfolgte Aufgeben der geliebten Heimath, kann nur von ängstlichen Gemüthern als eine damals dringende Nothwendigkeit betrachtet werden. Ich bin fest überzeugt, daß der brave Richter Flandreau nie daran gedacht hätte, nach dem erfolgreichen Zurücktreiben der Indianer die Stadt einer handvoll Marodeure zu überlassen, wenn er nicht durch Leute, welche vielleicht einen anderen Vortheil bei dem Aufgeben New Ulm's im Auge hatten, gewissermaßen dazu gedrängt worden wäre. Hatte er doch den Vorschlag einiger seiner Freunde, die Stadt schon am Donnerstag vor dem Kampfe zu verlassen und sich in der Richtung nach St. Peter oder Mankato zurückzuziehen, entschieden zurückgewiesen, und darauf hingedeutet, daß eine Handvoll Indianer in den Niederungen des Cottonwood-Thales Tod und Verderben den Abziehenden bringen könnten. Nein und abermal nein! Ich bin fest überzeugt davon, Richter Flandreau würde niemals seine Einwilligung zu dem schmählichen Abzuge gegeben haben, hätte man ihn nicht dazu überredet. Ein triftiger Grund für das Aufgeben der Stadt, das Zurücklassen werthvollen Eigenthums, das denn auch zum größten Theil, wie nicht anders zu erwarten, in die Hände maraudirenden Gesindels fiel, war nie vorhanden.

Die Annahme Einzelner, daß man die Frauen und Kinder in Sicherheit bringen wollte, ist so abgeschmackt, daß es sich wahrlich nicht lohnt, viele Worte darüber zu verlieren. Warum brachte man denn die Frauen und Kinder nicht früher in Sicherheit? Warum setzte man sie erst dem ganzen Schrecken einer Belagerung durch die Indianer aus? In dieser Beziehung werden wir in Nachfolgendem klar und deutlich beweisen, daß die Frauen und Kinder während der ganzen verflossenen Woche sich in so keiner großen Gefahr befanden, als auf dem Rückzug von New Ulm nach Mankato.

Der freundliche Leser wird mir nun an dieser Stelle erlauben, die Gegend, durch welche der gefährliche doch den Umständen angemessen noch glücklich ausgeführte Rückzug stattfand, ein wenig näher zu beschreiben. — Ungefähr eine Meile von dem Centrum der Stadt New Ulm macht die Straße eine ziemliche Senkung, geht aber dann noch immer durch die offene Prairie. Doch nach einem abermaligen Marsche von circa einer halben Meile in der Richtung gegen Mankato zu geht es, aber nicht sehr bedeutend, wiederholt Bergab gegen das Ufer des Cottonwood. Der Fluß selbst ist im Sommer weiter nichts als ein kleiner Bach und deshalb gut zu überschreiten, aber seine Ufer sind an beiden Seiten, wenn auch in keiner großen Ausdehnung, mit Holz bewachsen, und stellenweise sehr steil. Von hier aus ist der Kamm eines Hügels von über 400 Fuß Höhe zu erreichen, ehe man sich auf der Straße nach Mankato hin einigermaßen frei umblicken kann. Wenn man nun bedenkt, daß die Abzugscolonne wenigstens 140 bis 150 Wagen aufzuweisen hatte, welche mit Frauen, Kinder, Kranken und Verwundeten angefüllt waren, wenn man weiter bedenkt, daß der bewaffnete Schutz für dieselben den Umständen entsprechend ein sehr bedenklicher war, so kann man sich leicht vorstellen, daß, wenn die halbe Zahl der Indianer, welche am vorhergegangenen Samstag New Ulm angegriffen, in den Niederungen des Cottonwood=Thales oder auf der erwähnten Anhöhe gelauert, ein Morden stattgefunden hätte, wie in der Geschichte der Vereinigten Staaten vielleicht kein zweites zu verzeichnen ist. Der Augenzeuge dieser diminutiven Völkerwanderung wird sich wohl noch zu erinneren wissen, welches Durcheinander bei dem Ueberschreiten des kleinen Flusses herrschte. Jeder wollte mit seinem Wagen die gefährliche Niederung zuerst passiren, und da konnte es nicht anders kommen, als daß ein vollständiges Ineinanderfahren stattfand, und es die größte Mühe kostete, die Ordnung einigermaßen wieder herzustellen. Hätten, wie schon gesagt, in den Gebüschen an dieser Stelle nur hundert Indianer gelegen, dann wäre ein entsetzliches Blutbad nicht zu vermeiden gewesen, und wer, fragen wir, wer würde für ein solches verantwortlich gewesen sein? Doch genug!

Wir wollen die ihre Heimath Verlassenden nebst ihrer Bedeckung nicht Schritt um Schritt auf ihrer gefährlichen Reise begleiten, und nur erwähnen, daß nach dem Passiren noch einiger solcher gefährlichen Stellen, wie die oben beschriebene, die ganze Colonne am nächsten Morgen den Umständen nach glücklich und wohlbehalten in Mankato angekommen. Hier ward nun Alles gethan, was in der kurzen Zeit für die Hülfsbedürftigen zu thun möglich war, doch mußten, nachdem alle erquickt, ein Theil der Heimathlosen, weil die Stadt von ihnen überfüllt, sogleich den Vormarsch nach St. Peter antreten, wo sie ebenfalls wie in Mankato mit offenen Armen und warmen Herzen empfangen wurden. Es läßt sich nun nicht hinwegläugnen, daß das bittere Gefühl, die geliebte Heimath verlassen zu müssen, sich manchmal in lauten Klagen Luft machte, welche bei einigen insofern doppelt gerechtfertigt erschienen, weil sie fast Alles verloren, und theilweise nur das nackte Leben gerettet hatten; aber Diejenigen unter ihnen konnten sich doch noch glücklich preisen, welche mit ihren Angehörigen ihr unfreiwilliges Exil gesund und wohl erreichten. Wie anders sah es aber bei Denen aus, die krank oder verwundet meistens in offenen Wagen die Strapazen dieser Reise auszuhalten hatten! Wie mancher hauptsächlich Derjenigen, welche später an ihren vernachlässigten Wunden gestorben, hätte gerettet werden können, wenn ihm die nöthige Pflege nicht gemangelt hätte! Doch wozu die düsteren Bilder einer traurigen Vergangenheit nochmals an unserem geistigen Auge vorüberziehen lassen? Sehr viele der heimathlosen New Ulmer wandten sich nach St. Paul, wo sie von der ganzen Bevölkerung, doch insbesondere von der deutschen, auf das Herzlichste bewillkommnet und in guten Quartiren untergebracht wurden.

Doch lassen wir jetzt die Flüchtlinge sich von ihren Strapazen erholen, und kehren wir zu der verlassenen Turnerstadt New Ulm zurück, um auszufinden, ob dieselbe vollständig in Trümmern liegt oder nicht, und ob es überhaupt nöthig gewesen, dieselbe über Hals und Kopf so schnell zu verlassen.

Am Mittwoch den 27. August, also kaum einen Tag nach dem Verlassen der Stadt, kam Capitain Dean mit seiner Compagnie Ver. Staaten Volontäre und nahm Besitz von derselben. Mit welchen Gefühlen die „Boys in blue" in den verlassenen Ort, der einer sogenannten Todtenstadt nicht unähnlich sah, damals einrückten, kann nur Derjenige beschreiben, der persönlich zugegen gewesen. Sämmtliche Gebäude, welche während des Kampfes den Flammen nicht zum Opfer gefallen, standen auch jetzt noch unversehrt auf derselben Stelle, und von Indianern war keine Spur mehr zu entdecken. Die Compagnie bezog ein Lager inmitten der Stadt auf einer Anhöhe und verlegte ihr Hauptquartier in eines der vorhandenen, aber selbstverständlich von seinem früheren Inhaber verlassenen, Hotel. Der Tag und ebenso die folgende Nacht verlief ruhig, weder Weiße noch Rothhäute ließen sich sehen.

Am nächsten Tage, Freitag, den 29. August, erschienen die ersten Bewohner aus New Ulm und Umgegend wieder in der Stadt. Es waren die Herrn George Jacobs, Rudolph Kiesling und Hochhausen. Die Namen dieser Avantgarde verdienen der Oeffentlichkeit übergeben zu werden, denn es war kein Kinderspiel, was diese Leute unternommen hatten, vielmehr war es ein muthiges Vordringen, das dem tapfersten Soldaten alle Ehre gemacht hätte. Die genannten drei und ein Farmer aus Courtland, Names Gerboth, verließen St. Peter bereits am Donnerstag Morgen, den 28. August, der Eine auf einem kleinen Pony, die Anderen zu Fuß. Der Berittene sprengte jedesmal, wenn eine Anhöhe oder ein Hügel in der Nähe ihres Marsches war, voraus, um genaue Umschau zu halten. So kamen sie bis in die Nähe von Gerboths Farm, wo der letztere, trotz der Warnung seiner Reisegefährten, welche vereint weiter vordrangen, vorläufig zu bleiben entschlossen war. Diesen Entschluß sollte er mit seinem Leben büßen, denn von einzelnen noch immer in der Gegend herumstreifenden Indianern ward er schon am nächsten Tage in seinem Kornfelde ermordet. Die drei Andern erreichten noch am Donnerstag Abend die Farm und das Wohnhaus von Rudolph Kießling, gegenüber der Stadt New Ulm auf der anderen Seite des Minnesota-Flusses. Hier machten sie Halt und brachten die Nacht abwechselnd Wache stehend zu. Am folgenden Morgen gingen sie in der Richtung gegen New Ulm an den Minnesota-Fluß, und wer beschreibt ihren Schrecken, als sie da oben auf dem Hügel, wo jetzt das Gerichtsgebäude steht, eine kleine Zeltstadt erblickten. Ihr erster Gedanke war natürlich der, daß Indianer da drüben lagerten, doch um Gewißheit zu erlangen beschlossen sie den Fluß zu überschreiten, und sich so nahe als möglich gegen die Zelte heranzuschleichen. Man kann sich leicht denken, daß es den drei muthigen Männern unaussprechliche Freude verursachte, als sie ausgefunden, daß die Bewohner der erwähnten Zeltstadt keine Indianer, sondern Weiße in der Uniform Onkel Sam's waren. So schnell, als sie ihre Füße nur tragen konnten, eilten sie nun zu den Soldaten, und wurden von denselben auf das herzlichste bewillkommnet.

Das war die Avantgarde der in ihre verlassene Heimath zurückkehrenden New Ulmer, welche letztere nun auch nicht mehr lange auf sich warten ließen. Tag auf Tag trafen die Zurückkehrenden jetzt ein und bald herrschte in der Stadt selbst wieder ein reges Leben. Die Zurückgekommenen bezogen die leerstehenden Häuser, die Straßen und Nebenstraßen wurden gereinigt und Alles so weit es anging wieder in gute Ordnung gebracht, und schon drei Wochen später war nichts mehr von den hier stattgehabten Kämpfen zu sehen, als die in Schutt und Trümmern liegenden Gebäude. Auch diese wurden im darauffolgenden Jahre, nachdem Entschädigungsgelder seitens der Ver. Staaten Regierung ausbezahlt worden waren, meist wieder aufgebaut, auch andere neue dazu, und einige Jahre darauf waren die Spuren der furchtbaren Katastrophe vollständig verwischt. Die Turnerstadt hatte sich dann wieder erholt, frisch und froh, stark und treu war sie wieder erstiegen, wie der Phönix aus der Asche.

Sehen wir nun, da wir jetzt die nöthige Zeit dazu erübrigen können, was aus den am 24. August von New Ulm abgezogenen Rothhäuten geworden. Wieder zogen sie, wenigstens ein großer Theil derselben, die Straße nach Fort Ridgely entlang, doch hüteten sie sich wohlweislich dieses Mal dem Fort zu nahe zu kommen. Dennoch konnte sich der tapfere Sergeant Jones, als sie am Fuße des Hügels, auf welchem das Fort liegt, vorbeizogen, das Vergnügen nicht versagen, seine Geschütze abermals und zum Abschiede auf sie spielen zu lassen. Aber die feigen rothen Canaillen, jetzt doppelt niedergeschlagen durch die in der vergangenen Woche erlittenen Niederlagen, wagten nicht auf die Abschiedsgrüße der Kanonen des Forts eine einzige bleierne Antwort zu geben, sondern machten sich in der Richtung nach der unteren Agentur so schnell als möglich aus dem Staube. Aber die Göttin der

Rache hängte sich, wie wir später erfahren werden, an ihre Fersen, und ließ nicht ab, bis die rothen Teufel in Menschengestalt ihr einen guten Theil des ihr gebührenden Tributs bezahlt hatten.

Man sollte nun denken, daß nach den erfolglosen Versuchen der Rothhäute, New Ulm und Fort Ridgely in ihre Gewalt zu bekommen, man sollte meinen, daß nach den großen Verlusten, welche sie bei ihren Angriffen auf beide Plätze erlitten, die blutdürstigen Bestien eingesehen hätten, daß ein Fortsetzen des Kampfes gegen die Bleichgesichter ihnen von jetzt ab nur noch mehr verderbenbringend sein könnte, und schließlich mit ihrem vollständigen Ruine den diabolischen Ausbruch zum Abschluß bringen würde; man sollte denken, daß die Sioux, durch ihre sonstige Schlauheit geleitet, zu der Ueberzeugung gekommen seien, daß von jetzt ihr Heil in schleuniger Flucht auf britisches Gebiet bestehe, — doch man irrt sich mit dieser Annahme. Die rothen Teufel hatten sich bisher mit Wollust im Blute der Weißen gebadet, sie hatten in den letzten zwei Wochen Hunderte und abermals Hunderte der verhaßten Bleichgesichter nach Herzenslust abgeschlachtet, sollten sie daher nicht, um sich für die Niederlage vor New Ulm und Fort Ridgely zu rächen, versuchen einen kleineren, vielleicht nicht so gut vertheidigten Platz in ihre Hände zu bekommen? Und sie versuchten es.

Hutchison, ein Städtchen in McLead County, Minn., war der Platz, den sie zur Rache für ihre bisherigen schweren Verluste heimsuchen wollten. Bevor sie dahin aufbrachen, bestanden sie ein Gefecht mit einer Compagnie Ver. Staaten-Freiwilliger bei Birch Cooly, oberhalb Fort Ridgely. Hier waren die Rothhäute zum zweiten Male einem gut bewaffneten, wenn auch nicht sehr zahlreichem Truppe Soldaten gegenüber siegreich. Von einem militärisch unfähigen, seiner Aufgabe nicht gewachsenen Offizier kommandirt, hatten die letzteren in einem kleinen engen Thälchen, welches von mehreren Seiten von steil abfallenden Hügeln umschlossen ist, ihr Lager aufgeschlagen, und wurden sie denn auch in dieser Mausfalle von den in der Nähe sich befindenden Indianer angegriffen. Nur durch noch rechtzeitig eingetroffene Hülfe ward, nachdem ein Theil dieser Soldaten von den Rothhäuten, von den oben erwähnten Hügeln aus, erschossen war, der Rest der Compagnie vor dem gänzlichen Untergange bewahrt.

Ermuthigt durch diesen kleinen Sieg, den ein militärisch ungebildeter Offizier ihnen so leicht gemacht, zogen sie jetzt nach dem oben genannten Städtchen Hutchison. Doch die Bewohner dieses damals kleinen Platzes hatten sich gut verschanzt, und trieben, unterstützt von den Farmern der Umgegend, welche sich mit ihren Familien hierher geflüchtet, nach einem hartnäckigen Kampfe die Wilden mit blutigen Köpfen zurück. Von jetzt an, nachdem sie noch einige ihrer gewohnten Schandthaten begangen, zogen sich die rothen Mordbrenner vollständig entmuthigt vor den von Fort Snelling heranrückenden Streitkräften unter Kommando von General Sibley eiligst zurück. Bei Wood Lake, ungefähr 60 engl. Meilen von Fort Ridgely wurden sie eingeholt, und in dem darauffolgenden Treffen erlitten die Rothhäute eine vollständige Niederlage, welche ihnen endlich die Ueberzeugung beibrachte, daß ihr Aufstand ein gänzlich mißlungener, und ihre Sache eine verlorene sei, und so traten sie nun ihren Rückzug gegen die britische Grenze an. Da nun die sich zurückziehenden Indianer viele gefangene weißen Frauen und Kinder mit sich nahmen, deren Schicksal jedenfalls ein schreckliches gewesen, hätte man sie nicht aus den Händen der letzteren befreien können, so mußte man vor allen Dingen darauf sehen, diese Unglücklichen von ihren Peinigern ausgeliefert zu bekommen. Unter den Gefangenen befand sich u. A. der damals 11jährige Benedict Juni, nunmehr als Lehrer an den öffentlichen Schulen von New Ulm thätig, der den Rothhäuten beim Treiben des gestohlenen Viehes behülflich sein mußte. Wie Herr Juni dem Verfasser mitgetheilt, wurde er leidlich gut behandelt, doch die meisten der anderen weißen Gefangenen waren nichts als Sclaven ihrer Peiniger und wurden demgemäß auf die grausamste Weise von den rothen Bluthunden behandelt. Das herbe Schicksal derjenigen unglücklichen gefangenen weißen Frauen welche zum Theil mit kleinen Kindern in die Hände der rothen Teufel in Menschengestalt gefallen waren, nur annähernd zu beschreiben, vermag keine Feder.

Da aber auch die rothen Hallunken wohl wußten welchem Elend durch Hunger, Kälte u. s.w. sie entgegen gingen, da ferner die Zeit der Büffel=Jagd jetzt vorüber, und von dem großen Vater, Onkel Sam, nichts mehr zu erwarten war, so war man beiderseits darin bald einig gegenseitige Unterhandlungen anzuknüpfen, welche schließlich zu einem Resultat führten, das wenigstens einen Theil der Mörder der gerechten Strafe für die begangenen Gräuelthaten nicht entschlüpfen ließ.

Man sollte nun denken, daß diese Kerle, welche innerhalb eines Zeitraumes von höchstens fünf Wochen die scheußlichsten Grausamkeiten begangen, Hunderte von unschuldigen Menschen, die ihnen nie etwas zu Leide gethan, abgeschlachtet hatten, die während der kurzen Periode ihres Ausbruchs mehr als eine Million Dollars werth an Eigenthum zerstört und außerdem während dessen den ganzen Staat Minnesota in Angst und Schrecken versetzt hatten, man sollte meinen, daß diese Mordbrenner sich unter den obwaltenden Umständen auf keine Unterhandlungen eingelassen hätten, da sie doch zum Voraus wissen mußten, daß der Galgen für die Einen schon errichtet, die Zuchthäuser für die Andern geöffnet waren; doch man irrt sich in dieser Annahme.

Wer Gelegenheit hatte, die Natur des Indianer ein wenig zu studiren wird beobachtet haben, daß er ein Raubthier der blutdürstigsten und grausamsten Art ist. Der einzige Unterschied zwischen ihm und seinem thierischen Collegen besteht darin, daß er eine menschliche Gestalt sein eigen nennt, unter welcher die stets Unheil brütende Bestie sich birgt. So wenig das Raubthier sich daraus macht, einem Feinde den Garaus zu machen und sich an seinem Opfer den Hunger zu stillen, ohne sich weiter darum zu kümmern, ob es für die begangene That zur Rechenschaft gezogen wird oder nicht, eben so wenig bekümmert sich der Indianer nach vollbrachter Mordthat darum ob er dafür verantwortlich gemacht werden kann oder wird.

Die angeborene Schlauheit der höheren Bestie, sollte sie ja einmal wegen begangener Scheußlichkeiten von den zuständigen Gerichten zur Rechenschaft gezogen werden, verläßt sich darauf, durch Lügen und andere zweckdienliche Manöver den Hals aus der Schlinge zu ziehen, und oft, sehr oft gelingt es der Rothhaut, sich vor dem Gesetze von dem begangenen Verbrechen rein zu waschen, da ja in der Regel die nöthigen Zeugen zur Ueberführung fehlen. So und nicht anders kann man sich das massenhafte Uebergeben der rothen Mörder auf Gnade oder Ungnade, nachdem vorher alle Gefangenen bis auf einige wenige, die schon vorher von den Indianern fortgebracht, ausgeliefert waren, an General Sibley in Camp Release erklären. Wo wollte man denn auch Zeugen gegen sie auftreiben? Sie alle waren mit einer und derselben Farbe bemalt und meistens in dem Naturkostüm gekleidet, ein Weißer konnte sie mit Gewißheit nicht erkannt haben, und Diejenigen, welche vielleicht den Einen oder den Andern dennoch erkannt hätten, waren sammt ihren Familien abgeschlachtet. So konnten es die Spitzbuben schon wagen, sich mit der Miene der vollständigsten Unschuld dem General zu übergeben. Nur die Schlauesten und deswegen auch die Bekanntesten unter ihnen, wie Little Crow selbst, Shakopee, Little Six und Andere mehr hüteten sich, ihre Haut in dem Lager der Truppen abzuliefern. Sie wußten nur zu gut, daß ihre einzige Rettung in den Uebergang auf britisches Gebiet bestand, daß sie von den Vereinigten Staaten nichts weiter mehr zu erwarten hatten, als einen gut gedrehten hänfenen Strick. Doch wir werden bald sehen, daß auch die von den Truppen gefangen gehaltenen Indianer sich theilweise sehr im Irrthum befanden, wenn sie darauf rechneten, baldigst in Freiheit gesetzt zu werden. War man in ganz Minnesota darüber im Klaren, daß die ganze männliche Mörderbande der gefangenen Rothhäute sofort ins Jenseits gesandt werden sollte, weil sie insgesammt an den schrecklichen Gräuelscenen des vergangenen Monat August und September betheiligt waren, so war man in Washington, wo der Einfluß der Quäker und anderer Fanatiker sich sofort zu Gunsten der gefangenen rothen Bestien erklärte, ganz anderer Meinung, und beschloß man dorten, die ganze Angelegenheit vor die zuständigen Gerichte zu bringen. Demgemäß wurden nun alle Gefangenen, Weiber und Kinder mit einbegriffen, unter starker militärischer Eskorte nach Mankato transportirt, wo sie in einigen zu dem Zwecke erbauten großen Blockhäusern untergebracht und Tag und Nacht durch Militär streng bewacht wurden.

Daß man auf dem Wege nach obiger Stadt die blutdürstigen Todfeinde New Ulm's bei hellem Tageslicht auf über fünfzig von Soldaten umgebenen Wagen gerade durch die von den rothen Bluthunden so furchtbar heimgesuchte Stadt transportirte, war eine Gefühlsverletzung der Bewohner dieses Platzes und eine nicht zu rechtfertigende Tactlosigkeit der betreffenden Militär=Behörden. Es konnte daher nicht anders erwartet werden, als daß bei dem Erblicken ihrer Peiniger die durch die Indianer so schwer geschädigten Bewohner der Turnerstadt auf das Aeußerste gereizt, mit Steinen, Aexten, u. s. w. einen wüthenden Angriff auf die Rothhäute machten, von welchen viele einen guten Gedenkzettel mit nach ihrem vorläufigen Bestimmungsort, der Stadt Mankato, nahmen.

Thatsache ist, daß unter den Angreifenden sich viele Frauen befanden, Frauen welchen die rothen Canaillen einen oder den anderen ihrer geliebten Angehörigen gemordet, ihre Heimath zerstört oder sonst andere teuflische Unbill zugefügt hatten. War es unter den obwaltenden Umständen den Armen zu verdenken, daß sie sich in ihrem gerechten Zorne an ihren Peinigern, an den Zerstörern ihres Glücks vergriffen? Gewiß nicht! Daß aber nachher nativistische und puritanische Schmutzblätter, welche New Ulm von jeher mit gehässigen Blicken angesehen, und es stets zu verdächtigen suchten, in ihren Spalten behaupteten, in New Ulm hätten nur die Frauen gekämpft, und so wissentlich den Angriff auf die gefangenen Indianer mit dem Angriffe der letzteren auf die Stadt verwechselten, das ist eine ebenso feige Lüge, als diejenige, daß die New Ulmer einstens Jesus Christus in Effigie verbrannt.

Statten wir jetzt den gefangenen Rothhäuten in Mankato einen Besuch ab. Sie sind hier in den warmen Blockhäusern ganz comfortabel eingerichtet, und was ihre Kost anbelangt, so läßt dieselbe für sie wenigstens nichts zu wünschen übrig. Sie werden im Allgemeinen gut behandelt, und denken gewiß nicht daran, daß man sie für das bischen Morden, Plündern, Brennen und Sengen das sie sich im Monat August und September erlaubten, noch zur Rechenschaft ziehen würde. Zudem wußten sie nur zu gut, daß kein Mitglied ihres Stammes, um seinen eigenen Hals mit der hänfenen Cravatte nicht in Berührung zu bringen, den Verräther spielen, sich zum Staatszeugen einschwören lassen würde, sie wußten gut genug, daß von dieser Seite keine Gefahr für sie vorhanden, und daß jeder der Ihrigen eher unter den grausamsten Martern verenden würde, als einen seiner Stammesgenossen zu verrathen. Das alles wußten sie, die rothen Gurgelabschneider. Was sie aber nicht wußten war, daß dennoch unter ihnen selbst einer der grausamsten Mörder, ein Teufel in Menschengestalt, ein Hallunke, der zwanzigfach den Tod verdient, sich dazu hergeben würde, als Staatszeuge gegen sie alle aufzutreten. Es war dies ein Mulatte, der mit einer Frau ihres Stammes verheirathet, seit Jahren von dem letzteren adoptirt, und deswegen so gut wie einer der Ihrigen selbst von ihrer Seite betrachtet wurde. Von dem Tage des Ausbruches an war dieser schwarzgelbe Neger der Grausamste unter den Grausamen der rothen Mörderbande. Haarsträubende Geschichten von begangenen Greuelthaten wurden von diesem Ungeheuer berichtet, doch jetzt einmal eingefangen zitterte die feige Canaille vor dem zwanzigfach verdienten Tode und trat, um sein elendes Leben zu retten, gegen seine Mitschuldigen, gegen die Männer des Stammes, dem er seit Jahren angehörte, als Staatszeuge auf.

Schon gut, sagte Pascha Mustapha während des griechischen Befreiungskampfes zu einem Griechen, der ihm als Spion und Verräther gegen seine Landsleute und Glaubensgenossen treffliche Dienste geleistet hatte, schon gut, deine Dienste waren uns von großem Nutzen, und hier hast du auch die dir zugesicherte Belohnung für dieselben, doch jetzt nachdem alles sonst in Ordnung ist und du deinen Sündenlohn empfangen und eingesackt hast, lasse ich dir den Kopf abschlagen, denn ein Kerl wie du, der seine Landsleute und Glaubensgenossen verrathen, verräth mich und die Meinigen um so eher bei der ersten besten Gelegenheit. Und so geschah es, der Verräther ward sofort hingerichtet. Schade daß Präsident Lincoln kein Pascha Mustapha war, und den schlechten Mulatten ebenso abfertigte wie es der Türke mit dem schlechten Griechen gethan. Der Mulatte erwies sich übrigens als trefflicher Zeuge, denn er brachte es dahin, daß 38 seiner Schandgenossen zum Tode und eine Anzahl Anderer zum Zuchthaus verurtheilt wurden. Unter den zum Galgen Verurtheilten befanden sich allerdings einige der blutigsten Mörder, wie Cut Nose, White Dog und andere mehr; doch die Bevölkerung von St. Peter, New Ulm, Mankato und die der Umgegend war schon längst einig darüber, daß alle männliche gefangenen Indianer den Tod mehrfach verdient hätten. Und so kam es, daß man in verschiedenen geheim abgehaltenen Versammlungen sich dahin einigte, in einer bestimmten Nacht von allen Seiten nach Mankato aufzubrechen, die Wachen zu überrumpeln, und sich alsdann der gefangenen Indianer zu bemächtigen, um sie alle in ihre ewigen Jagdgründe zu spediren. Doch das Militär-Kommando in Mankato erhielt Kunde von dieser Verschwörung a la sicilianische Vesper, und verdreifachte die Wachen um die Blockhäuser, in denen die Rothhäute gefangen gehalten wurden, und als sich eine Parthie der Rächerschaar in Mankato blicken ließ, ward sie von ausgesandten Patrouillen sofort aufgehoben, um natürlich den nächsten Tag, nachdem sie versprochen, die Stadt zu verlassen und das Massenabschlachten der Indianer aufzugeben, wieder in Freiheit gesetzt zu werden. Unter den Verschworenen selbst, welche das Abschlachten der gefangenen Indianer als

Devise auf ihre Fahne geschrieben, befanden sich viele Soldaten, welche hauptsächlich den fünf Compagnien der „Minnesota Mounted Rangers" angehörten, die zum größeren Theil im oberen Minnesota=Thale angeworben, in St. Peter und der Umgegend damals ihre Standquartiere hatten. Von diesen Leuten hatten die meisten mehr oder weniger durch die Mordbrennereien der rothen Bestien gelitten, und war es ihnen nicht zu verdenken, daß sie die gefangenen Indianer nicht als Kriegsgefangene anerkennen wollten, sondern als das, was sie in Wirklichkeit waren, eine Räuberbande der grausamsten Art. Eine Untersuchung dieser Vorfälle hätte daher von vornherein einen Schrei der Entrüstung im ganzen Minnesota=Thale hervorgerufen, und so fand man es höheren Ortes für angemessen, die ganze Geschichte todt zu schweigen. Doch da man auf die Rangers, die nur gegen Indianer zu kämpfen in die Dienste Onkel Sam's eingeschworen waren ("against any Indians at war with the Government of the United States of North America") zum Bewachen indianischer Gefangenen sich nicht verlassen konnte, so ward zu der schon vorhandenen noch mehr Infantrie nach Mankato beordert, um womöglich derartige Vorkommnisse wie die eben geschilderten künftighin zu verhüten. Weitere Versuche, die rothen Teufel dem Richter Lynch zu übergeben, wurden indessen nicht mehr gemacht, und ließ man von jetzt ab, trotz des furchtbaren Hasses gegen die gefangenen Indianer, dem Gesetze seinen Lauf. Während dessen rückte der Tag, welcher zur Hinrichtung der 38 zum Tode verurtheilten Indianer bestimmt war, näher und näher heran. Die Verurtheilten befanden sich in einem abgesonderten Gebäude, in dem sie alle, um ihre Flucht zu verhindern, mit Ketten an den Fußboden angeschlossen waren. Es war allerdings keine leichte Aufgabe für den verrätherischen Mulatten, daß er die von ihm Verrathenen während der letzten Tage ihres Lebens bedienen mußte, und die Verachtung, welche ihm von Seiten seiner Mordgenossen bei jeder passenden Gelegenheit zu Theil wurde, so wie die stets auf ihn gerichteten zornflammenden Blicke, waren nicht geeignet, ihm das Leben während dieser Zeit zu versüßen.

Mit meiner Compagnie „Minnesota Mounted Rangers" am Tage vor der Hinrichtung nach Mankato beordert, um bei der Aufrechthaltung der Ordnung mitzuhelfen, hatte ich Gelegenheit, den 38 zum Tode Verurtheilten einen Besuch abzustatten. In Begleitung eines Ordonnanz=Offiziers des damaligen Militär=Kommandanten der Stadt und späteren Gouverneurs von Minnesota, Colonel Miller, machte ich mich auf den Weg, und bald darauf stand ich den angeschlossenen verurtheilten Verbrechern gegenüber. Es waren menschliche Gestalten, die da, nach Indianerart zusammengekauert, am Boden saßen, doch aus allen Poren des menschlichen Körpers blickte die blutdürstige Bestie heraus, und mich überlief es eiskalt, als ich daran dachte, welch entsetzliches Elend diese 38 Mordbuben über so viele friedliche Familien gebracht; doch ich beruhigte mich bei dem Gedanken, daß wenigstens diese Meuchelmörder den kommenden Tag am Galgen enden mußten.

Unter den Verurtheilten befanden sich Einige, die ich in früheren Jahren schon gekannt hatte. In Fort Ridgely war es, wo ich in meinem Hause und in dem des braven Dollmetschers Quinn dieselben zum Oefteren sah und kennen lernte. Besonders zwei von ihnen kannte ich ganz genau.

White Dog, ein schön gebauter junger Indianer von ungefähr 24 Jahren und eine ältere ungefähr 45 Jahre alte Rothhaut sah ich dorten verschiedene Male. White Dog war, nebenbei gesagt, ein indianischer Don Juan, von dem man damals behauptete, daß er nicht nur jungen Indianerinnen den Kopf verdrehte, sondern auch Glück mit seinen Don-Juanaden bei einigen weißen Frauen hatte. Er war übrigens ein sehr wilder Geselle, der wenn er von irgendeinem weißen Schufte, natürlich für zehnfache Bezahlung Feuerwasser ergattern konnte, sich viehisch betrank, und deswegen in dem dark hole (dunklen Loch) der Hauptwache im Fort öfters und mehr als ihm lieb war, sein Quartier aufschlagen mußte. Er war denn auch, wie es sich von einem solchen Hallunken nicht anders erwarten ließ, einer der allergrößten Spitzbuben unter den übrigen rothen Spitzbuben beim Indianer-Aufstande. Daß er, der sonst so schlaue Indianer, in die Falle ging, und sich in Camp Release auf Gnade oder Ungnade an General Sibley übergab, wurde dem Umstande zugeschrieben, daß eine unter den weißen Gefangenen der Indianer sich befindende Dame, mit der er ein kleines Liebesverhältniß während der Dauer der Gefangenschaft der letzteren unterhielt, ihm die Versicherung gab, sie werde ihn durch ihren Einfluß und ihr Zeugniß sicher und gewiß frei bringen. Doch die Dame hatte sich verrechnet. Dem rothen blutbesudelten Schurken wurden seine begangenen Schandthaten so klar bewiesen, daß ihn das Bitten, Händeringen und die vergossenen Thränen seiner weißen Duenna vom Galgen nicht erretten konnten.

Der andere ältere Indianer, dessen ich erwähnt, war vielleicht nicht ganz so schlecht, als White Dog, doch immerhin ein Hauptspitzbube unter den anderen rothen Spitzbuben. Näher bekannt ward ich mit dieser Canaille an einem kalten Wintertage des Jahres 1860 in Fort Ridgely. Durch die Fürsprache des Dollmetschers Quinn bekam er damals für sich und seine hungernde Familie zwei Säcke angefüllt mit Lebensmitteln verschiedener Art, hauptsächlich aber mit gesalzenem Fleisch, aus dem Magazin des Fort, natürlich unentgeltlich, verabfolgt. Da nun die Rothhaut im Allgemeinen seine Ponies, wo es angeht, mehr schont als seine Frauen, so belud er mit je einem dieser Säcke, welcher jeder wenigstens seine 50 Pfund schwer war, eine von seinen zwei ihn begleitenden Squaws. Er selbst bestieg sein starkes Pony und war eben im Begriffe fortzureiten, sich nicht darum kümmernd, ob seine beiden Lastthiere von Weibern ihm mit ihrer schweren Last durch den tiefen Schnee folgen konnten oder nicht. Aber der damalige Kommandant des Postens, Major Morris, ein gutmüthiger braver Herr, der gerade anwesend, war mit dieser Art von Frauenbehandlung nicht ganz einverstanden, und befahl der Rothhaut abzusitzen, dem Pony die beiden Säcke über den Rücken zu legen, und dasselbe am Zügel zu führen. Da der Indianer gegen diese seine indianische Ehre verletzende Zumuthung protestirte, ward er auf einen Wink des Kommandanten von einigen eben vorbeigehenden Soldaten schneller abgesetzt, als ihm lieb war, und dem Pony wurden alsdann die beiden Säcke, nachdem sie mit einem Seile aneinander gebunden waren, über den Rücken gelegt, und mußte sich der Indianer dazu bequemen sein Pferd zu führen, da ihm ausserdem zu wissen gethan ward, daß, wenn er die Säcke nicht bis zu seinem ungefähr zwei Meilen von dem Fort entfernten Zelte durch sein Pony tragen lasse, er sich nie wieder in Fort Ridgely sehen lassen sollte.

Augenzeuge während der ganzen Zeit des eben beschriebenen Vorfalles konnte ich natürlich nicht anders, als mit noch mehreren anderen Anwesenden über die komische Scene tüchtig zu lachen. Als ich nun am Abend vor seiner Hinrichtung diesen Indianer wieder sah und ihn fragte, ob er mich noch kenne, sagte er ja und gab mir gleichzeitig die Versicherung, daß es ihm das größte Vergnügen gemacht hätte, mich in seine Gewalt zu bekommen, um seinen Gürtel mit meinem Scalp zieren zu können. Ich dankte ihm natürlich im Namen meiner Kopfhaut für die ihr zugedachte Ehre, und versicherte ihn, daß als Gegenbeweis meiner Freundschaft ich mich morgen auf dem Richtplatz einfinden würde um zuzusehen, wie er gehenkt würde. Ein diabolischer Blick, ein wildes Aufblitzen seiner Augen war die Antwort, welche ich von der Rothhaut erhielt; denn das Aufhängen ist für den Indianer der schimpflichste Tod, den es nur geben kann, und er würde sich, wenn er die Wahl hätte, am Marterpfahl lieber langsam zu Tode rösten lassen, als sein Leben am Galgen zu enden.

Es war ein schöner Wintertag, der 26. December 1862, der Hinrichtungstag der 38 verurtheilten Indianer. Das für diese Jahreszeit ungewöhnlich milde Wetter hatte nicht wenig dazu beigetragen, daß Tausende von Zuschauern von nah und fern erschienen, um sich das seltene, wenn auch schaurige Schauspiel mit eigenen Augen anzusehen; denn es war gewiß eine Seltenheit, daß 38 schwere Verbrecher an ein und demselben Galgen zur gleichen Zeit in das Jenseits befördert wurden. Es war nicht allein Neugierde, sondern auch ein gewisses Gefühl der Befriedigung, daß hier wenigstens ein Theil der verhaßten rothen Mordbrenner, von ihrem Schicksal ereilt, ihre wohlverdiente Strafe empfingen, was die meisten der Zuschauer zum Theil aus weiter Entfernung hierher gebracht. Der Galgen war ein kreisförmig gebautes Gerüst, dessen Platform, auf welche die verurtheilten Verbrecher in kleinen Zwischenräumen zu stehen kamen, durch ein einziges starkes Seil festgehalten wurde. Jetzt wurden die Todeskandidaten unter starker militärischer Bedeckung herangebracht, und nahmen auf der Platform unter dem Absingen schauriger Todtenlieder diejenige Stelle ein, welche ihnen angewiesen wurde. Da ich zu Pferd ganz in der Nähe des Galgens hielt, so hatte ich Gelegenheit die 38 Mordbrenner bevor die verhängnißvolle Platform fiel, auf der sie, den Strick kunstgerecht um den Hals gelegt, standen, genau zu beobachten, und ich muß zugeben, daß die Kerle im Angesichte des Todes demselben muthig ins Auge schauten. Fest und gleichmäßig ertönte ihr schauriger Gesang, da — ein einziger Hieb mit einem scharfen Beile, der das die Platform haltende Seil durchschnitt, und die 38 rothen Mörder hingen wie Puppen an den eisernen Haken. Nein nicht alle! Bei dem Einen, einem großen schweren Kerl, war der Strick gerissen, und die Rothhaut lag zuckend auf dem Boden. Aber nicht lange, denn einige Minuten später hing sie kunstgerecht und leblos neben ihren todten Kameraden.

Während der Hinrichtung waren die in den Blockhäusern untergebrachten andern Indianer, durch den Gesang der Todeskandidaten auf den verhängnißvollen Augenblick aufmerksam gemacht, in die Kniee gesunken und hatten — gebetet. Da sieht man nun so recht, was das bischen Belecken der Civilisation, das Bekehren zum Christenthum aus diesem Gesindel gemacht; denn dieses Beten kam ja doch nicht aus einem von Reue und Gewissensbissen gequälten Herzen, sondern war nur der heuchlerische Deckmantel ohnmächtiger Wuth, daß sie ihren verurtheilten Mordgenossen nicht zu Hülfe eilen konnten, daß es ihnen nicht gestattet war, sich abermals, wie sie es während ihrer vierwöchentlichen Schreckensherrschaft so oft gethan, in dem Blute der Bleichgesichter zu baden.

Besonders war es das weibliche Personal der rothen Galgenkandidaten, das im verhängnißvollen Augenblick (der Galgen war ganz in der Nähe ihres Gefängnisses errichtet und waren, wie schon erwähnt, die Insassen des letzteren durch das Singen der Verurtheilten auf den schaurigen Akt aufmerksam gemacht) nebst Beten, seinem Schmerze und seiner ohnmächtigen Wuth in lauten Klagen Luft machte. Eine alte Squaw, deren Sohn, ein Halbindianer Namens Henry Milford und ein hervoragender Hallunke unter den anderen Hallunken, heute seine irdische Laufbahn an dem Galgen beschloß, geberdete sich wie rasend, raufte sich das Haar aus und schrie beständig, daß der Vater ihres Sprößlings ein hoch angesehener weißer Herr in Minnesota sei, der seinen Sohn hätte retten können, wenn er nur ein Wort zu seinen Gunsten gesprochen hätte. Ob die alte Indianerin die Wahrheit gesprochen, kann ich nicht behaupten, doch so viel ist gewiß, daß jener Henry Milford einer jener Halfbreeds war, die in wilder Ehe erzeugt, und weil vaterlos, von dem

Stamme der Mutter angenommen und erzogen werden. Man darf sich übrigens vor allen Dingen nicht durch sentimentale Gefühlsduselei bei dem verzweiflungs= vollen Ausbruche des wilden Schmerzes der Indianerinnen beeinflussen lassen, denn derselbe hält in der Regel, wie wir später erfahren werden, gleichen Schritt mit der wilden Grausamkeit dieser Megären.

Man erlaube mir nun an dieser Stelle einige Worte über die indianische Frau (Squaw) zur besseren Erläuterung des Charakters der letzteren einzuschalten, da man gewöhnlich annimmt, das indianische Weib sei ein von ihrem Manne nieder= gedrücktes, zur beständigen Arbeit verurtheiltes, aber sonst gutmüthiges Wesen.

Es ist wahr, die Indianerin ist die Sklavin ihres Mannes, der wenn er nicht gut gelaunt oder sonst keine andere Zerstreuung hat, seine Frauen, wenn er deren mehrere besitzt, eine nach der anderen gehörig durchprügelt. Die Squaw ist vollständig entrechtet, muß sich also die grausamste Behandlung von ihrem Manne gefallen lassen, ohne zu murren. Es ist wieder wahr, daß das indianische Weib die gesammte Arbeit verrichten muß, denn der Indianer beschäftigt sich blos mit der Jagd oder dem Krieg, durch jede andere Arbeit, welche er verrichten soll, glaubt er seiner Manneswürde etwas zu vergeben, und er würde sich in gewissen Fällen lieber todtschlagen lassen, als eine Handarbeit zu verrichten. Er ist eben Nomade und daher arbeitsscheu, wie alle Nomaden in der Regel sind. Der Sohn der Wildniß will von keiner anderen Beschäftigung etwas wissen, als auf seinem flüchtigen Pony die Prairie zu durchjagen, das Wild zu erlegen oder—Scalpe zu nehmen. Hier ist er in seinem Element. Die Jagd, der Kampf mit seinem Feinde, oder vielmehr das hinterlistige Abschlachten desselben, gehen ihm über Alles, jede andere An= strengung ist ihm zuwider, er betrachtet sie als entehrend, und überläßt aus diesem Grunde alle, selbst die anstrengendsten Arbeiten seinen Frauen.

Der Verfasser dieses war vor langen Jahren in Fort Ridgely Augenzeuge einer Scene, welche ihm unvergeßlich bleiben wird, und die ihm damals schon die Ueber= zeugung beigebracht, daß es sehr schwer zu bewerkstelligen ist, einen Indianer irgend eine, wenn auch nur geringe, Arbeit verrichten zu lassen.— Es bestanden von jeher und bestehen heute noch Gesetze, welche bei strenger Strafe verbieten, einer Rothhaut „Whisky" oder sonst eine Art „Feuerwasser" zu verkaufen.

Trotz alledem begegnete man in früheren Zeiten in hiesiger Gegend sehr häu= fig betrunkenen Indianern, welche-den ihnen verbotenen Schnaps entweder von ehr= losen Weißen zu sehr hohen Preisen erstanden, oder ihn durch Vermittelung der Mischlinge (Halfbreeds) welch letztere, nebenbei gesagt, zum Theil noch schlechter als die Vollblut=Indianer sind, bekamen.

Der Halfbreed war, weil etwas weißes Blut in seinen Adern rollt, in Be= treff des Ankaufs geistiger Getränke vor dem Gesetze mit der Vollblut=Rothhaut

nicht auf die gleiche Stufe gestellt, vielmehr hatte er das Recht von dem verderb=
lichen Feuerwasser so viel zu kaufen als er Lust und Geld hatte. Diese rothgelben
Hallunken machten nun von diesem ihrem Rechte den weitgehensten Gebrauch,
kauften Whisky und verkauften ihn wieder an ihre rothen Stammesgenossen zu
sehr hohen Preisen, und da dieser verbotene Handel stets außerhalb der Agenturen
betrieben wurde, so war es in den meisten Fällen sehr schwer, diese schuftigen
Schnapshändler den Gerichten zu überliefern.— Es war also an einem schönen
October=Nachmittage des Jahres 1859 als ein betrunkener Indianer in das Fort
gesprengt kam und sein Pony auf dem Paradeplatz tummelte. Der wachthabende
Offizier ließ die betrunkene Rothhaut sofort verhaften und in das sogenannte
dunkele Loch der Hauptwache bringen. Hier konnte der Wilde nun seinen Rausch
ausschlafen, und als er endlich erwachte, war er verurtheilt, unter Begleitung
einer Wache einen ganzen Tag lang zwei an der Quelle unten im Thale mit Was=
ser gefüllte Eimer auf das Fort zu tragen. Da nun zu jener Zeit beständig eine
Anzahl Rothhäute, insbesondere aber Squaws auf Fort Ridgely bettelnd herum=
lungerten, so konnte dem betreffenden Indianer keine härtere Strafe zuerkannt
werden, als die, unter den Augen seiner Stammesgenossen, hauptsächlich der
Squaws, ihn seiner Meinung nach entehrende Arbeit verrichten zu lassen. Und
so kam es, daß der verurtheilte Indianer weder durch gute Worte noch durch Droh=
ungen dazu zu bewegen war, die beiden verhaßten Wassereimer zu ergreifen und sich
damit in Bewegung zu setzen. Da nun alles Zureden nichts helfen wollte, ließ der
dienstthuende Offizier des Tages vier Mann mit aufgeflanztem Bayonett antre=
ten, welche die Rothhaut so in ihre Mitte nahmen, daß ihr von allen Seiten, von
der Front, dem Rücken und den beiden Flanken je ein Bayonett entgegen starrte.
Und noch immer weigerte sich die arbeitscheue Canaille, ihre Strafe anzutreten.
Doch als auf das Commando: Vorwärts! Marsch! der Zug sich in Bewegung
setzte, und selbstverständlich das Bayonett des im Rücken marschirenden Soldaten
den Rücken des Indianers berührte, da erst trat unter dem allgemeinen Gelächter
der Umstehenden der feige Schuft seine Strafe an, zu welcher er aber in derselben
Weise, selbstverständlich mit öfterer Abwechselung der betreffenden Mannschaften,
den ganzen Tag über gezwungen werden mußte. Dies theilweise zum Beweise,
wie unendlich schwer es hält, die Indianer zu civilisiren, das heißt, ihnen vor
allen Dingen das vagabondirende Nomadenleben abzugewöhnen, und sie zu seß=
haften, ruhigen, arbeitsamen Menschen heranzubilden. Wir haben nun nach den
obigen Schilderungen zur Genüge gesehen, daß der arbeitscheue Indianer alle,
auch die härtesten Arbeiten seiner Frau aufbürdet, und dieselbe obendrein zum
Danke für die geleisteten Dienste von Zeit zu Zeit gehörig durchprügelt. Daraus
ergibt sich, daß die Squaw ein unterdrücktes, armseliges Dasein fristet. Wer aber

behaupten will, daß die Indianerin in der Regel eine gutmüthige Creatur ist, dem muß ich einfach erwiedern, daß er sich in großem Irrthume befindet, denn ein grausameres Geschöpf kann es auf dem ganzen Erdenrunde nicht geben, als das Weib einer Rothhaut. Die zurückgedrängte Wuth durch die manchmal übergrausame Behandlung ihres Mannes bricht sich bei der ersten besten Gelegenheit furchtbar Bahn, und wehe den Unglücklichen, an denen diese schrecklichen Megären ihren verhaltenen Zorn auszulassen in der Lage sind.

Das langsam zu Tode Martern der Gefangenen ist in der Regel den Weibern der rothen Bestien überlassen, und diese entmenschten Creaturen betreiben diese grauenvolle Arbeit mit einer raffinirten Grausamkeit, daß man bei den haarsträubenden Schilderungen derselben in Versuchung geräth, steif und fest zu glauben, daß diese furchtbaren Weiber keine menschlichen Geschöpfe, sonderen der Hölle entstiegene Dämonen sind.

So viel nun über die arme, unterdrückte, und so gutmüthige Squaw des Indianers, welch letztere Tugend ihr hauptsächlich von den Blaustrümpfen angedichtet wird, da dieselben ein für allemal nicht gelten lassen wollen, daß die blutdürstige Bestie eben so gut in dem Inneren des Weibes ihren Wohnsitz haben kann, wie bei dem Manne.

Nach der Hinrichtung der 38 indianischen Mordbrenner in Mankato verlief der Rest des Winters so ziemlich ruhig, obgleich dann und wann Gerüchte auftauchten, daß die gegen die britische Grenze zurückgedrängten Indianer einen zweiten Ueberfall der Ansiedelungen in dem oberen Minnesota-Thale bald in Scene zu setzen entschlossen seien. Unter den nöthigen Vorbereitungen für eine starke militärische Indianer-Expedition, welche die Aufgabe haben sollte, den Rest der feindlichen Sioux kommendes Frühjahr unschädlich zu machen, das heißt, sie entweder gefangen zu nehmen oder, was allerdings das Beste gewesen wäre, sie wenn möglich vollständig zu vernichten, kam das mit Sehnsucht erwartete Frühjahr heran. Da, es war im Anfang des Monats April 1863, erscholl der Schreckensruf, eine Bande Indianer habe ihr Erscheinen am Watonwan-Fluße in der Nähe von Madelia, ungefähr 30 Meilen von Mankato entfernt, gemacht, mehrere Ansiedler, meistens Norweger, in der dortigen Gegend ermordet, andere verwundet und die zur Hülfe herbeieilende, aber nicht sehr starke Besatzung eines in der Nähe angelegten kleinen Forts in ihre Befestigungswerke zurückgetrieben. Sofort erhielt der Verfasser dieses, damals mit seiner Compagnie "Mounted Rangers" in St. Peter stationirt, den Befehl mit fünfzig Mann sogleich nach der bedrohten Gegend aufzubrechen, um den dortigen Ansiedlern den nöthigen Schutz zu gewähren und womöglich die rothen Bestien für ihre wiederholt begangenen Gräuelthaten zu züchtigen.

Die Vorbereitungen waren schnell getroffen, und eine Stunde nach der erhaltenen Ordre saßen wir, mit Munition für die Carabiner und Revolver reichlich versehen, im Sattel und fort ging es, nachdem Mannschaft und Pferde bei sehr stürmischem Wetter glücklich über den Minnesota=Fluß gebracht waren im scharfem Trabe nach Mankato, wo die Proviantwagen bereits auf unsre Ankunft warteten. Es war schon Abend als wir Mankato verließen, und doch hatten wir noch ohne Aufenthalt über 30 engl. Meilen zu reiten, um das vorher erwähnte kleine Fort am Watonwan=Fluß zu erreichen. Als wir den Blue=Earth=Fluß einige Meilen oberhalb Mankato überschritten, begann es bereits dunkel zu werden, und ungefähr eine halbe Stunde später umgab uns dichte Finsterniß. Es war, wie man zu sagen pflegt, eine wilde Nacht. Der Sturm tobte immer stärker und stärker, und dabei war es so finster, daß man die Hand vor den Augen nicht sehen konnte, aber vorwärts ging es über Stock und Stein auf dem meistens holperigen Wege in die Nacht hinein, denn es galt ja, den bedrängten armen Ansiedlern dort hinten so schnell als möglich die ersehnte Hülfe zu bringen. Auch war es das Verlangen mit den rothen Hallunken baldigst zusammen zu treffen, um ihnen mit unsren haarscharf geschliffenen Säbeln die Bestie aus dem verruchten Körper zu hauen, was uns das stürmische Wetter, und die stockfinstere Nacht vergessen ließ. Unser "Scout", ein Infanterist, welcher im Hauptquartier zu Mankato den Auftrag erhalten, uns, da er den Weg genau kannte, zu begleiten, war kein Reiter, und in Folge dessen schon auf dem halben Wege so wund geritten, daß er jämmerlich aufschrie, und daher auf einen der Proviantwagen untergebracht werden mußte. Es war dies bei der herrschenden Dunkelheit doppelt unangenehm, da die Fuhrwerke im Rücken unsrer Colonne fahren mußten, und wir so den des Weges kundigen Führer an unsrer Spitze verloren hatten. Dennoch ging es vorwärts durch Sturm und Finsterniß, denn wir hatten im Hauptquartier unser Wort gegeben, so rasch als möglich und ohne irgend welchen Aufenthalt vorzudringen.

Endlich, etwas nach 1 Uhr des Nachts, erreichten wir das kleine Fort. Reiter und Pferde waren von dem Parforceritte todtmüde, denn wir hatten, und den größten Theil davon in einer finsteren und stürmischen Nacht, 45 engl. Meilen ohne irgend einen merklichen Aufenthalt zurückgelegt. Daß wir von der schwachen Besatzung des kleinen Postens — es waren ihrer in allem ungefähr 20 Mann — froh und freundlich begrüßt wurden, läßt sich leicht denken. Wußte diese Handvoll Soldaten doch nicht, ob die Rothhäute, nachdem sie dieselben einmal zurückgeschlagen, in verstärkter Anzahl bald wieder kommen würden, um sie zu überwältigen und abzuschlachten. Hier hörten wir nun auch das Nähere über das Erscheinen der Indianer und ihre etwaigen Absichten.

Ich erlaube mir daher, dem freundlichen Leser auseinander zu setzen, was die so ziemlich in Sicherheit befindlichen Indianer bewogen hatte, ihr sicheres Asyl zu verlassen, selbst auf die Gefahr hin abgefangen und ihren in Mankato hingerichteten Schandgenossen in die Ewigkeit nachgeschickt zu werden. Die erste und Hauptursache war allerdings der Gedanke, an den Bleichgesichtern den Tod der 38 gehängten Hallunken zu rächen, und nebenbei so viele Pferde zu stehlen, als sie deren habhaft werden konnten. Dann war es auch allerdings die Sehnsucht, ja ich möchte fast sagen das Heimweh, das jeden Menschen, selbst den ruhelosesten Nomaden immer wieder und wieder nach dem Stückchen Erde treibt, auf dem er den größten Theil seiner Jugendzeit zugebracht hat. — Wer nun in damaliger Zeit im Sommer die Gegend, wo heute das Städtchen Madelia, der Countysitz von Watonwan County, liegt, besuchte, und sich von da aus, sei es nun um dem Vergnügen der Jagd obzuliegen, oder um anderweitige Geschäfte zu erledigen, nach der kleinen Ansiedlung am Lake Shetek begab, wer für Naturschönheiten sich ein empfängliches Gemüth bewahrt, das durch das hier zu Lande so gebräuchliche rastlose Jagen nach dem allmächtigen Dollar noch nicht total verknöchert ist, der wird es leicht begreiflich finden, daß es zum Theil immerhin eine gewisse Sehnsucht war, welche die oben erwähnte Bande Indianer im Frühjahr 1863 bewog, die unwirthliche Gegend an der britischen Grenze zu verlassen, um ihrer alten Heimath einen Besuch abzustatten. Es war ein schönes Stück Erde, diese damals von der Civilisation noch wenig oder gar nicht beleckte Gegend zwischen Madelia und Lake Shetek. Ein einziger großer Blumengarten, angefüllt mit klaren fischreichen Seen, welche meistens von kleinen aber herrlichen Waldungen umgeben waren, lag hier ausgebreitet vor den Blicken des für Naturschönheiten empfänglichen Reisenden. Heute sieht es in der betreffenden Gegend ganz anders aus. Farm reiht sich hier an Farm, ein großer Theil dieses Bodens ist cultivirt; wogende Halmfrucht=Felder, Wiesenland, auf dem das Vieh der umliegenden Farmen zu Hunderten weidet, mögen wohl Zeugniß ablegen von dem Wohlstande der in der Gegend angesiedelten Landwirthe, aber das wogende Blumenmeer ist ganz und der die Seen umgebende Wald zum größten Theil verschwunden, mit ihnen jedoch auch, — und dies muß uns gewissermaßen mit der fortschreitenden, die ehemaligen Naturschönheiten vernichtenden Civilisation versöhnen, — der raub= und mordlustige Indianer. Die früheren Herren dieser Gegend, die räuberischen Rothhäute haben ihre Tipis jetzt in einer weit von hier gelegenen Gegend aufgeschlagen, und der jetzt auf seinem Felde beschäftigte Landwirth, der Jäger oder Fischer, sie alle haben nicht mehr zu fürchten, bei dem Ausüben ihrer verschiedenartigen Thätigkeit durch die mörderische Kugel eines rothen Hallunken gestört zu werden. Anders war dies natürlich, wie wir gleich erfahren werden, in früheren Zeiten.

Es war an einem schönen Morgen Anfangs April 1863 als ein Norweger, in der Gegend von Crystal Lake wohnhaft, mit Apparaten zum Fischen versehen und begleitet von seinem fünfzehnjährigen Sohne nach dem besagten See zum Fischen ging. Weder Vater noch Sohn dachte daran, daß hinter hohem trockenem Gras und Gesträuchern verborgen, die heimtückische Rothhaut begierig auf die beste Gelegenheit wartete, den beiden Ahnungslosen das mörderische Blei als Morgengruß zuzusenden. Plötzlich fielen 10 bis 12 Schüsse, der alte Norweger stürzte von mehreren Kugeln durchbohrt todt zu Boden, der Sohn konnte sich, obschon verwundet, noch retten und die Besatzung des kleinen Forts alarmiren. Die braven Soldaten, meistens Norweger, zögerten trotz ihrer geringen Zahl keinen Augenblick und zogen, das Fort unter Bewachung von nur zwei Mann lassend, muthig und pflichtgetreu gegen die rothen Mordbrenner. Sie konnten aber den dreifach überlegenen Hallunken in dem nun beginnenden Kampfe nicht lange Stand halten, und zogen sich, um den letzten Anhaltspunkt für die in der Umgegend wohnenden Ansiedler nicht zu verlieren, nach dem Fort zurück und erwarteten hier stündlich den Angriff der Indianer. Und dieser Angriff ließ auch nicht lange auf sich warten. Die Rothhäute, siegesstolz die von ihnen so gehaßten in die Uniform Onkel Sams gekleideten Soldaten zurückgetrieben zu haben, folgten den letzteren auf dem Fuße und griffen die kleine Befestigung augenblicklich an. Doch auch hier, wie früher bei New Ulm und Fort Ridgely, scheiterten ihre oft wiederholten stürmischen Angriffe an dem kaltblütigen Muthe der kleinen Besatzung. Die Indianer zogen sich nun zurück, und da man ihrer nicht mehr ansichtig werden konnte, überließen sich die umwohnenden Farmer, welche bisher in dem kleinen Fort Zuflucht gesucht und auch gefunden, der gewöhnlichen Sorglosigkeit und kehrten nach ihren Heimstätten zurück. Doch diese Sorglosigkeit sollte Einzelnen theuer zu stehen kommen.

Ich habe im Anfange dieser Geschichte darauf hingewiesen, daß gerade dieses Sichgehenlassen, ja ich möchte sagen dieser dumme Leichtsinn bei dem Herannahen der Gefahr des Ausbruchs der Indianer so vielen Weißen verderbenbringend werden sollte, und selbst nach dem Ausbruche der Rothhäute spielte dieser dumme Leichtsinn immer noch seine Rolle. Besonders war es das unüberlegte Wagniß vieler Farmer, welche sich mit ihren Familien vor den mörderischen Streichen eines blutdürstigen Feindes nach einem sicheren Zufluchtsorte gerettet, sich einzeln oder in kleinen Trupps nach ihren Farmen zurückzubegeben, um nach ihren—Schweinen oder einigen Stück Hornvieh zu sehen, ein Wagniß, das so Mancher mit seinem Leben bezahlen mußte. Und in der Regel waren dies Leute, denen man im gewöhnlichen Leben nicht nachsagen konnte, daß sie tollkühn seien, vielmehr waren mehrere unter ihnen, die bei einer anderen Gelegenheit dem Tode nicht allzumuthig ins Auge geschaut hätten.

Weder durch gute noch böse Worte konnte ein Theil dieser leichtsinnigen

Starrköpfe von ihrem unseligen Beginnen, einer Kuh oder eines Schweines wegen ihr Leben auf das Spiel zu setzen, abgehalten werden; alle wohlgemeinten vor der Gefahr warnenden Worte waren in den Wind gesprochen. Manche wurden denn auch schon auf dem Wege dahin, andere auf ihren Farmen selbst durch die Kugeln der in einem Hinterhalt liegenden rothen Mörder niedergestreckt. Diese unglücklichen Opfer eines grenzenlosen Leichtsinnes waren stets zum größeren Theil Familienväter, und vergeblich warteten die Gattin und die Kinder in ihren sicheren Zufluchtsorten auf die Rückkehr des Gatten und Vaters. Viele wußten es nicht oder wollten es nicht wissen, daß man es in der Person des Indianers mit einem heimtückischen, hinterlistigen Feinde zu thun hatte, bei dem man stets auf seiner Hut sein muß und die nöthige Vorsicht nie außer Acht lassen darf.

Man hatte zur Zeit des Indianer-Ausbruchs im Sommer 1862 im oberen Minnesota-Thale weder Eisenbahnen noch Telegraphen. Um dringende Depeschen schnell zu übermitteln mußte man in damaliger Zeit zu einem guten Pferde und einem guten Reiter seine Zuflucht nehmen, und daher kam es, daß etwa 24 Stunden vor jener stürmischen Nacht, in welcher unter den oben erwähnten Hindernissen der Verfasser mit seinen 50 Mann so schnell als möglich vorwärts drang, um den bedrängten Ansiedlern am Watonwanflusse die nöthige Hülfe zu bringen, die Indianer, wohlwissend, daß die Rächer für ihre abermaligen Bluttaten bald auf der Bildfläche erscheinen würden, vor der Ankunft der letzteren wiederholt so viele Gräuelthaten begingen, als es ihnen nur irgendwie in der kurzen Zeit möglich war zu begehen.

Abermals, wie im vergangenen Sommer, drangen sie in die Wohnungen der Farmer, und mordeten Alle deren sie in der Eile habhaft werden konnten. In einem zwei Meilen von dem Fort gelegenen Hause war die junge Frau eben zu Bette gegangen, als drei der rothen Schufte die Thüre zertrümmerten und in das Schlafgemach eindrangen. Der Mann selbst, ein junger Norweger, hielt sich zur Zeit in Mankato auf, um einige dringende Geschäfte zu erledigen. Zum Glücke für seine Familie hatte er aber, ehe er sich von seiner Heimath entfernte, den Kommandanten des kleinen Postens ersucht, während seiner Abwesenheit zwei Mann zur Beschützung seiner Angehörigen in seinem Hause einzuquartiren. Dem Verlangen war entsprochen worden, und zwei handfeste Söhne des Nordens bildeten die kleine Besatzung seines Hauses. Alle lagen schon im tiefen Schlafe, da ertönte plötzlich ein Krach, die Thüre ward aufgesprengt und das Krachen derselben, sowie einige gegen das Bett der Frau abgefeuerte Schüsse erklärten den beiden Soldaten, daß ihre Hülfe nicht umsonst verlangt worden sei. Mit Blitzesschnelle sprangen sie von ihrem Lager, doch ihre Gewehre standen im Schlafzimmer der Frau, in welches die Indianer schon eingedrungen waren. Die Rothhäute konnten im Dunkel der

Nacht zum Glücke für die Ueberfallenen die geladenen Waffen der beiden Soldaten nicht erblicken, und beschränkten sich nun darauf, als die letzteren auf dem Kampfplatze erschienen, da sie ihre eigenen Flinten abgeschossen, und ihnen keine Zeit zum Laden übrig blieb, den beiden Norwegern mit ihren Pfeilen, welche sie, aber ohne Bogen bei sich trugen, zu Leibe zu gehen. Doch da kamen sie schlecht an. Der Faustschlag eines der Nordlandsrecken streckte einen Indianer sofort zu Boden, und die wuchtigen Hiebe, welche ein anderer erhielt, machten diesen sowohl als den dritten daran denken, so schnell als möglich das Haus zu verlassen, und ihr Heil in der Flucht zu suchen. Der bewußtlos am Boden liegende Indianer war nun vollständig in der Gewalt der beiden Soldaten, und was diese, als sie ausfanden, daß die arme junge Frau durch einen der drei abgefeuerten Schüsse schwer verwundet war, mit dem rothen Spitzbuben angefangen, läßt sich leicht denken. Als er wieder zum Bewußtsein kam, wurde er mit einigen gutgezielten Schüssen in seine ewigen Jagdgründe geschickt.

Gegen Morgen, als wir uns eben zum Aufbruch fertig machten, nachdem Mannschaften und Pferde einige Stunden geruht hatten, kamen unerwartet von Fort Ridgely her noch 50 Mann von unserem Regiment, um sich mit uns zur weiteren und besseren Verfolgung der Indianer zu vereinigen. Der damalige Kommandant des genannten Forts, Oberst-Lieutenant Wm. Pfänder, gewiß fast jedem Turner der Ver. Staaten rühmlichst bekannt, hatte, auf die erste erhaltene Nachricht von dem Erscheinen der Indianer am Watonwan-Flusse, sofort diese Mannschaft abgeschickt, um eine Vereinigung mit den von St. Peter aus beorderten Leuten des Regiments zu bewerkstelligen. Zudem wußte man ja nicht und konnte es auch nicht wissen, ob diese nicht sehr starke Bande Indianer, welche so plötzlich ihr blutiges Erscheinen am Watonwan-Flusse gemacht, nicht etwa die Avantgarde einer größeren Masse der rothen Bestien sei, die den schimpflichen Tod ihrer 38 Genossen am Galgen nicht vergessen konnten. Doch die Befürchtung, daß die vertriebenen Indianer ihre immerhin noch nicht zu verachtenden Streitkräfte an einem Punkte vereinigt haben könnten, um abermals verheerend und zerstörend unter den Bleichgesichtern zu erscheinen, war eine unbegründete, denn die Bande der am Watonwan-Flusse so plötzlich erschienenen Rothhäute hatte den Zug auf eigene Faust unternommen.

Little Crow, der schlaueste unter den schlauen rothen Spitzbuben, hatte seine Krieger ermahnt, von jetzt ab in nicht allzugroßer Anzahl zusammen auf den Kriegspfad gegen die Bleichgesichter zu ziehen, sondern in kleineren Abtheilungen, welche sich eher zwischen den, jetzt von der Grenze des Staates Jowa bis Fort Ridgely und von da weiter gegen Fort Ripley zu, angelegten Befestigungswerken durchschleichen könnten. Der weiße Mann hat viele Soldaten in Minnesota, hatte dieser Häuptling zu seinen Untergebenen gesagt, die euch, wenn ihr in größerer Zahl erscheint, leicht den Rückzug abschneiden können, und dann ist, wie ihr wohl wißt, euer Schicksal besiegelt. Und der alte Häuptling hatte Recht; denn die manchmal in Banden von vier bis fünf an der Grenze erscheinenden Indianer hatten fast jedesmal Erfolge zu verzeichnen, da es ihnen oft gelang, einzelne auf ihrem Felde beschäftigten Farmer aus einem Hinterhalt zu erschießen, und nebenbei Pferde zu stehlen. Höchst selten konnte man einen der rothen Raubmörder für die begangenen Gräuelthaten zur Rechenschaft ziehen, denn so schnell als sie, hauptsächlich im Schutze der Wälder, gekommen, eben so schnell waren sie auch wieder verschwunden. Doch mit dem Beginn der wärmeren Jahreszeit im Jahre 1863, als der Grenzcordon mit mehr Militär, hauptsächlich Kavallerie, besetzt werden konnte, ward den rothen Buschkleppern ihr blutiges Handwerk gelegt, denn mehrere wurden bei der Ausübung des letzteren erschossen, und unter denselben einige durch begangene Gräuelthaten hervorragenden Persönlichkeiten.

Am Morgen des 9. April saßen wir, mit Proviant auf fünf Tage versehen, nunmehr hundert Mann stark und alle gut beritten, zur Verfolgung der rothen Mörder im Sattel. Doch da die Indianer einen Vorsprung von fast 30 Stunden hatten, so durften wir unter keiner Bedingung ihnen direkt auf dem Fuße gegen Lake Shetek hin folgen, sondern mußten, sollte unsre Bemühung, sie einzuholen und zu züchtigen, von Erfolg gekrönt sein, uns mehr seitwärts in die um diese Jahreszeit noch ganz kahle Prairie schlagen, um wo möglich der Räuberbande ihren Rückzug durch die letztere abzuschneiden. Der freundliche Leser, dem die Bedeutung des Wortes Prairie oder Steppe nicht so recht bekannt ist, wird mir hier gewiß erlauben, ihm eine kleine Aufklärung darüber zu geben. Für Vergnügungsreisende, welche aus Neugierde oder um dem Vergnügen der Jagd sich hinzugeben, die ungeheueren Ebenen des Nordwestens der Vereinigten Staaten im Sommer besuchen, mag der Reiz der Neuheit seine Wirkung nicht verfehlen, aber dennoch werden auch sie in den meisten Fällen geblendet durch das immerwährende Einförmige der Natur, sowie durch die scheinbar endlose Fernsicht; auch sie werden sehr oft von dem sogenannten Prairie-Fieber befallen, welche Krankheit mehr eine Krankheit der Seele als des Körpers und als eine Art von Heimweh zu bezeichnen ist. Doch Derjenige, welcher an den Aufenthalt in dieser großen Ebene, welche man Monate lang durchstreifen kann, ohne einen Baum oder nur ein kleines Gesträuch anzutreffen, gewohnt ist, kann sich schwer trennen von der ihm lieb gewordenen Einförmigkeit. Der Verfasser dieses traf im Sommer 1864 im nördlichen Theile des Territoriums Dakota mit einem alten Trapper (Fallensteller) zusammen, welcher schon über 30 Jahre in seiner Erdhütte in dieser unendlichen Einsamkeit zugebracht, und sich nur wenn er Munition, Tabak und Salz gebrauchte, höchstens einmal im Jahre nach einem entfernten Militär-Posten begab, um gegen Felle diese ihm unentbehrlichen Gegenstände einzuhandeln. Auf die Frage, ob er keine Sehnsucht nach seiner früheren Heimath in Illinois oder dem gesellschaftlichen Zusammenleben mit Menschen dann und wann verspüre, schüttelte der Alte den Kopf und meinte, er möchte um keinen Preis seine liebgewonnene jetzige Heimath, diese scheinbar enblose Prairie, verlassen.

Es ist nun allerdings wahr, daß das wogende Blumenmeer der Prairie einen eigenthümlichen Eindruck auf das Gemüth des fühlenden Menschen ausübt. Man denke sich eine Ebene so weit als das Auge reicht, heute in Roth, nach dem Verlaufe von zwei oder drei Wochen in Gelb, dann wieder in Blau schimmernd, und man hat ein Bild der Steppe der Vereinigten Staaten im Sommer. Doch wie anders sieht es in diesen Gegenden im Winter oder auch noch früh im beginnenden Frühling aus. Furchtbare Schneestürme rasen zeitweise mit diabolischer Wildheit über die unabsehbare Fläche und wehe dem armen Wanderer, der die Grenze der Steppe überschritten, und dem entfesselten Elemente preisgegeben ist. Die ganze weite Ebene ist dann weiter nichts als ein riesiges Leichentuch das alles Leben mit erstarrendem Hauche unter sich begräbt. Hauptsächlich waren es in früheren Jahren, als die Militär-Posten der Vereinigten Staaten manchmal einige hundert engl. Meilen von einander entfernt lagen, und Truppenverschiebungen im Anfange des Winter und öfters selbst mitten in demselben zur dringenden Nothwendigkeit wurden, Soldaten, welche, auf ihren Märschen von solchen eisigen Stürmen überrascht, denselben zum Opfer fielen.

Im Winter 1864 ward eine auf dem Wege nach Fort Wadsworth befindliche Compagnie Cavallerie in der Steppe von einem Schneesturm überrascht, und fielen ein Drittel der Leute nebst einem Theil der Pferde dem eisigen Winde zum Opfer. Wer jemals von einem Schneesturm, selbst in schon bewohnten Gegenden, doch fern von einem schützenden Walde, überrascht wurde, und das Glück hatte mit dem Leben davon zu kommen, der wird in seinem ganzen Leben die Schreckenszeit, welche er in dem rasenden Durcheinander von eisigem Wind und wirbelndem Schneegestöber zugebracht, nicht vergessen. Gegen den Sturm selbst anzukämpfen, ist eine reine Unmöglichkeit und nur dadurch kann der von ihm Ueberfallene sich vielleicht retten, daß er mit dem rasenden Element zurück geht, und durch stetige Bewegung seinem Körper die nöthige Wärme erhält; doch wehe dem Unglücklichen, der ohne einen schützenden Wald oder eine menschliche Wohnung zu erreichen, ermattet zusammensinkt; er ist in kurzer Zeit eine starre Leiche. Das Eigenthümliche bei diesem furchtbaren Naturereigniß ist, daß, wie der Blitz bei einem Gewitter, ein sekundenlanges Aufleuchten die dichte Finsterniß durchbricht, und es dem von einem solchen Schneesturm überraschten Wanderer ermöglicht, aber auch nur auf einen Augenblick, Umschau zu halten. Glücklich, wenn er alsdann einen schützenden Punkt erspäht, welchen er zu erreichen im Stande ist. Dies, lieber Leser, ist annähernd eine Darstellung eines Schneesturmes im Winter oder früh im Frühjahr in der Prairie; doch diese furchtbare Naturerscheinung in ihrer ganzen Ausdehnung zu beschreiben, vermag eine Feder nicht, nur wer mit dem Herrn Boreas persönlich Bekanntschaft gemacht, und so glücklich war, seiner eisigen Umstrickung sich noch rechtzeitig zu entwinden, weiß, was ein Schneesturm da draußen in der Ebene zu bedeuten hat.

Es war also am Morgen des erwähnten Apriltages, als wir das kleine Fort am Watonwan=Fluß verließen, um die flüchtigen rothen Mordbrenner einzuholen, und sie für die früheren und jetzt wieder begangenen Greuelthaten zu züchtigen. Und vorwärts ging es so rasch als die Pferde ausgreifen konnten, denn wir mußten ja ungefähr die Gegend nach der sie sich hingewendet, und gedachten sie längstens am nächsten Tage einzuholen. Doch auch die Indianer waren gut beritten und zündeten in unsrer Front beständig das trockene Gras der Prairie an, so daß wir für unsre Pferde keine andere Nahrung hatten, als das mitgenommene Korn, das aber auf die Dauer zur Fütterung nicht genügend war. Dennoch dauerte die wilde Jagd fünf volle Tage, und es waren, um mit den Vorräthen für Menschen und Thier auszukommen, die Mannschaften sowohl als auch die Pferde schon seit 2½ Tagen auf halbe Rationen gesetzt. Am Abend des fünften Tages, als wir todtmüde von dem heutigen Parforceritte, zu unserem Glücke in einer Schlucht lagerten, welche mit etwas Holz bewachsen war, brach ein Schneesturm mit einer Heftigkeit los, wie ein solches Unwetter nur in der Steppe, wo sich kein Wiederstand seinem rasenden Laufe bietet, vorkommen kann. Doch wir hatten Feuer und das zur Unterhaltung desselben nöthige Holz, mußten aber alles Mögliche thun, um die, die Menschen und Thiere erwärmende Glut stets mit neuer Nahrung zu versorgen. Es stürmte die ganze Nacht und an Schlafen konnte nicht gedacht werden. Wir lagerten um die riesigen Feuer, denen Baum nach Baum zum Opfer fiel, und gedeckt durch die Wände der tiefen Schlucht war unsre Situation unter den obwaltenden Umständen immerhin noch eine erträgliche zu nennen. Aber an eine weitere Verfolgung der Indianer konnte jetzt nicht mehr gedacht werden. Wüthend, die rothen Schufte nicht erreicht zu haben, traten wir am nächsten Tage durch Schneewehen unsren Rückmarsch an; ein in Bezug auf Feindesnähe zwar nicht gefährliches, aber doch trauriges Zurückgehen.

Der Proviant für Menschen und Thiere war zusammengeschmolzen auf Rationen für höchstens noch 2½ Tage, und doch war die Stadt New Ulm, wo wir unsren Proviant ergänzen konnten, unmöglich schneller als nach 5 Tage zu erreichen. Dabei die niedergeschlagene Stimmung, die rothen Mordbrenner nicht eingeholt zu haben, um sie für die neuerdings begangenen Gräuelthaten zu züchtigen. Doch der Trieb der Selbsterhaltung gab sehr bald keinem anderen Gedanken Raum, denn die nun zu überwältigenden Strapazen waren derartig, daß sie die Feder nicht leicht beschreiben kann. Doch wir näherten uns jetzt New Ulm und waren zu guter Letzt noch so glücklich am letzten Abend unsrer Expedition, ungefähr 30 Meilen von der genannten Stadt zwei alte verlassene Blockhäuser anzutreffen, deren halbverfaulten Strohdächer zum Futter für die Pferde ein willkommener Artikel waren, und die nebenbei in ihren Innern einen kleinen Vorrath von gefrorenen Kartoffeln bargen. So widerlich das Gericht, nachdem es in der heißen Asche gebraten, auch schmeckte, der Heißhunger ist ein sehr guter Koch, es ward mit Begierde gegessen, denn in den letzten 24 Stunden hatten wir per Ration auf den Mann das Letzte, was wir an Lebensmitteln noch besaßen, einen „Cracker" zu verzehren. Wir hätten nun allerdings eines unsrer Pferde abschlachten können, doch so lange die dringendste Noth zu diesem letzten Mittel nicht aufforderte, nahm man Abstand von demselben, denn von der ganzen Mannschaft wollte keiner das ihm liebgewordene Thier zum Verzehren hergeben. Allerdings, Noth kennt kein Gebot, und hätten wir an dem Abend des naßkalten Apriltages die erfrorenen Kartoffeln nicht gefunden, welche, eine widerliche Nahrung, dennoch dem leeren Magen etwas Ruhe geboten, dann hätte das Loos entscheiden müssen, welches von den Pferden unsrem Hunger zum Opfer fallen sollte.

Oberst Marschall, später Gouverneur des Staates Minnesota, welcher mit jenen von Fort Ridgely abgeschickten 50 Mann am Watonwan-Fluß zu uns stieß, und als höherer Offizier das Kommando über die Expedition übernommen hatte, war ein jovialer Herr, der durch seine Leutseligkeit und besonders durch seinen Humor nicht wenig dazu beitrug, die Mannschaft, trotz aller Wiederwärtigkeiten und Strapazen, in beständig guter Stimmung zu erhalten. Wer heute von denjenigen, welche diese Expedition mitgemacht, zum ersten Male wieder in die Gegend kommt, wo wir unser letztes trauriges Nachtlager aufgeschlagen, der wird sich ganz sicher hier nicht mehr zurecht finden. Es ist derselbe Platz, auf dem gegenwärtig das blühende Städtchen Springfield in Brown County liegt. In gedrückter Stimmung, weil es uns nicht vergönnt war, die rothen Räuber einzuholen und zu züchtigen, verließen wir früh am nächsten Morgen die Jammerstelle, auf der wir die letzte Nacht hungernd und schlaflos zugebracht, doch immerhin hatten wir das Bewußtsein, unsre Pflicht erfüllt zu haben, und daß wir nur durch die Ungunst der Witterung und durch den Mangel an Proviant dazu gezwungen wurden, von einer weiteren Verfolgung der rothen Mörder abzustehen.

In New Ulm angekommen, fanden wir die Bevölkerung der Stadt in großer Aufregung. Gerüchte von auf der Bildfläche abermals erschienenen starken Banden von Indianern, welche selbst die jetzt in guten Vertheidigungszustand gesetzte

Turner-Stadt bald anzugreifen gedachten, waren in Umlauf gesetzt, und alle waren der Meinung, daß ein erneuerter Kampf mit den rothen Bestien in kurzer Zeit stattfinden würde. Mit welchem Jubel wir daher empfangen wurden, läßt sich leicht denken; denn brachten wir ja doch die sichere Kunde, daß die Anzahl der Indianer, welche am Watonwan-Fluß die neuesten Gräuelscenen begangen, eine sehr geringe, und daß ein abermaliger Angriff der Rothhäute auf New Ulm nicht zu befürchten sei. Nachdem nun vor allen Dingen der bellende Magen befriedigt war, wofür jeder der Unsrigen dem freundlichen Wirthe des Dakota Hauses, Herrn Adolph Seiter, zu Dank verpflichtet ist, und Mannschaft und Pferde 24 volle Stunden geruht hatten, begaben wir uns nach unsrem Standquartier St. Peter zurück, wo wir ebenfalls, da die falsche Nachricht in Cirkulation gesetzt war, wir seien durch die uns in Masse überfallenden Indianer vollständig aufgerieben worden, von den Einwohnern jubelnd empfangen wurden.

Ruhige Zeiten kamen jetzt, keine neue beunruhigende Gerüchte von Indianer-Ausbrüchen tauchten auf; doch diese Ruhe dauerte nicht lange, denn schon nach ungefähr drei Wochen kam die die Gemüther abermals aufregende Nachricht nach St. Peter, daß Indianer plötzlich auf der Farm von Oberst-Lieutenant Wm. Pfänder in Milford (nur drei Meilen von New Ulm) erschienen, einen mit Pflügen beschäftigten Arbeiter Namens Bosche erschossen, und zwei werthvolle Pferde gestohlen hätten. Sofort erhielt der Verfasser den Befehl, mit dem größten Theil seiner Compagnie nach New Ulm aufzubrechen, die Stadt zu besetzen und Jagd auf etwa in den angrenzenden Wäldern sich aufhaltende Indianer zu machen. In New Ulm angekommen erfuhren wir sofort, daß ein großer Theil der Bevölkerung in der Nachbarschaft der Stadt, nach dieser neuen Unthat der rothen Hallunken, fest entschlossen sei, ihrer sonst so lieb gewonnenen Heimath auf Nimmerwiedersehen den Rücken zu kehren. Doch durch dem Zwecke vollständig entsprechende Anordnungen (bei den entfernt wohnenden Farmern wurden je zwei bis vier Soldaten, welche selbstverständlich die zustehenden Rationen von der Compagnie bezogen, einquartirt, in der Nähe selbst wurden die Leute durch das fleißige Absuchen der Gegend und der Tag und Nacht erscheinenden Patrouillen so ziemlich beruhigt), gelang es diese abermalige Völkerwanderung bis auf den Abzug einzelner Wenigen zu beschränken.

Ruhe und Vertrauen kehrten nach und nach wieder, und wenn auch manchmal beunruhigende Gerüchte von hier oder dort erschienenen Indianern auftauchten, so waren solche Gerüchte stets derartig, daß sie bald widerlegt und als Unwahrheiten erklärt werden konnten. Den Bemühungen des Commandanten von Fort Ridgely, Oberst-Lieutenant Wm. Pfänder, gelang es denn auch den zum hauptsächlichen Zwecke des Pferde-Diebstahls sich der Grenze nähernden Indianern, das von den Rothhäuten so geliebte Gewerbe vollständig zu verleiden, und ausgesandte größere militärische Expeditionen trieben weit draußen in den Ebenen das rothe Gesindel so zu Paaren, daß ihm alle Lust verging, sich der Grenze noch einmal zu nähern. So athmete denn Alles wieder ruhig auf, und der Hoffnungsstern des Vertrauens in eine schönere Zukunft leuchtete wieder allen Gemüthern.

Bevor ich nun meine Geschichte des Indianer-Ausbruches schließe, werde ich mir erlauben zu berichten, was aus dem Haupthallunken der rothen Mörderbande, dem Häuptlinge Little Crow, geworden. Genau ein volles Jahr nach dem durch den blutgierigen Hauptspitzbuben der Dakota-Sioux angeschürten furchtbaren Ausbruch, welchem so viele Menschenleben zum Opfer fielen, erschienen zwei Indianer, Vater und Sohn, in dem riesig großen Walde in Minnesota, welcher unter dem Namen der Big Woods bekannt, um wilde Beeren zu suchen, und auch neben diesem friedlichen Geschäfte, wenn die Gelegenheit dazu günstig, Pferde zu stehlen. Zwei zufällig in der Gegend anwesende norwegische Jäger, ebenfalls Vater und Sohn, sahen ohne von ihnen bemerkt zu werden die beiden Indianer, und wohlwissend, daß ein guter Preis für das Einbringen des Scalps einer Rothhaut ausgesetzt war, schossen sie den Alten sofort nieder, der junge Indianer floh, ward aber später eingefangen, und in Fort Snelling in sicheren Gewahrsam gebracht. Allerdings mußten die beiden Norweger damals nicht, wer der rothe Spitzbube war, den sie eben in seine ewigen Jagdgründe befördert, doch später bei der genaueren Untersuchung der Leiche ward die Thatsache festgestellt und von dem gefangenen Sohne auch bestätigt, daß der Erschossene kein Anderer, als der blutdürstige Häuptling der Dakota-Sioux, Little Crow selbst, war. Er ward an einem alten Armbruche und einer eigenthümlichen Form der Zähne erkannt.

Schließen wir nun unsere Geschichte mit dem theilweise befriedigenden Bewußtsein, daß wenigstens ein Theil der rothen Mordbrenner von ihrem Schicksal erreicht, den schimpflichen, aber hundertfach verdienten, Tod am Galgen gestorben, und daß zu guter Letzt der Hauptanführer der Hallunken, Little Crow, hungernd umherirrend, verlassen von Allen, die ihm früher nahe gestanden, nur von seinem Sohne begleitet, und nicht an der Spitze seiner sonst so stolzen Kriegerschaar, in tiefer Waldeinsamkeit von den Kugeln zweier weißen Jäger getroffen, seine mörderische Laufbahn zum richtigen, wohlverdienten Abschluß brachte.

Anhang.

Zur besseren Orientirung des geneigten Lesers über die wichtigsten Oertlichkeiten, welche in dem vorstehend beschriebenen Ausbruche der Indianer eine hervorragende Rolle spielten, halte ich es für meine Pflicht, dieselben etwas näher zu bezeichnen.

Beginnen wir also mit New Ulm, welches dem ersten Ansturm der Indianer die Stirne zu bieten hatte, denn die auf den beiden Agenturen am 18. August von den Indianern Ermordeten waren, wie fast alle von ihnen getödtete Landbewohner, von den rothen Teufeln meuchlerisch überfallen und ohne Widerstand leisten zu können, abgeschlachtet worden. Die mit sehr wenigen Ausnahmen von Deutschen bewohnte Stadt New Ulm war und ist heute noch die Hauptstadt von Brown County, Minnesota. Die ersten Ansiedler und Gründer des Platzes kamen bereits im Jahre 1854 hierher und da die meisten von ihnen früher in der Umgegend von Ulm in Würtemberg ihre Heimath gehabt und die Erinnerung an ihr früheres Heimathland bewahrt hatten, so ward der neugegründeten Stadt, zu Ehren der altehrwürdigen Reichsstadt im alten Vaterlande, der Name New Ulm gegeben. Diese Würtemberger und einige andere Deutsche gehörten größtentheils zu einer in Chicago gegründeten Gesellschaft, welche hier oben an der Grenze der Indianer-Reservation eine Colonie gründeten und schon damals von den umherschweifenden Rothhäuten, obgleich sie ihnen alles nur mögliche Gute erwiesen, viel zu leiden hatten. Im Jahre 1856 wurde zwischen der genannten Gesellschaft und dem Ansiedlungsverein des nordamerikanischen Turnerbundes ein Uebereinkommen getroffen, in Folge dessen viele Turner aus den größeren Städten der Union, hauptsächlich aber von Cincinnati in Ohio herbeikamen, um sich hier dauernd nieder zu lassen. So kam es, daß diese Turner-Colonie, wie der Platz von jetzt ab häufig genannt wurde, bald zu einem blühenden Städtchen heranwuchs und im Sommer des Jahres 1862 bereits über 200 Gebäude mit mehr als 900 Einwohnern sein eigen nennen konnte. Die Lage von New Ulm ist eine reizende, doch ist die Stadt selbst zu weit ausgedehnt, was selbstverständlich die Vertheidigung derselben erschwerte. Auf drei Terrassen erbaut, konnte nur der Geschäftstheil auf der mittleren Terrasse und ein Theil der oberen vertheidigt werden. Der untere Theil mußte gleich bei dem Beginne des Kampfes, weil nicht genügende Streitkräfte vorhanden, aufgegeben werden, wie auch viele der außerhalb der Vertheidigungs-Linie zerstreut liegenden Häuser. Diesem Umstande war es daher auch zuzuschreiben, daß bei dem zweiten Angriff der Indianer nur etwa 40 im Centrum gelegene Gebaude gerettet werden konnten, während der übrige und größere Theil in Flammen aufging.

Fort Ridgely liegt 18 englische Meilen oberhalb New Ulm und war in der Zeit des Indianer-Ausbruchs ein Militär-Posten und nichts weniger als eine Festung. Es ist schon seit langen Jahren aufgegeben und liegt gegenwärtig in Ruinen. Vor dem Bürgerkriege hatte es regelmäßig eine Besatzung von vier Compagnien der regulären Armee der Ver. Staaten, welche bei dem Ausbruch der südlichen Rebellion nach dem Kriegsschauplatze beordert und durch verhältnißmäßig schwache Streitkräfte der Freiwilligen ersetzt wurden. Die Lage des Forts selbst ist zur Vertheidigung eine sehr ungünstige, und bei dem zweitägigen Kampfe mit den Indianern hatte es nur seinen Kanonen und der trefflichen Bedienungsmannschaft derselben seine Rettung zu verdanken.

Die beiden Agenturen, die Civilisations-Fabriken für die Rothhäute, lagen oberhalb des erwähnten Forts, die untere Agentur 12 Meilen, die obere ungefähr 40 engl. Meilen von demselben entfernt. Hier waren eine Anzahl Regierungsgebäude, Wohnungen für die Beamten, Schmiede- und Wagner-Werkstätten, u. s. w. errichtet. Außerdem hatten die privilegirten Händler, welche das alleinige Recht hatten, den Indianern ihre schlechten Waaren zu einem guten Preise zu verkaufen, ihre Wohn- und Lagerhäuser hier stehen. Alle diese Gebäulichkeiten sind schon seit langer Zeit verschwunden, und der Boden auf dem sie einst gestanden ist in Privat-Besitz übergangen, ebenso die Ländereien, wovon ein Theil durch die Regierung für die rothen Tagdiebe umgeackert und angepflanzt waren.

Zwischen diesen Agenturen und Fort Ridgely auf der einen Seite und nach New Ulm zu auf der anderen Seite des Minnesota-Flusses wurden von den wilden Bestien die meisten Mordthaten begangen. Hauptsächlich waren die Ortschaften auf dem linken Ufer des Flußes der Schauplatz vieler Gräuelscenen. Hier fielen ganze Familien der Blutgier dieser Teufel in Menschengestalt zum Opfer.

Die Stadt Mankato, wo die 38 Bluthunde ihren hundertfach verdienten Lohn am Galgen erhielten, liegt 28 Meilen unterhalb New Ulm und hätte, wäre die letztere Stadt von den Indianern genommen worden, sich gegen dieselben nicht halten können, da ihre Lage zur Vertheidigung eine höchst ungünstige ist. Dies sind so ziemlich die Oertlichkeiten, welche mit dem Ausbruche der Sioux-Indianer im August 1862 mehr oder weniger in Erinnerung gebracht werden müssen, da theilweise in und zwischen ihnen das furchtbare Drama sich abspielte.

❋❋❋❋

PART TWO—ENGLISH EDITION (1994)

❋❋❋❋

To the Brave Defenders
of the City of New Ulm
On the Occasion
of the 25th Anniversary
of the Sioux Uprising

–Table of Contents–

1. Introduction
2. The Cause of the Sioux Uprising
3. Warnings to the Winds
4. The Cry of Horror
5. Captain Marsh
6. New Ulm
7. Nix Appointed Commandant of New Ulm
8. The 19th of August 1862
9. "To Your Posts! Get Ready to Fight!"
10. The Plan of the Attackers
11. The Battle of New Ulm
12. Honor to Whom Honor is Due!
13. Fort Ridgely
14. The Second Attack on New Ulm
15. Colonel Flandrau Appointed Commander-in-Chief
16. Victory or Death
17. Trenches
18. The Indian Retreat from New Ulm
19. The Departure from New Ulm
20. Conditions in New Ulm
21. Hutchinson
22. Retreat and Defeat
23. Trial in Mankato
24. The 38 Murderers and Rapists
25. Crime and Punishment
26. April 1863—A Second Reign of Terror?
27. The Prairie
28. The Watonwon River Expedition
29. Peace
30. Appendix

–1.–

INTRODUCTION

The rising sun of the 18th of August 1862 beamed mildly and friendly upon the Turner town of New Ulm and the surrounding territory in the upper Minnesota Valley. Peaceful silence rested upon the magnificent landscape, interrupted only by the chirping of the feathered songsters that jubilantly greeted Aurora as it appeared on the firmament.

Here and there now, things began to stir. Yet neither the lonely wanderers along the country roads, nor the farmers setting out for their work in the fields had any idea that this peaceful silence would soon be broken by the painful moaning of the wounded and the groans of the dying, intermingled with the fiendish war cries of the Sioux Indians. To be sure, those who were better informed knew that the Indians had had disagreements with the agents of the U.S. Government when their annual payments were to be delivered to them and, as a result of this, had been unusually excited. Full well did most of the officials at both agencies know that the Indians went about sullenly for several days and that in their secret meetings, terrible threats had been uttered against the white man. Full well did many know these ill feelings, because of reports and warnings which had come to them through several Indians who were friendly to the white man. But in spite of all this, the agents of the Government paid very little attention to these warnings. With unpardonable carelessness they calmed their fears with the thought that the handful of soldiers stationed at the two meeting places of the Indians would be far superior to the Redskins. Things turned out differently.

The officials and dealers at both agencies would only too soon regret their blissful sense of security under the blows of the tomahawk of the red man. However, we do not wish to record events which followed later, but rather desire to discover first and foremost what caused the Redskins, who had always appeared to be calm and quiet on the days when they were paid, to change to veritable beasts, compared to which the tiger of the East Indian jungles might be considered a sympathetic creature.

The contract made between the U.S. Government and the Sioux Indians contained the clause that the U.S. Government was to pay to the Redskins annually sums of U.S. money in gold coins in return for the large tract of land which they had given up, and so much was to be paid per person. Now whoever has at any time had business dealings with the Indians, such as the purchase of pelts, maple sugar, etc., knows that the red man will only on very rare occasions agree upon barter. He sells and buys only for ready cash. One must realize also that the Redskin has had traditionally a superstitious, and in most cases a justified dread of all paper money, which at that time seemed to grow like mushrooms in U.S. and Canadian banks. We do not mean to maintain that all villains and swindlers are Indian agents, but no sensible human being, even though he may be only partially familiar with the Indians and their relations to the agencies, could deny that a large number of the Indian agents might be worthy of the honorary title of "rogue."

To date, no statistics have been compiled to show how many attacks of the Redskins on the settlements of the white man, accompanied by murder and fire, may be blamed upon Indian agents. However, the number is quite significant. Every person of feeling will and must deplore the unshaken fact that the Moloch of contemptible bain, who in the shape of illegal enrichment appeared in a number of scoundrels, has made a sacrifice of thousands of brave and industrious white settlers. Also, here in Minnesota the desire to gain wealth played an important role in bringing about the scenes of horror which took place in the last half of the month of August 1862. No one can deny that the greed of one of the government officials of that time had a great deal of responsibility for the terrible outbreak of the Sioux Indians in the Upper Mississippi Valley. In fact, the same person who was possessed of only one thought, to squeeze a maximum of dollars out of the Indians, bears sole blame for the horrible fate of many brave settlers.

—2.—

THE CAUSE OF THE SIOUX UPRISING

I shall now attempt to prove beyond doubt that with the above assumption the nail has been squarely hit on the head, and that all other intimations regarding the cause of the Sioux uprising belong to the realm of fiction. The total silence with regard to the underlying facts, however, is a blatant falsification of history, for no intelligent person can accept the explanation that it is impossible to discover what induced the red man to suddenly go on the warpath against the whites and slaughter more than seven hundred of them. Everyone must see that there must have been some reason for these crimes. The opinion expressed by certain persons that the question of money did not play a role in the terrible drama is downright ridiculous; and so is the rumor that the Indians were incited by several visiting representatives of the Confederacy who had promised them the help of the South. This proves that someone wished to hush up the truth, even though the facts and the proof of the real cause of the uprising were obvious. Notwithstanding my personal dislike of the southern rebels, I cannot subscribe to the statement that it was they who caused the Indian uprising of that time.

Other Day, one of the few Indians under whose red skin beat a human and thankful heart, knew that the uprising was not caused by the southern rebels. Other Day has established for his name an honorable place in the history of Minnesota, because the bearer of that name, in grateful remembrance of the ever open hand of the white man in times of need, had continuously advised his tribesmen against going on the warpath against the pale face. When he was later asked whether any representative of the southern rebel government had, at that time, appeared among the Indians and had incited them by means of deceptive pretense to make war against the white man, Other Day declared that this was not the case. If this were still insisted upon, he would have to declare it to be an infamous lie. This brave Indian had attended all the secret meetings of his tribesmen, in which he always arose as a friend of his white brothers and advised peace. Again in the meeting held the day before the outbreak, he protested against all violence. Other Day, and we cannot mention the name of this brave man often enough, when he was convinced that the bloodthirsty desires of his dehumanized tribesmen could not be stilled by words of reconciliation, left his coat and hat behind as he took flight from this last and decisive council of the Redskins. Besides, at this meeting, Little Crow had repeatedly declared him to be a traitor of his tribe and, hence, an outlaw.

The brave man, knowing full well that the lives of many whites depended upon him, now hurried as rapidly as he could to the Upper Agency, which was most distantly located from all places of refuge. He saved the lives of sixty white men, women, and children, by taking them along remote paths through the prairie to a place of safety. Honor be to his memory!

The reader will now permit me to move directly toward my goal, that is, to prove by means of facts, that the avarice, greed, and the unscrupulousness of certain individuals must be considered the central cause of the Sioux uprising.

The scheduled time for the 1862 payment had come, and the Indians were assembled at the two agencies, the so-called Upper and Lower Agencies. The paymaster had arrived and that part of the annual payment which dealt with munitions, woolen blankets, etc., had begun. Up to this point everything was going smoothly, but now came the time to pay out the cash. The official had paper money. The Indians, however, wanted gold, to which they were entitled according to the agreement with the U.S. Government, and the explanation that paper money was of the same value as gold, they did not accept. Then the paymaster left the agency with the promise to return in a short time and give them their annual payment in hard cash. The Sioux were satisfied for the time being, but they were soon to find out that they had been deceived with regard to the promised speedy return of the particular official who was to pay them in gold, as had always been done before. Days and weeks went by, but the paymaster did not return. The obvious purpose behind the delay was to break the spirit of these obstinate Indians, and thus force them to accept the paper money. Gold at that time already had a premium value of 12%, and kept rising from day to day. Somebody was out to make a buck in this shady deal, but who was it?

In the meantime, the merchants at the agencies refused to grant the Indians credit, which had heretofore always been extended willingly. Yes, rumor has it that some of the merchants, when asked to give provisions on credit, scornfully laughed at the Indians and said, "You can eat grass." As a result of this pinch, living conditions of the Indians became desperate. Eyewitnesses later assured us that many small Indian children literally died of starvation.

–3.–

WARNINGS TO THE WINDS

The farmers in the vicinity and the inhabitants of the little towns located nearby did their utmost to mitigate this misery. The begging Indians were given every possible help. The inhabitants of the Upper Minnesota Valley, therefore, believed that the Indians, with whom they had been on the friendliest of terms and to whom they had repeatedly shown kindness, would not consider the settlers living near the agencies responsible for their present misery. But whoever has come in contact with savages, whether in Africa, Australia, or America, or elsewhere on earth, and whoever has had the opportunity to observe them closely knows that the brute only slumbers in the savage, and, once aroused, may pounce with tigerlike bloodthirstiness upon the nearest victims. The tragic confidence of the inhabitants of the Upper Minnesota Valley in the hypocritical friendship and the submissive manner of the Indians whom they had so willingly helped in time of direst need, even sharing with them their last provisions, this blind confidence led to the ruination of a large number of the settlers. All warnings of precaution were in vain. In vain, too, were the gesticulations of several friendly Indians who tried thereby to portray the scenes of horror which were soon to make a bloody red appearance. Each and every warning was as if spoken to the winds. "The Indians are our friends; we have shown them so much kindness and they will under no circumstances lay violent hands on the farmers of the neighborhood and their families."

Oh, how the bloodthirsty Redskins betrayed the confidence of their white friends and helpers in times of need! The tomahawk of the inhuman savage separated with one blow the hand of the white man and the white woman from the body—the same hand which a few days before had sympathetically given refreshing alms to him and his hungry children. The beast awakened which had, up to now, been slumbering in the bosom of the Redskin, the wild scoundrel, who now treated the devoted white friend as if he were the bitterest enemy. All this is sufficient proof that the suddenly unfettered fury of the Indian knows no distinction between friend and foe. The Redskin, controlled by this diabolical power only wants to reckon with his bloodthirsty desires.

It is part of the nature of the son of the wilderness to release, from time to time, the beast of his innermost being upon his fellow man. Woe to the one who becomes his victim! Of mercy there is not a trace. The savage knows as little about this, as does the tiger, for the latter, at least, does not take time to torture his victim long, but immediately crushes it between his teeth. For that reason, it is a double crime on the part of the officials appointed for the Indians by the Government, if they incite the sullen but repressed fury of the Redskins to a terrible rage by means of committing injustices. This fury then breaks upon the heads of unsuspecting settlers with the rapidity of lightning, bringing destruction, just as lightning would.

But sneers and fiendish laughter! Why would one not from time to time grant the Indians the pleasure of massacring several hundred whites? After a while one will overpower them again, crush them, in most cases though only after a wearisome and very costly war, and then finally bring the captives to newly erected reservations. These are but the almshouses for the superfluous office-seekers of the political party which is at the time in office, and which aims to satisfy these political moles by an appointment, since in newly erected Indian reservations one also needs to have new officials. But as long as corrupt political leaders in this great Republic are at loggerheads with one another during elections, and as long as the politicians of the victorious party adhere to the motto "To the victor belong the spoils," Indian agencies will appear to be especially suitable for political appointments. But let us now give the political birds of prey a chance to rest, for the time being, in their captured nests, and let us return, in spirit to that quiet beautiful morning of 18 August 1862.

—4.—

THE CRY OF HORROR

On the day before the fateful summer morning, on the 17th, the Turner town of New Ulm was full of activity. A company of volunteers which consisted, in fact, of half-breeds and which had enlisted for Uncle Sam at one of the two agencies, appeared suddenly and was jubilantly received by the patriotic inhabitants. Only a few, who were well informed in regard to the conditions existing at that time in the meeting places of the Indians, were surprised that just now one of the highest ranking governmental officials should leave the agencies behind and take to Fort Snelling, located 100 miles from New Ulm. Didn't this man know that during the past days the starving Indians had assumed a more than threatening attitude, or did he not wish to know? This has been an unsolved riddle up to the present time. Several persons are still insisting that the gentleman wished to escape the threatening thunderclouds in order to save his hide before lightning struck. Comments concerning the possibility of an attack by the Indians upon farms near the two agencies were indignantly rejected, for after all, one said, this official would never have dared to leave his post at such a critical time. Therefore, in the night of the 17th/18th of August and on the following morning, the people of New Ulm and the entire surrounding territory were carefree and unconcerned, unsuspecting of death and destruction which was threatening the two agencies. Suddenly, like a bolt of lightning from a clear blue sky, the cry of horror resounded, "The Indians have gone on the warpath and are murdering all the settlers."

A cry of horror, but also of indignation and righteous anger over the negligence of the Government which had left the two agencies and almost the entire Upper Minnesota Valley at the mercy of the tomahawk of the red beasts, resounded through the entire state of Minnesota. One knew only too well what the few expressive words signified, "The Indians have gone on the warpath." With the arrival of many refugees and wounded, Fort Ridgely was first to learn about the horror caused by the uprising. Fort Ridgely is located on a plateau of the chain of hills which stretches along on the left side of the Minnesota River and is 18 miles away from New Ulm. Here there was only a weak garrison which consisted of a company of the 5th regiment of the Minnesota Volunteers, only strong enough to surround this military station with a chain of sentries. Instead of the four companies of regular troops which had been stationed there in former times, among which there was also a battery with six light field guns, there was now only a garrison composed of a handful of volunteers who had enlisted only a few months before. But the brave commander of the Fort, Captain Marsh, did not hesitate a moment to bring help to the distressed and, immediately after receiving the report, started out with 50 men toward the Lower Agency, a distance of 12 miles.

—5.—

Captain Marsh

This dutiful officer and most of his brave men were never to see Fort Ridgely again. Pressing forward along the country road on the left shore of the Minnesota River, the agency was located on the right, these few soldiers succeeded in protecting many refugees, mostly women and children from small roving bands of Indians. These poor and homeless had attempted to get to the shelter of the Fort.

After a dangerous and fatiguing march of several hours, the small group of soldiers arrived near the little ferry which connected the two shores of the Minnesota River not far from the Lower Agency. On the right shore of the little river there appeared, immediately upon the arrival of the soldiers, several Indians who asked the former to come over since they, the Indians, had been sent by the majority of their tribesmen to come to a friendly understanding with the soldiers. "We have always been," cried the Redskins, "friends of the white man, and are friends of him today. You must, therefore, not hold us responsible for the crimes which some miserable scoundrels of our tribe have committed." Captain Marsh, not sufficiently familiar with the treacherous character of the Indian, and knowing full well that he with his small unit could do little when facing this entire band of Indians, believed the deceitful red villains and gave, in spite of the warning of the interpreter, the immediate command to cross to the other shore. Foreseeing no danger, the small group of soldiers then left their protected position and moved toward the ferry on the bank of the river. They had hardly arrived there, the greater number of them had come into the ferry, when over 100 shots were fired from the opposite bank of the narrow river by the traitors and mortally or seriously wounded the soldiers—37 soldiers lay in their own blood.

The red beasts, more than 100 in number, had hidden, unnoticed by the soldiers, behind bushes and wood piles. Captain Marsh, who was one of the first to step into the ferry, jumped, whether wounded or not could not be determined, into the river to save himself by swimming. But several bullets of the Redskins struck and killed him at once. Only thirteen, one-fourth of the original number of brave soldiers, reached Fort Ridgely, after many further hardships.

Among those who were killed, was the interpreter of the post, by name of Quinn, born in Ireland, who knew the language of the Sioux thoroughly. He had married one of the women of the tribe and had lived with and among the Indians for many years. That the savages did not spare him but that he was shot down as one of the very first men, verifies the fact that the Indians in general with very few exceptions, have no sense of gratitude and spare neither friend nor foe once they begin to murder. Quinn was for many years the friend of their villainous chieftain, Little Crow, and in times of direst need the heart of this brave old man beat warm for the tribesmen of his wife, for whom he often secured, from the military officials at Fort Ridgely, provisions of all kinds. But for the time being, let us move from Fort Ridgely with its cannons, its soldiers and their fate, and turn to New Ulm, which had to endure the first attack of the Indians.

—6.—

NEW ULM

About 10 A.M. on 18 August, a recruiting party accompanied by a band with several wagons left the town and drove, in order to enlist recruits for the U.S. Army, first toward Milford, which was located on the border of the Indian reservation, and was one of the earliest settlements and therefore one of the most densely populated in Brown County.

The conflict with the Confederacy raged unabated and the recent call for 500,000 more men proved definitely that Uncle Sam was in deadly earnest to fight the rebels with all possible means at his disposal. From Brown County, and especially from New Ulm, its County Seat, many young men had already followed the Stars and Stripes. Now again, for the purpose of organizing another company, more recruits were needed. It was hoped to secure voluntary enlistments whenever possible, thus forestalling the hated draft. So this recruiting party left on the morning of 18 August 1862, a departure that was to be fateful to many of the group.

The inn of Mr. Anton Henle, 8 miles from New Ulm, located in the town of Milford, was designated as the first stop. Here was to begin the recruiting effort. About 1/2 mile from this place, on the road to New Ulm, a small bridge spans a ravine. Every spring the torrents rushing down there have made its sides, especially at the right side of the bridge on the Minnesota River side, quite steep. Trees and shrubs growing along its slopes have pretty well hidden the bridge. Whoever has had any experience in Indian wars will admit that the Indians, even though they don't know anything about conducting regular-type warfare, are nevertheless the best skirmishers in the world. Any small elevation, grass which is hardly a foot high, every shrub, no matter how small, is cover for them, and crawling along on their stomachs in snake-like fashion they wind their way close to the ground. Woe unto him who faces them in combat and even for a moment doesn't watch out. In the next second, the inattentive one is hit by the whirring arrow or the whizzing bullet, and the scalping knife then, as a rule, does its final and horrible duty. In open combat the

Redskin is usually a cowardly scoundrel. Only in rare exceptions, when a chief or a beloved personality of their blood relations is shot or wounded, does the Indian rush into the line of fire, into the heavy rain of bullets and tries, in heroic disregard of death, to secure from the enemy his dead or wounded one.

But let us end this discussion and return to our recruiting party. The first wagon had hardly arrived at the fateful little bridge which led across the ravine close to Henle's Inn, when a volley of shots resounded and several occupants of the wagons fell dead or mortally wounded. The others escaped the fire line in hasty flight. The murderous bullets of the savages had found their mark, because the Redskins had been hidden by the underbrush of the little ravine and were almost directly opposite the unsuspecting white men. Three of the latter remained on the spot where they fell, several others, though seriously wounded, were picked up and saved by men who followed in other wagons. These teams now hurried back to New Ulm as quickly as possible, because no one could undertake to resist the Indians here, for almost all the men in this expedition were unarmed. But the three New Ulmers, Fenske, Dietrich, and Schneider, who had been murdered at this place, as well as all the participants in the recruiting party helped greatly to slow down the murdering mood of the Redskins. They knew that the surrounding territory was now alarmed and that they would meet resistance, something the cowardly scoundrels avoid whenever possible.

The terrible news of the uprising and the acts of horror committed by the Indians in the area spread with lightning rapidity. From all directions came fleeing farmers with their families. They came by wagon, on horseback, and on foot, hoping for shelter in New Ulm.

As soon as the Sheriff of Brown County, Mr. Charles Roos, a brave and courageous man, was informed of the situation, he and a body of well armed men went to the place of the murders to investigate. At that point, people were still of the opinion that only small bands of Redskins had made the attack on the recruiting party and the farms nearby. But here, too, it became obvious that the savages will only choose ambush for their murderous actions, or when their side is 10 times stronger than the other. In cowardly fashion the Indians turned away from the small armed group of the Sheriff, and he had the satisfaction of saving and bringing to New Ulm a number of women and children who had hidden in the cornfields. Several wounded persons were also brought back.

–7.–

NIX APPOINTED COMMANDANT OF NEW ULM

In the late afternoon of the same day the writer of this narrative was appointed by the Sheriff as Commandant of New Ulm, and as such took the military oath to the State of Minnesota. Now began the real military organization, as well as this could be done in the short time which remained before the suspected attack of the Indians.

Among the citizens of New Ulm and the farmers who had taken flight to the town, there were very able men to be organized into small military units. But still as every sensible person knows, it was no small task to bring some basic military order into this confusion. Only by means of organization would it be possible to meet, with vigor, the bloodthirsty enemy who would doubtless attack the town soon. We were well aware that during a mass attack of the Indians, who had over 900 well-armed warriors, the limited military forces of New Ulm and the deficient arms of its defender would not be sufficient to seriously resist the bloodthirsty savages. If New Ulm were to be destroyed, the entire Lower Minnesota Valley would be imperiled, particularly the two low-lying neighboring cities of Mankato and St. Peter, because they were strategically rather vulnerable. The Commander, who realized that these neighboring cities would immediately answer New Ulm's cry for help, sent several messengers there who asked the citizens to hurry to the aid of New Ulm, since the Indians had gone on the warpath and the town was in extreme danger. Promptly, the call was answered with the reply that as soon as possible all available forces would be sent to help the threatened city. The first armed men, however, did not make their appearance until Tuesday, 19 August, shortly before 7 P.M. We shall return to this part of the account later.

In the meantime, those men and youths of New Ulm who had volunteered were distributed and organized. Also, as an aid to better defense the building of a number of barricades was begun and completed by the light of bonfires during the night. The men with their variety of weapons were placed in the following groups so that military operations could be begun at least to some degree:

I. Riflemen: About 14 men, consisting largely of former Cincinnati Turners, commanded by Louis Theobald.
II. Men with two-barrel guns: 18 men commanded by E. F. Brunk.
III. Men with simple, mainly poor shotguns: 12 men commanded by J. Chaikowitz.

To these men were added some 15 to 18 men, who were armed with guns of various types, but who did not join any of the groups above. [Ed. note: a total of 59/62 men.]

This, then, was the armed force of the town of New Ulm, on Tuesday, 19 August 1862, shortly before the attack of the Indians. A number of the above mentioned arms proved to be useless. But there was also a reserve equipped with pitchforks, axes of every description, and several revolvers. This group, however, was only to be put into use in case the Indians should succeed in forcing their way into the city. When one considers that at this time, there were in New Ulm over 600 local and refugee women and children, that many wounded from the surrounding territory sought shelter here, one can easily imagine that it was not an easy task to provide safe temporary shelter for so many helpless persons. Women and children were quartered in brick houses and others, which were secure against the bullets of the Indians, but space here was very limited indeed.

During these preparations and with the knowledge that the next day would decide the survival or destruction of New Ulm, that perhaps on the following evening the town might be reduced to a pile of ashes and its inhabitants buried beneath it, the Commander and the Sheriff spent many worried hours. It was in that small Sheriff's office on Minnesota St. that the two Turners, Sheriff Roos and Commandant Nix sat at a small table and conferred with one another. From time to time, also, they inspected the defense preparations, which continued through the night.

–8.–

THE 19TH OF AUGUST 1862

Finally, morning began to dawn; a beautiful morning, as the morning of the preceding day, 18 August, but still what a difference! Then joyous laughter and confidence in the future, now gloomy thoughts in spite of all assurances and comments by the Sheriff and the Commandant to the military units. If all of us worked together, we might easily prevail against the no-good rabble. It was a beautiful, but nevertheless sad morning. After all, did not nearly every defender have a wife and family to protect? But this very fact caused many a man, who might not have fought half as well for his petty prince in the old Fatherland, to conduct himself as a hero. Now he had to rescue his beloved wife and dear children from the hands of the red brutes. This was not a matter of fighting to protect a prince and his dominions but to protect one's own cherished home. That home now had to be defended by just a handful of brave men, since most of the young people were already in the service of the U.S. against the southern rebellion. It meant to put forth a total effort, for the Indian, if victorious, would have struck the word "mercy" from his vocabulary.

In his youth, the author had read with much interest the novels of Cooper. Especially *The Last of the Mohicans* aroused in him enthusiasm for the Redskins. But, unfortunately, novels have always been playing on the imagination instead of dwelling on truth and reality. Had Cooper known the real nature of the Indian, he would perhaps have preferred to put a bullet through his brain rather than writing such crazy nonsense about the red bloodhounds. No one can imagine dirtier dogs than the Indians with whom I have come in contact; they were not the last of the Mohicans, a tribe of Indians I have never seen, but tribes of Redskins in Wisconsin, Minnesota, Dakota, Idaho, Montana, and other northwestern sections which I got to know a little better. Treacherous of character, proud, and cold of bearing in response to the honest friendliness of the white men, yet begging when hungry and humbly receiving the desired gift and with a "Ho! Ho!", shaking the hand of his benefactor and then cowardly shoot him at the first opportunity, these are just about the main characteristics of our red brothers.

The Redskins hate the palefaces and their hatred has been glowing for centuries ever since the first white man appeared on this continent. And one should not believe that the present generation of Indians has forgotten, or does not know, that the entire, spacious territory of the U.S. once belonged to their ancestors and that their hunting grounds were alive and filled with all kinds of game. The savage knows this as well as we know it, and this is the reason for his unforgivable hatred of the paleface, a hatred which only waits for an opportunity to destroy the latter.

One should not, of course, have provoked the Indians with injustices, but they also should not have made the inhabitants of an entire region pay for the wrongs committed by specific individuals by murdering, burning, and scorching the earth, and attacking settlers, destroying everything—men and women, old people and children—which came before their rifles and bows and arrows. Then, of course, there suddenly appeared the fanatics who immediately took up the cause of the captured red murderers after the defeat of the uprising. The following momentous words from the Bible should have been cast before these crazy, hypocritical puritans: An eye for an eye! A tooth for a tooth! That means: Immediately after the capture of the red scoundrels, one should not have wasted any time in shooting or hanging every one who took part in the horrible crimes which occurred in the summer of 1862 in Minnesota.

But let us continue with the thread of our story. After a night filled with anxious forebodings, the rising sun again shone upon the picturesquely situated town, but it looked entirely different from 24 hours ago. Then peaceful silence, now the sound of arms, calls of patrolling soldiers, inner and outer pickets, barricades, and so on. The town of New Ulm, still so peaceful today was busy with armed men. Even though they were not in uniform, even though they did not march up and down with flags unfurled and to the sound of martial music, one could see at the roll calls that they realized why they had to exchange roles so rapidly: Yesterday, quiet citizens or peaceful farmers, today, soldiers. At first glance, one could see what the carrying of arms meant to the brave defenders of New Ulm. It meant the defense of their homes, of their loved ones. The morning passed rather quietly. But rumor had it that a number of Indians were assembled near Milford and that our town was to be attacked today. All preparations for a warm reception of the Redskins had begun, the barricades were well manned, the number of men at the inner and outer pickets were doubled, and one looked forward to what might happen with a certain degree of confidence.

About 2 P.M. a report reached town that a group of farmers near Cottonwood, a neighboring town, who had intended to flee to New Ulm with their families, had been surrounded by the Indians about 1 mile from the center of New Ulm. They would certainly be lost if not helped out of this dreadful situation. There could be armed help from New Ulm, but how could any man be spared now, not knowing which direction and when the Redskins would make their attack! The Commandant at first emphatically rejected the request, but was finally induced, by the urgent pleas of many, to help these poor people. Louis Theobald and his men were sent out but were advised not to stay away too long. If possible, they were to rescue the people and then return to New Ulm with them as hurriedly as possible.

However, more than a half an hour passed and neither the entrapped Cottonwooders, nor the men who had been sent to help them, appeared in sight. Because their absence was cause for concern that the latter had been cut off, E. F. Brunk and his men were ordered to march double time so as to lend Theobald and his men a helping hand, but then both units were to return to New Ulm as quickly as possible. It is sad but true that the lives of many have been placed as risk because of false report or a base lie, and it later turned out to be that there was not a trace of any entrapped Cottonwooders.

Now it was almost 3 P.M. when Engineer Brockmann stationed with field glasses on the flat roof of a tall building, sighted the first Indians. On horseback they were coming from Milford and down the elevation which extends above the town's cemetery. Near the cemetery they split into two formations and rode in wide semicircles around the town.

—9.—

"To Your Posts! Get Ready to Fight!"

"To your posts! Get ready to fight!" The command resounded, and now one did not have to wait long for the beginning of combat. The savages who were now to meet their first resistance were fuming with rage. They approached the barricades with infernal cries and fired the first shots. Within moments, a bitter struggle raged in every direction leaving the first dead and wounded among the defenders, as well as among the Redskins. In spite of strict orders that no one who was not directly engaged in the defense was to leave the shelter of houses during the shoot-out, a 13 year-old girl, unnoticed, stepped from a doorway behind the Commandant and half a minute later was a corpse, shot in the forehead by the bullet of the enemy. The Commandant incidentally, hit by one of the first bullets, had the ring finger of his left hand torn off.

More and more Indians came into view, all well armed, and more and more furious were their attacks. And the best armed of the defenders were still outside of the line of defense! Did they hear of the shooting? They had heard it. Through his spyglass the Commandant saw them very distinctly.

"Hold out, people, we shall soon be the master over the red rabble," he cried, and courageously they fought. Since their first attack, the wild beasts had not advanced an inch closer to the barricades. Ha! Now the defenders rushed in a long expanded line, headed by their riflemen (Louis Theobald, John Spenner, John Hauenstein, Ernst Brandt, Charles Pfau and others). Then came those who were armed with double-barrel guns, commanded by Brunk. They sent their bullets right and left into the flanks of the cowardly retreating Indians, possessed only by the thought of bringing much needed aid to their distressed fellow combatants. This aid was necessary, for more and more Indians appeared near the barricades and other places of defense. But the oft repeated attacks of the enemy, accompanied by bestial cries, which often rose to a frenzy, were crushed by the well aimed shots and the courage and unflinching perseverance of the defenders.

Wilder and wilder now raged the combat on all sides of the attacked town. The Indians, generally splendidly armed and sufficiently supplied with ammunition, were ahead of the white men on that score. Yes, the defenders' supply of ammunition was getting low. But one knew what to do. There still was quite a supply of gunpowder but not sufficient bullets. Now all bags of buck shot, with their contents, were brought from the stores and at designated places the small round buck shot was cast into full weight bullets of any needed calibre. With grim determination the fight continued. The one side realized with rising anger that in spite of all their desperate attacks no further ground could be gained. The other side was conscious of the fact that if the red murderers should succeed in forcing their way into town, the same would be reduced to a pile of rubble and the fate of their fellow men would be indescribable.

–10.–

The Plan of the Attackers

Chief Little Crow had promised his brother, Little Priest, the chief and arch-rogue of the Winnebagos, to take New Ulm with only one-fourth of his warriors. The mutual agreement of the two villains had this end result as a goal: Following the taking of New Ulm by the Sioux, Mankato was to be taken by the Winnebagos, then the two united tribes were to bring murder and fire to the entire Minnesota Valley.

The author of this narrative, who in the spring of 1863 was stationed at St. Peter, located 30 miles downstream from New Ulm, with his company of Mounted Rangers, one morning received orders from the Government to block off the usual landing place for small steamers which plied the Minnesota River. This was ordered so that the Winnebago Indians who were being brought by steam boat from Mankato, into other regions, might be transported without harm. This was indeed a hard command to obey, for every Ranger would rather have killed a half dozen of the red scoundrels than to protect them against attacks by the inhabitants of St. Peter and the surrounding area. At this time, I had the opportunity to meet that no good Little Priest, who now was not on very good terms with his former killer friend, Little Crow, and I heard from his own lips the confirmation of the pact between him and Little Crow. This fellow, Little Priest, sat playing cards on the deck of the little steam boat with other Indians of his tribe, and stated, in answer to my inquiry, that if Little Crow had kept his word and had taken New Ulm on Tuesday, 19 August, it would have been his, Little Priest's, greatest delight to have taken as many scalps as possible in Mankato and other points of the Minnesota Valley.

The reader will pardon the deviation from the main story, but it proves beyond any doubt that the actions of the brave defenders of New Ulm on 19 August 1862 checked the violent uprising of the Winnebagos and thus prevented a catastrophe of the kind that has never before struck this beautiful countryside and hopefully will never occur. And now, let us return to our brave defenders of New Ulm.

–11.–

THE BATTLE OF NEW ULM

Here the struggle raged on unabated. Furious and often repeated attacks of the red beasts followed one upon the other. But whenever the Indians, as a result of their rapid firing, had gained a little headway over the besieged, they were thrown back from the sections they had gained within just a short period of time.

The rage of the savages reached a climax. Their terrible cries, which one must have heard in order to be able to judge them, horrified even men whom one certainly could not brand as cowards, and who showed much bravery and courage during the combat. The fiercest fighting took place over the possession of the barricades which had been built at the southern part of the town. Several times the Indians tried to take this bulwark with heavy attacks, but each time the defenders forced them back with bloody heads. Also, from the northwest the savages attacked in blind fury, but their attempts were shattered by the well aimed gunfire and levelheaded courage of the men stationed at this point. It was here that the red rascals set fire to the houses located outside the barricades. These three buildings were the only ones that were destroyed in the attack of the Sioux Indians on New Ulm on 19 August 1862.

The assertion that the Redskins took the town during the first attack, burnt down the greater part of it, murdered many of the inhabitants, and that the survivors were saved by help from outsiders, is—stating it mildly—a colossal error.

Had New Ulm been taken by the Indians on that fateful August day, had the courage of the brave defenders not sent the savages away with bloody heads, then surely and certainly the program planned by the robber chieftain of the Sioux, Little Crow, and the robber chieftain of the Winnebagos, Little Priest, would have been carried out.

The catastrophe mentioned earlier in these pages, which was to have befallen the greater number of the inhabitants of the Minnesota Valley would then have followed shortly.

The 19th of August of the year 1862 will, therefore, always be a memorable day in the history of New Ulm and have the same significance as the 23rd of August of the same year.

The Indians driven back on the northwest section of the town, now tried their luck on the northeast section. But also here they met with heavy resistance after they had crept through high grass and some cornfields planted in German Park. They were forced to retreat, after taking with them, according to their custom, a number of their dead and wounded.

From now on and very likely after they had received further reinforcements, the Redskins changed their battle plan. With horrible war cries they attacked the town simultaneously from all directions. Now a murderous struggle began. The assailed fought with might and held their ground. Then about 4:30 P.M. unexpected help, of whom no one had thought before reached the assailed: Nature itself turned to their favor. A thunderstorm came from the southeast, at first slowly and barely audible, then grew in intensity as it approached the distressed town. Finally, it broke above with the violence that is characteristic of this natural phenomenon in the Minnesota Valley. Terrific thunder and streaming rain, intermingled with the howling of the accompanying storm interrupted the combat. The unfettered elements had, by their attacks, commanded the attackers to stop. Less and less frequently one heard the shooting of the Indians, until at last, shortly after 5 P.M., the shooting stopped completely.

The struggle was over for today. The assailed were relieved, and the confidence of the victors, the realization of having driven away from their town a powerful, bloodthirsty enemy better equipped than themselves, this realization tempered their nerves with immense strength. The opposite was true of the Redskins. They who had met with no opposition since their attack began yesterday, they who could murder, burn and commit all possible deeds of horror, they were driven away, they knew, by a handful of courageous men. With bloody heads, they were driven away from the place which they had promised to capture on 19 August. How would the Winnebagos, their allies, take it that the almost contractual promise had turned out to be a failure?

Opinions vary as to the extent to which the rolling thunder and streaming rain, combined with the bravery of the besieged, aided in the ultimate victory. Some believe that because the powder of the Indians became wet and because they were fully exposed to the storm they were forced to give up their struggle. Others regard the giving up of the struggle by the Indians from another point of view, and the author sides with this group.

Superstition has always played a prominent role among all savages, no matter on which part of the globe they may dwell. Common natural phenomena, as eclipses of the sun or moon, earthquakes, lightning and thunder, yes, even the beginning of twilight, shatter the nervous system of uncivilized peoples, more or less. "Manitou is angry and leaves us to the power of the evil spirit," the Indian says, as a rule, during a severe thunderstorm. Many Indian tribes cease fighting and let their weapons rest, even though the struggle is to their advantage, as soon as night begins to fall and the first stars appear in the firmament. The weird cult of the Indian's religion, his medical lore and many other things are squarely based on superstition. Let us not assume that the Indian who has embraced Christianity has lost this superstition, on the contrary, he is more firmly convinced that all phenomena, in the vastness of infinity, are guided by unseen spirits, and to his Indian God comes the Christian God, to his eternal hunting grounds are added Heaven and Hades, and since he cannot give up his old beliefs and should also believe the new, his senses are completely confused by these double impressions , and the wild son of nature, converted to Christianity is more superstitious than ever before.

What happened at the two above mentioned agencies proves definitely that the newly converted Indian is an equally bad, in some instances even a much worse, individual than the wildest of the Redskins. Many Indians lived there who had embraced Christianity, but they took part in the slaughtering of the white man just the same as Indians who had not been converted, showing no mercy to their own Christian minister and doctor or any other Christian white man. Only by means of good, sensibly conducted schools, which will make it a point to enlighten and influence the Indian, will it be possible to eventually bring up and educate a better generation of Redskins. But the so-called converted old Indian is what he has always been, an Indian in whom the slumbering beast will be aroused, as soon as there is an opportunity, just as it is aroused in the unconverted Indian.

And now to show the factual proof that the Redskin in general leaves his place of combat during such natural phenomena as a heavy thunder storm or the approach of night, even though he is gaining victory, the author wishes to tell of a little episode in his own life.

It was in August 1864, late in the afternoon, on the border of Dakota and Montana that I received orders to dismount with 15 to 20 of my men, leave the horses behind with the remainder of the company and, armed with carbines and revolvers, to march to a designated region quite familiar to me and search for a patrol which had been sent out and had not returned. The terrain was the characteristic rough and fissured lava deposits of the plains. Cautiously, and on the lookout with every step, we approached a small lava hill which we knew the patrol must have crossed. At the very moment in which we leaned against the rocky wall in order to be fairly hidden in case of an attack, we saw the Indians who had been lying in wait for us, coming from ravines and crags. Instantly, they had cut off our retreat and had completely surrounded us. Whoever knows the Redskin, knows of the delight with which they slowly torture their captives to death. Whoever knows them can realize that we did not consider surrender despite being outnumbered by them twenty to one. Now the struggle meant life or death; the last bullet of the carbine or revolver was reserved for one's own skull.

In the meantime, the Indians closed in on us more and more. But we were hidden in rocky terrain and equipped with the best of arms, Sharp's carbines, Colt's Navy revolvers (swords had been left behind with the company because they hinder the dismounted cavalryman when on the march), and we had plenty of ammunitions. So we could and had to, anyway, face the attacks of the Indians calmly. There was no other choice. Besides we knew that this great number of savages, which approached us with their usual and hellish screaming, consisted of a bunch of cowards, and most of them were only armed with bows and arrows and a few old shot guns. From childhood the Indian is taught to handle bow and arrow well, and if he possesses a good bow and knows how to use it, he seldom misses his mark at a distance of up to 70 to 80 feet, but at a distance of 120 to 130 feet it falls harmlessly to the ground.

The Redskins who now were attacking us were mostly from the Blackfoot tribe. They approached us with all the cunning of their race. One group crept through the boulders like snakes, while another large number pressed forward on the less protected side of our position and with murderous cries. Contrary to their usual custom and for whatever reason, they came within our shooting range. And responding to the quietly given command, "Aim, Fire!" 18 carbines cracked and 10 to 12 Indians lay in a pool of blood, some of them dead with their ponies. But since an Indian chief was among those who had fallen, they renewed their attack upon us from all sides with such murderous cries of rage and so furiously that it still resounds in my ears today. Closer and closer became the circle about us. We fired shot upon shot but without much harm to the Redskins who now were hiding behind boulders. Out situation was becoming desperate. True, our uninterrupted firing kept the Indians at bay, but we were running short of ammunition. Now from the east a thunderstorm drew close. Darkness spread earlier than usual, and before reinforcements came to our aid, the Indians gave up the struggle, even though they knew that our ammunition was well nigh spent. Later I was told by our half-breed scouts, to whom I had explained the details of this battle, that the Redskin fears a battle at night, and if a rising thunderstorm teams up with night, then the Indian lets his weapons rest and withdraws unconditionally from the place of combat. His superstition leads him to believe the Great Spirit is against him and is now exposing him to the evil spirits.

This may elucidate my opinion that it was more on account of the thunderstorm, which came to the aid of the brave defenders of New Ulm on the afternoon of 19 August 1862, than on account of the rain soaked gunpowder that the Indians quit fighting. But be this as it may, the Indians had been driven away after a desperate struggle shortly after 5 P.M. on that day, knowing that it was not so easy to destroy the Turner town of New Ulm as Little Crow had promised Little Priest. Now, nearly an hour after the fighting had ceased, the first relief came to New Ulm.

–12.–

HONOR TO WHOM HONOR IS DUE!

It was Boardman's Cavalry, or to be more precise, about 25 mounted citizens of St. Peter and the surrounding territory. There is no denying, the hurriedly dispatched help from our neighbors of St. Peter was greeted joyfully and doubly so, when we also heard the good news that in the course of the night several hundred men from the St. Peter area would arrive here. It never occurred to us that one might want to belittle the merits of fine assistance rendered to us by the neighboring towns of St. Peter and Mankato, and especially so by brave Judge Flandrau.

However, we must and shall evermore protest the notion that the arrival of Boardman's Cavalry at the battle scene decided the outcome favorably for New Ulm, because this is not the truth. When the 25 mounted men appeared, the struggle was virtually at an end, and immediately following their arrival, they were quartered in the two inns, the Dakota House and the Minnesota House, and their horses were cared for.

Among those citizens from St. Peter who were in New Ulm during the first engagement, from its beginnings to its close, I wish to mention Mr. Swift, who later became the Governor of Minnesota, and who, with his long Kentucky rifle gave splendid service in the struggle. Possibly others from St. Peter were here at that time as well, but I cannot affirm it. Justice to everyone, but also honor to whom honor is due!

The main battle for the defense of the settlers in the Minnesota Valley was fought in New Ulm on the 19th of August 1862. This battle, the outcome of which gave notice to the Indians: "This far and no further," was almost exclusively fought by Germans.

The German town of New Ulm was defended and saved by Germans on the 19th of August, and as long as New Ulm exists this will be a memorable day in its history.

Some 13 to 15 Anglo-Americans, who had fled to New Ulm on Monday, formed their own unit and were all splendidly armed. But contrary to the protests of the Commandant, they left New Ulm on the morning of the decisive day, only to return towards the end of the battle with the Indians hot on their trail. They were forced to leave behind them 4 or 5 dead and a number of wounded and again sought help in New Ulm which was promptly given.

It is the duty of the historian to bring before the public the names of those whose services of benevolence are worthy of being remembered. Without overstating or underestimating anybody's merits, we can say that what Dr. Alfred Mueller meant to the people of Fort Ridgely during the Indian War, Dr. Carl Weschke meant to the people of New Ulm. It was late in the evening of this day which will always be recorded with red ink in the annals of New Ulm that the author stepped into the office of the young doctor in order to have the wound dressed which he had received shortly after the Indian attack had begun. What I saw will never be erased from my memory. All along the walls, on beds and mattresses, lay severely and lightly wounded persons. One man was unconscious and struggling with death, which in that very night came to his relief. On a mattress in the midst of the wounded lay the dutiful doctor, dead tired from the sorrowful work of the day that had passed. Slowly as I had come, I left the doctor's office, determined to entrust the treatment of my wound to less skillful hands rather than to rob this brave young man of one moment of his well-earned and necessary sleep. The name of Dr. Carl Weschke, whose bearer is at present Mayor of New Ulm, shall always occupy an imminent position in the history of our city. Honor to whom honor is due!

Beginning that night and early the following morning the Indians began to retreat, but only to unite with other robbing and murdering bands in the neighborhood of Fort Ridgely in an attack on the Fort. Let us give New Ulm a chance to recoup from its battle and let us follow the red devils to the scene of their next murderous activity at the Fort and find out how they there were received and treated.

–13.–

FORT RIDGELY

After brave Captain Marsh and his 50 men had marched off, of whom, as we have mentioned, only 13 again reached the Fort alive, the 1st Lt. of the company took command of the place. In reality, however, Sgt. Jones, later Captain of the Third Minnesota Battery, who belonged to the regular army and was stationed there, was the commander. At this point, the entire garrison consisted of hardly more than 20 trained and healthy soldiers. To this number were soon added a large number of farmers and others who had fled to the Fort and now also had to perform duties. A few of these had been in the military before and worked out excellently. Among them was Werner Bösch, now a long-time resident of New Ulm. Fifty men under Lt. Sheehan, who had been dispatched to the two agencies from Fort Ripley, located near the upper Mississippi in Minnesota, were on their return march to that fort when they were reached by courier with orders to turn to Fort Ridgely.

They arrived there safely on the day preceding the Indian attack and even more help followed. Now the defenders, who also had their own cannons and excellent gunners, could look forward to the attack of the Redskins with confidence. The Indian really fears cannons. And this may be the reason why several nights before the outbreak of the red scoundrels a band of them stuffed the cannons of the fort with rags so that they did not function when fired. When one discovered the cause, they had to be cleaned out again. How the rascals could sneak up on the cannons is, and remains, a riddle. Naturally, we cannot go into the details of the terrible and bloody two-day struggle for the possession of the Fort. The repeated and sometimes frenzied attacks of the Indians were subdued by the iron courage and well-maintained artillery fire of the defenders.

Thanks especially to brave Sgt. Jones, his cannons and the splendid gunners of the same, the Redskins were also repulsed here and driven back with bloody heads. Among the ranks of the white defenders of this military outpost were several half-breeds whose services were excellent.

Repeatedly, these half-breeds were urged by the attacking Indians to come over to their side because blood of the red man flowed in their veins. But every request was answered by shots which seldom missed their mark. Finally, the arch-scoundrel, Little Crow, personally appeared in order to induce the brave half-breeds to desert their posts, but several bullets whizzed by his head, teaching him that this was not the suitable place to display his talents as an Indian speaker. The brave half-breeds could not be induced to leave the ranks of their white friends and they fought with heroic courage, and to the end of the battle, for the preservation of the Fort and the cause of their white allies. However, one should not get the impression that all half-breeds of the Sioux were on the side of the white men at that time. On the contrary, large numbers of these fought in the ranks of the Redskins and some of them were just as cruel ruffians as the Indians themselves. Noteworthy is the fact that those part-Indians who in times of direst need fought faithfully and devotedly at the side of their white friends were, with few exceptions, of part-French descent. This is evident in their names. On the other hand, many of those who stood shoulder to shoulder with the Indians and murdered and burned, bore English names.

In order to explain the reasons for the facts just stated, we must again permit a short excursion which may shed some light on the many questionable goings on at the Indian agencies and the morally unjustifiable behavior of some of the whites who sought contact with the Redskins there. The Frenchman who lives in the western and northwestern part of the U.S., and especially the French Canadian is, as a rule, married to an Indian woman. Even though such a union is not considered legitimate from the view of the state and of the church, in most of these cases living together lasts a lifetime. The children who are the offspring of such a union are more attached to the white man than to the red race since they are brought up under the guidance of a white father and are much attached to him. The mother has only a small part in rearing such children, and the sons especially are under the direct control of the father. Different, however, is the situation among half-breeds who, on their father's side, are not of French descent. A goodly number of these do not, as a rule, know their own father. And even if they do know him, the father, in most cases, pays little or nor attention to the child of such a concubinage. Such children are always brought up in a red tribal environment. Fatherless half-breeds of this kind are therefore very often more embittered opponents of the white race than the Indians themselves. The very bitter thought of having been driven helplessly and namelessly into the arms of their red tribesmen by their no-good white procreators, cannot fail to cause these half-breeds, in case of combat, to deal more cruelly with the white men than the full-blooded Indians would. This again shows that because of the injustices committed by some scoundrels of the Caucasian race, peace-loving white settlers have to suffer.

With homage, we wish to praise here the noble self-denial of Dr. Alfred Mueller and his wife, Mrs. Elisa Mueller, in caring for the wounded and the sick, and how in particular this brave lady may be regarded as the guardian angel of the Fort.

One would think that the Indians, after two defeats they had suffered at New Ulm and Fort Ridgely, would seriously have thought of giving up the struggle; one would think they should have realized the futility of continuing the same. But this supposition is false, for the red beasts had smelled blood and were, like the tiger when he has tasted this, more bloodthirsty than ever before. They had attacked New Ulm with only a part of their warriors.

If they would now, after they had united, repeat their attack, wouldn't the town certainly fall into their hands? What satisfaction at the very thought of it! For then one could enjoy murdering, burning, and plundering. This was approximately the sense of the message of Little Crow to this warriors after their departure from Fort Ridgely. Therefore, without delay on to New Ulm.

–14.–

THE SECOND ATTACK ON NEW ULM

Imagine now that we are back in this German town and at the time when the unsuccessful Redskins began their retreat to Fort Ridgely. It was about 12 P.M., the night after the desperate struggle on Tuesday, 19 August 1862. The guards, stationed along the road to St. Peter and Mankato, heard the regular tread of marching men. These could be Indians, but nevertheless they had to answer the "Who's there?" And joy! It was the longed-for help from St. Peter and other places, we had hoped would come. We had heard from the Boardman Cavalry that a group was to be expected. At their head was brave Judge Flandrau, trusty friend of the people of New Ulm. Cheers and a hearty welcome greeted the brave men, for in New Ulm one knew only to well that only a contingent of Little Crow's warriors had attacked the town the day before and that the red rascals would soon attack again with twice the manpower. On the next day, too, more help came from all directions.

Among the fairly well organized companies, which in time of greatest need hastened to the aid of New Ulm, I wish to mention especially: St. Peter Company under Captain Flandrau; Mankato Company under Captain Bierbrauer; and LeSueur Company under Captain Saunders. Besides these, many farmers from the surrounding countryside had come to New Ulm, and organized as best they could under the following: Milforders under Captain F. Meile; Cottonwooders under Captain William Winkelmann; and New Ulmers under Captain J. Bell. Other organized groups which may have existed besides the above named I cannot indicate, as practically the entire set of muster-rolls has since been lost.

Naturally, we cannot expect that this historian list all the names of all those who more or less distinguished themselves in a conflict of the kind that was waged in New Ulm on the 23rd of August 1862. The collecting of the materials took place in a short period of time, so that the record is still not quite accurate. We can only assure the reader that the defenders of New Ulm during the second Indian attack fought just as bravely and courageously as those who repelled the onslaught of the Redskins in the first battle on the 19th of August.

Errors in descriptions of exciting events over which no actual control can be exerted do occur, as here with the second siege of New Ulm by the Indians. An example of this is the error already mentioned, namely that the greater part of New Ulm was burned by the Indians on 19 August, although on that day of the conflict only three houses were destroyed by flames, while on the 23rd, during the second attack of the Redskins, many buildings had to be destroyed in order to deprive the Indians of vantage points and cover. Among other buildings lost, were two large steam mills, Subilia's distillery, the Turner Hall, a church and a number of scattered dwellings which were reduced to ashes by the red firebugs while the brave defenders of New Ulm could do nothing to prevent the destruction.

Today's New Ulm is still located, and in those days considering the size of the town even more so, on terrain which would require a small army of several thousand well-trained soldiers to defend it, if one were to form a line of defense that would include all buildings up to one mile from the center part of town. But more about this later. Let us return to the morning following the arrival of outside help.

–15.–

COL. FLANDRAU APPOINTED COMMANDER-IN-CHIEF

On Wednesday, 20 August, the defense system was considerably extended by barricades and other measures. The arrival of outside help permitted lots of changes from the defense posture we had during the first battle. Judge Flandrau, formerly an Indian agent and well informed about the customs and warfare of the Redskins, was appointed Commander-in-Chief. Everything possible was done which was deemed necessary for the protection of the city.

On Thursday morning a reconnoitering squad was sent out with orders to escort to New Ulm those farmers and their families who were now helplessly cut off from the town. At the same time, they were to find out where and what positions the Indians had taken. One can easily realize that in spite of the help which had arrived, excitement in town ran high. As is to be expected, there were timid souls even among those who had come to help. Not every one, of course, is fit to be a soldier and the deeds of horror which the red scoundrels had committed within the last days were not suited to work as a pacifier for everyone. But in spite of everything the majority of the defenders looked forward to the approaching fight with a courageous enthusiasm that would have done honor to old battle-hardened soldiers. The rumbling sound of cannon fire up there in Fort Ridgely, which could be distinctly heard from here, did not leave the slightest doubt that a tough struggle was raging there. Some were afraid that the Indians might succeed in taking the Fort and with the captured cannons would attack New Ulm. What then? New Ulm had not a single cannon at its disposal. But it was not to come to this; the Redskins, as previously mentioned, were driven away with bloody heads by Fort Ridgely's brave soldiers.

Thus, in preparation of a life-and-death struggle, Saturday, 23 August 1862, finally dawned, that memorable day which likewise is recorded in blood in the history of New Ulm. Again, the rising sun shone brightly and friendly upon the Turner town. But the small town and its idyllic surroundings, which a week before had been peaceful, now had a warlike appearance. Indeed, it seemed even more warlike than on that noteworthy morning of the 19th of the same month, for the traces of the struggle of that past Tuesday were not yet erased, and again one had to be prepared to meet, for the second time, and within a few hours, the onslaught of a cruel and bloodthirsty enemy. The returning scouts reported that the Indians were coming from Fort Ridgely, along both sides of the Minnesota River, to attack New Ulm.

–16.–

VICTORY OR DEATH

The defense preparations and the many armed men on the streets clearly emphasized that there was a state of war and that soon events of far-reaching consequences would unfold. The sun rose higher and higher, then, at nearly 10 A.M. the columns of smoke that rose around the town announced that the red beasts were approaching New Ulm with fires and blazes marking their way. Shortly thereafter the first shots resounded and fighting began on several sides, accompanied by the bestial cries of the Redskins.

The Indians, infuriated by the heavy losses which they had suffered during recent days in their attacks on New Ulm and Fort Ridgely, and incited by the fiery speech of their chieftain, Little Crow, this time put forth the most desperate struggle to get the town into their power. At first, they drove back several advance guards to the main line of defense, which was on the open prairie with the back to the town. But soon the violent onslaught of the Indians was shattered by the tough resistance and the greater courage of the white man. But now the savages changed their methods of attack and, with the cunning characteristic of their race, sought shelter behind and in deserted buildings from where they could fire more effectively on the defenders. As mentioned before, the scattered houses and buildings lying beyond the barricades could not be occupied because of shortage of manpower. It was therefore easy for the wild enemy to take up positions in the buildings best suited for their siege and to burn those which they did not wish to occupy. It was therefore during the second battle, on the 23rd and not, as often erroneously reported, on the 19th of August, that the town of New Ulm was in serious danger of burning to the ground. While the red beasts now hurled the flaming torch into the homes of peaceful citizens who had never harmed them, the battle raged on with all the imaginable bitterness.

At the very beginning of the battle the Indians had, by means of a flank attack, taken possession of Turner Hall, but barely 400 or 500 feet from there, located on the same hill, was a large windmill in which a number of our men from the LeSueur and Mankato Companies had entrenched themselves and they, with their uninterrupted gunfire, kept the savages at a respectable distance on this side. The west side of the city was covered by a brick building, the post office at that time, which was held by good men who made it impossible for the enemy to advance there. The north side also had a good stronghold, a well garrisoned brick house. Only the south and southeast sides, the weakest points of defense, offered an opportunity for the Redskins to force through and into the central part of the beleaguered town.

The sly Indian chief knew this very well. Consequently, he had assembled his best warriors right there while at other points the less dependable ones had been given the task of keeping the defenders of New Ulm continuously on the alert through repeated attacks, for this could divert the latter's attention from the weakest defense positions. The part of German Park located in the southeastern part of the city was overgrown with tall grass. It was the task of the Indians to crawl through it in snake-like fashion. For this task they were highly qualified, for as we have mentioned before, the Indians are the best skirmishers in the world. Hidden by tall grass, sneaking up from the southeast toward the south, the Redskins succeeded in reaching Minnesota St. and took positions in the houses deserted by their owners. From here their advance was farther and farther to the north, directed toward the center of the town.

It was nearly 12 noon when Captain Dodd of St. Peter, accompanied by a man from Milford by the name of Krieger, dashed along Minnesota St. in a southerly direction to reconnoiter. He had paid no attention to his friends' words of caution. Hardly 50 yards from the barricades erected at this point, the Captain fell mortally wounded beside his horse which was shot at the same time. The Indians had shot from the houses they occupied. The severely wounded man was courageously carried away by several of our men who defied death in so doing. One of these brave men, Mr. Jacob Haeberle, a respected resident of Milford was also hit by an enemy bullet and died a couple of hours later. The other Milforder, Mr. Krieger, who accompanied the Captain on his fateful ride, was an old German soldier; he, too, was dangerously wounded but succeeded to reach the town with his horse. Several months later, however, he died of his wounds at the town's hospital.

In the meantime, the bloodthirsty enemy pressed forward, step by step. The defenders of New Ulm had already lost 6 dead and over 20 wounded. But what would happen to the 800 to 1,000 women and children if the Indians were to succeed in forcing their way into town? For the time being they were housed in safe buildings, but what fate was to await them if they were to be taken captive by the Redskins? "Under no circumstances! It must not happen! Over our dead bodies! Victory or death!" This was our battle cry, and woe to the coward who would now have taken flight from the onrushing enemy!

It was now 3 P.M. and the savages had taken possession of several houses on the south side of Minnesota St. From this splendid cover their gunfire could reach the barricades on Center St., which is the dividing line between the north and south sides of the town. Nearer and nearer came the hour of decision. Uninterrupted and with the greatest bitterness, the fighting continued on all sides. Who will be the victor? It is still undecided, even as it approaches the fourth hour of the afternoon. But it's got to be! They shall and must be forced back! More and more Indians now appeared on the south side of Minnesota St. They came from German Park under cover of their own people and the tall grass.

On the southeast corner of Minnesota and Center Sts. stood a large log house. The front part of this building was a blacksmith shop, the back part was the dwelling of the blacksmith, Mr. August Kiesling. This strong bulwark was located outside of the barricades but was occupied by our men. Suddenly, shortly before 4:30 P.M., the Indians, with terrible cries, attacked with increased manpower and took the blockhouse, the strongest position of the southeast side of the town. Now the moment had arrived which was to determine New Ulm's existence. If, within a quarter of an hour, the Indians could not be driven out of this position which was so advantageous to them and so dangerous to the defenders, then all would be lost, because the center of the town, between the two main barricades on the north side of Minnesota St. was now exposed to the gunfire of the Indians. And they did not hesitate for a moment to maximize the advantage they had gained.

At this critical moment, when all was at stake, one could not hesitate but only act at once. Judge Flandrau and the author of this work now quickly gathered a troop of 60 to 70 courageous men, and at the head of these stout-hearted soldiers, plunged over the barricades and with hurrahs that would have done justice to the wildest Indian cries attacked that strategically important blockhouse. Here ensued a terrible and bloody struggle which meant life or death. Here in just a few minutes, the fate of the town was in the balance. The Indians, even though they outnumbered us four to one, were driven out of the blockhouse and out of several other nearby buildings which they had taken during the afternoon. Their losses were heavy. The town was saved, but how great were the sacrifices.

During this short encounter, the defenders had lost 5 men and 15 to 18 wounded. But our men knew that this spot, drenched with blood, would proclaim to future generations how their small courageous number had here beaten an enemy that outnumbered them four to one. They knew that by this decisive victory over the bestial Indian hordes they had spared nearly 1,000 women and children from a terrible fate. Being aware of this encouraged the faith of the survivors in their own strength and permitted even the wounded to forget their burning pains. In order to completely discourage the Indians from further advances on the southeastern and southern side of the town, a number of vacant dwellings were immediately destroyed. The defenders with their small numbers, would otherwise not have been able to hold their ground at this point. By destroying these buildings they also hoped to avoid another encounter at this place.

With a tenacity which would have been worthy of a better cause, the Redskins, despite the loss of their strong position on Minnesota St., continued their struggle. But one thing could not escape the attention of the close observer, since their defeat at that street their strength had suffered immeasurably. Only from Turner Hall they rained their bullets uninterruptedly towards the windmill. But the defenders there had plenty of ammunition and good cover behind sacks filled with flour, etc., and therefore were not at a loss to answer the attack. But angered by the tenacity of the enemy at this point and enthusiastic over the victory on Minnesota St., again a squad of brave men gathered with the firm determination to storm Turner Hall. Since such an undertaking would again mean the loss of many lives if carried out in daylight, and since no immediate danger to the city existed at this point, one finally agreed to wait until evening before storming the building under the cover of darkness and paying a visit to the red murderers up there.

But nothing came of this, for the Indians full well knowing that they could not remain in the building during the night, set fire to it as darkness set in. Within an hour the beautiful Turner Hall was reduced to a pile of ashes. Who were the perpetrators? This is still an unsolved riddle today, for at almost the same day that the Turner Hall was engulfed in flames the windmill, so well defended up to this time, was also ablaze at all corners. It didn't take long before this building which had contributed so much to the defense of the town was also in ruins. The historian must avoid assumptions. I cannot definitely maintain that it was the Indians who sacrificed this bulwark of the defenders to the god of fire. The exchange of gunfire continued till evening, but it became weaker and weaker on the Indian side and then finally ended altogether.

The struggle of the red race against the white race, the war of murderous Indian firebugs against peaceable people who had never in any way harmed the red brutes, was halted for the day. The guns were silent. But here still was that unfettered element, the demon of fire. High towards the firmament whirled the bursts of fire spreading afar their light, turning night into day. A spectacle so terrible and frightful, it is impossible to express in words, yet it is impressed indelibly as a horrible memory on the minds of surviving eyewitnesses. Naturally, I am referring only to the combatants of the white race, for by today the survivors of the red race will look back upon their terrible work of destruction with entirely different feelings. One can easily imagine with what diabolical ecstasy the murderous firebugs looked down upon the burning city from the neighboring hills to which they had withdrawn on that gruesome evening of the 23rd of August. Today, Sioux Indians who took part in these scenes of horror in Minnesota in August of 1862 and who, at that time, escaped the bullets of the white man as well as the gallows which they deserved a hundredfold, will still rejoice having hauled the burning torch into New Ulm, the town they hated so much, and from which they had been driven away twice and with bloody heads.

But just as the brave defenders of New Ulm had stopped the Indians in the afternoon, so in the evening of that eventful day they mastered the fire, which by midnight was completely under control. The center of the town in which there were many women, children, and wounded, was now secured against any further danger from the fire. Toward morning, one also noticed with satisfaction that those buildings from which bright flames shot into the air the previous evening before were now only masses of tumbled, glimmering ruins. Not until now did one have the time to think about the errors committed by the defenders in the course of the preceding day. Finally, it became clear that one of the biggest mistakes was to order a company of over 100 well-armed men to cross the Minnesota River in order to fight the Indians on that fateful Saturday morning, the 23rd of August. They were completely cut off from the town by an overwhelming enemy force. Being the underdog in this struggle with the Indians, they lost their Captain and several of their men. Under these conditions they could do nothing but try to save themselves and thus were unable to contribute to the defense of New Ulm.

Most of these men promptly marched to St. Peter. They, like many fugitives, spread the report that New Ulm had been burned to the ground, and this for the second time within a week! That is the way wrong records are created; hearsay reports we later erroneously call "history"!

Of course, anyone looking from a distance at the leaping columns of flames in the town of New Ulm on the evening of the 23rd might have been deceived, for the town was at that time in the greatest of danger of being destroyed by fire. But anyone who might have approached this town on the evening of the 19th of August would have seen only a few small watch fires (bivouacs) of the besieged. The three buildings to which the Indians had set fire on the 23rd lay each and all a mass of smoldering ruins.

–17.–

TRENCHES

In the evening, then, the gunfire of the besieged was reduced to only single shots, which were either fired at random, or at any object which in the darkness one mistook for an Indian. In the cool and dark evening the baker of the besieged town, clad in a buffalo coat, was on his way to his bakery on Broadway. He was mistaken for an Indian and became the victim of friendly fire. The name of this dutiful man, who was tireless in his efforts during the siege of New Ulm, and who so sadly lost his life, was Jacob Castor.

Now one also had time to reflect on what the fate of those men might have been who had been ordered to occupy the so-called rifle-pits (trenches) which were widely scattered and thus of real significance for the defense of the town. This dangerous honor was to be shared by New Ulm citizens in particular. After some final thoughts on this matter, the conclusion was that had it not been for the energetic opposition of the author of these lines against the occupation of the rifle-pits, the city would have lost at least 50 more of its bravest citizens in this struggle. For the Indians paid no attention to these dugouts, which had no connection whatsoever with the town. With their ponies the Indians jumped across and among them, cut them off from the besieged town, and had they been occupied the men would, beyond a doubt, have fallen into the hands of the enemy, dead or alive.

By way of general comment on trenches, let us state here that in the case of a besieged town—even if only protected by mounds—or in the case of regular fortifications, trenches have always and only been used by the beleaguering parties. These so-called holes of death, thus named because their occupants seldom leave them alive, are moved forward from time to time. They are always dug out in the dark of night and are protected still more by the dug up ground and other materials up front. As a rule, they are occupied with excellent riflemen and serve as a protection to the advancing siege operations. As long as these trenches are located outside the range of shell fire of the besieged, they are not so dangerous because their occupants have only to guard against incidental sallies of the besieged. If, however, they can be shot at directly by the latter, then most of the occupants can from the very beginning be placed on the casualty list, for very few leave their self-dug graves alive!

During the siege of Sebastapol, during the Crimean War, these trenches played an important part, for with the cover they provided, the siege operations against the beleaguered were continuously moved forward. But how many lives did it take? The casualty lists of the English and particularly the French tell the story. When finally General Pelissier stormed and took Malakoff, over 10,000 French dead lay about this immensely strong bulwark. In spite of all that, he could report to Paris, "Better do this at once, than gradually." Therefore, no one need to have read and studied Vanban to know that trenches during sieges are only built by the besieger and are, as a rule, furthermore guarded by batteries. So much for trenches in general.

–18.–

THE INDIAN RETREAT FROM NEW ULM

During the afternoon and almost the entire night a staff of doctors cared untiringly and in loyal performance of their duty for the wounded. The author of this work considers it his duty to mention at this place the names of these brave men. They were Dr. McMahan of Mankato, Dr. Mayo and Dr. Ayer of LeSueur, Dr. Daniels of St. Peter, and Dr. Weschke of New Ulm. All these fine men did their utmost in performing their sad duties and they gave to the wounded the best possible care. Honor to these brave men!

Finally, as already mentioned, after a night spent without rest, the longed-for morning dawned. It was a beautiful morning. But how different things appeared here as compared to the Sunday before! Only a week had passed and yet such a terrible change. Last Sunday—a joyous mood, happy laughter and bright prospects for the future; today—gloomy seriousness on all faces, destruction in every quarter, smoldering ruins where a week ago had stood the most beautiful dwellings and business buildings of a happy people. Today there was only a desperate outlook for the future. This sad mood was certainly not banished when in the morning more bodies of murdered persons were brought in. But one did not have much time for sorrowful thoughts. Since daybreak, Indians were visible on all sides, possibly to renew attack any moment. But the Redskins were quite discouraged by the losses they had suffered on the preceding day, and they were without any cover due to the burning down of the houses located outside the barricades.

Yet, they gathered again outside of the town in small bands, and it already appeared as though they wanted to repeat their furious attacks. The attentive observer could easily notice, however, that the misfortunes of yesterday had broken their strength and energy. Nevertheless, the defenders had to be prepared to beat back any possible renewed attack of the Indians. Everyone knew how embittered the red scoundrels were and that their defeat yesterday made their hatred towards the palefaces even greater. Hence, one did not assume that they would peaceably turn their backs upon the town of New Ulm without any further attempt at overpowering the same. Indeed, for a moment it really seemed as though the Indians were determined to repeat their attacks. As the first shots resounded foretelling further trouble, the besieged had a lucky and original idea, which was quickly acted upon and greatly contributed to the fact that the Indians gave up further attempts to gain control of the town and began their retreat as rapidly as possible.

The roaring of cannons is not, as already mentioned, pleasant music to the Redskins, and it was the roaring of a cannon, even though innocent in itself as we shall find shortly, which struck the ears of the retreating red murderers. Two anvils were placed, one on top of the other, so that the holes of one would rest directly upon the holes of the other. These holes were filled with gunpowder which could easily be ignited without danger by means of a fuse hanging down on the wall of one of the anvils. In front of this curious looking gun a stove pipe was mounted upon a four-wheeled cart in such a manner that from a distance it looked very much like a cannon. This improvised "weapon" was pointed southward and was fired when several Indians appeared from that direction. As far as the roaring of the "cannon" was concerned, this anvil-cannon truly was impressive, for the latter disappeared immediately, without even sending off a single shot. Naturally, one did not hesitate any more to keep firing the anvil-stove-pipe-cannon. Shot followed shot, and the shooting continued until not a single Indian was in sight anymore. Several of the red scoundrels, who were among the more than 300 prisoners later interned in Mankato, informed the author that they had a deep respect for the anvil-stove-pipe-cannon because they thought it was for real. They thought that it had been sent to New Ulm from Fort Snelling or from Fort Ridgely to aid in more effective defense.

–19.–

THE DEPARTURE FROM NEW ULM

Shortly after noon, approximately an hour after the retreat of the Indians, a company under the command of Captain Cox, which had left St. Peter the day before, arrived to further help the town of New Ulm. The struggle had practically ended before they arrived. Whatever influenced the commander of this company to spend the night near Nicollet, which is 15 miles from New Ulm, instead of marching rapidly during the night to reach and help the distressed town is, and will remain, a riddle which is unsolved to the present day. That, however, the arrival of this last auxiliary troop had much, indeed very much, to do with the dangerous as well as humiliating departure from New Ulm and the complete abandonment of the town, is unfortunately the bitter truth.

The departure from New Ulm on Tuesday, the 26th of August, the giving up of the beloved soil over which there had been two victorious battles with the Indians, can only be considered as an urgent necessity by fearful souls. I am firmly convinced that brave Judge Flandrau, after the defeat of the Indians, would never have thought of leaving the town to a handful of marauders, if he had not been pressed to some extent by people who perhaps had thought to profit once New Ulm was given up. After all, had he not previously objected to the suggestion of a number of his friends to leave the town Thursday before the battle and to retreat in the direction of St. Peter and Mankato, pointing out that a handful of Indians in the level lands of the Cottonwood Valley might bring death and destruction to the departing people? No, and no again. I am firmly convinced that Judge Flandrau would never have given his consent to this miserable departure if he had not been prevailed upon to do so. A valid reason never existed for giving up the town, for leaving behind valuable property, which then, of course, to a large extent, as was to be expected, fell into the hands of the marauding vagabonds.

The assumption of some that it was done in order to bring women and children to a safe place is so absurd that it is hardly worthwhile to talk about it. Why were the women and children not brought to a safe place earlier? Why did they have to be exposed to the severe fright of an Indian attack? In this respect we shall use the following lines to prove clearly and definitely that during the entire preceding week the women and children were not in as great a danger as they were on the retreat from New Ulm to Mankato.

The reader will now permit me at this point to describe the region through which the dangerous, yet fortunate, retreat took place. About one mile from the center of the town of New Ulm there is quite a downhill section of the road, but it still continues through the open prairie. Then after another half a mile or so in the direction towards Mankato, it continues to go gradually downhill towards the banks of the Cottonwood River. In summer, the river is hardly more than a small brook and therefore easy to cross, but its banks on both sides are quite steep at some points and they are wooded to a great extent. From here one must reach the crest of a hill 400 foot before again reaching the more or less open stretch of road to Mankato. Let us remember that the departing colony consisted of at least 140 to 150 wagons filled with women, children, sick and wounded.

If we consider that the armed protection for these people was very inadequate under the circumstances, then it is easy to imagine what would have happened if half the Indians who had attacked New Ulm on the preceding Saturday had been lying in wait in the lowlands of the Cottonwood Valley or on the hill above it. A slaughter would have taken place as probably never before recorded in the history of the U.S. Eyewitnesses of this migration will surely remember the confusion that reigned at the crossing of the small stream. Everyone, with his wagon, wanted to be first in passing over the dangerous low region. As a result of this, many teams practically drove into one another and it took quite a bit of doing to restore some order. As mentioned earlier, had only a hundred of the Indians been lying in wait at this place, then a terrible blood bath would have been unavoidable. Who, may we ask, would have been responsible for this? But enough of this!

We are not going to cover everything of this dangerous journey of those who had to leave their homes and the men who went along to guard them. Let us just say that after passing a number of other places equally as dangerous as the one described above, the entire colony fortunately arrived at Mankato the next morning and in good condition. Here everything possible was done for the needy ones and in a very short time. After being refreshed, however, part of the homeless ones had to move on to St. Peter, because there were more people there than could be taken care of at Mankato. At St. Peter, as at Mankato, they were received with open arms and warm hearts. It cannot be denied that there was loud lamenting over the sorrow of leaving beloved homes. In some cases, this seems doubly justified because they had lost nearly everything and escaped merely with their bare lives. But still those among them, who with their relatives reached their involuntary exile in good health, could consider themselves fortunate. How differently did those fare who were ill or wounded and mostly had to endure the rigor of the journey in open wagons. How many of them, and particularly those who later died of neglected wounds, could have been saved had they received proper care? But why bring to the mind's eye again the dreary picture of a sad bygone day? Very many of the homeless New Ulmers turned to St. Paul where they were received by all inhabitants, but particularly by the Germans, in the heartiest fashion and provided with comfortable housing.

—20.—

CONDITIONS IN NEW ULM

Let us now allow the refugees to rest from their hardships while we return to the deserted Turner town of New Ulm to find out whether or not it is in ruins and whether it was at all necessary to leave it in such haste.

On Wednesday, the 27th of August, hardly a day after the town had been abandoned, Captain Dean and his Company of the U.S. Volunteers came and took possession. How the "boys in blue" felt when they marched into this deserted place, which very much resembled a ghost town, can be described only by those who were personally there. All buildings which were not sacrificed to fire during the struggle were undisturbed. Not a trace of Indians could be discovered anywhere. The company pitched camp on an elevation in the middle of the town. Headquarters were established in a hotel now deserted by its former proprietor. The day as well as the following night passed quietly. Neither white men nor Redskins put in an appearance.

The next day, 29 August, the first folks of New Ulm and vicinity appeared again in the city. They were the following gentlemen: George Jacobs, Rudolph Kiesling, and Hochhausen. The names of this vanguard deserve to be recognized. What these people had undertaken was not child's play but a courageous advance which would have done honor to the most valiant soldier. The three above named and a farmer from Courtland, named Gerboth, left St. Peter on Thursday, 28 August. One rode a small pony, the others were on foot. Whenever there was an elevation or a hill along their route, the rider dashed ahead in order to reconnoiter. When they came to the area of Gerboth's farm, Gerboth was determined to stay for the present, in spite of the warnings of his traveling companions who pressed on farther.

Gerboth's decision cost him his life, for he was murdered the next day in his cornfield by Indians who were still roaming about the country in small bands. By Thursday evening, the other three arrived at the farm and dwelling of Rudolph Kiesling, opposite the town of New Ulm on the other side of the Minnesota River. Here they stopped and spent the night, taking turns standing guard. Next morning, they went to the Minnesota River in the direction of New Ulm.

Who can describe their fright when they saw a small city of tents on the place where the courthouse stands today. Their first thought, of course, was that the Indians were encamped over there, but in order to be certain they decided to cross the river and to sneak as close as possible to the tents. One can easily imagine the indescribable joy of the three men when they discovered that the occupants of the tents were not Indians but white men in the uniform of Uncle Sam. As quickly as their legs could carry them they hurried to the soldiers and were most heartily welcomed by them.

That was the advance guard of New Ulm citizens who were to return to their deserted homes. Others did not wait long. Day after day people returned and soon the town was a busy place again. Those who returned, occupied the vacant houses. The main and side streets were cleaned and everything was put back in order as far as possible. Three weeks later nothing was to be seen of the struggle which had been waged here, only the ashes and ruins of the burned buildings were there as a reminder. These too were almost all rebuilt in the following year, after payment of reimbursements by the U.S. Government, and other new buildings were erected as well. A few years later the last of the traces of the catastrophe were completely erased. The Turner town recovered, hale and free, strong and loyal. It had risen, like Phoenix, out of the ashes.

–21.–

HUTCHINSON

Since we can spare some time now, let us see what happened to the Redskins after they retreated from New Ulm on the 24th of August. Again, they traveled, at least a large number of them, down the road to Fort Ridgely. But very wisely, they avoided getting too close to the Fort this time. Nevertheless, courageous Sgt. Jones could not deny himself the pleasure of allowing his guns to play them a farewell tune, as they traveled along the foot of the hill upon which the Fort was located. But the cowardly red scoundrels, now doubly beaten and suffering from the defeats of the preceding week, did not dare to answer the Fort's gun farewell with even a single shot. They kicked the dust as quickly as possible in the direction of the Lower Agency. But, as we shall find out later, the goddess of revenge followed closely upon their heels and did not let go until the red devils had paid her a goodly part of the tribute due her.

One would think that after the unsuccessful attempts of the Redskins to get New Ulm and Fort Ridgely into their power, and after the great losses which they suffered during the attacks at both places, the bloodthirsty scoundrels should have realized that a continuation of the struggle against the palefaces could, from now on, only be more ruinous to them. One would think they should realize that this would end their diabolic uprising with the complete ruin of their people. One would further assume that the Sioux, guided by their usual craftiness, should come to the conclusion that from now on their safety could only be restored through a hasty flight to British territory. But this assumption is in error. The red devils had, up to now, bathed with delight in the blood of the white man. In the last two weeks they had slaughtered, to their hearts' content, hundreds upon hundreds of the hated palefaces. Should they not, therefore, revenge their defeat at New Ulm and Fort Ridgely by attempting to get into their hands a smaller and perhaps not as well defended place? And they tried it!

Hutchinson, a small town in McLeod County, Minn., was the place upon which they wished to visit their revenge for the severe losses they had suffered up to now. Before they decamped to that place they fought a company of U.S. volunteers near Birch Coulee, beyond Fort Ridgely. Here the Redskins were, for the second time, victorious over a well-armed but not very large group of soldiers, commanded by an officer who was incapable from a military point of view and not equal to the task. The soldiers had pitched their camp in a narrow little valley which was shut in on several sides by steep sloping hills. In this mousetrap they were attacked by Indians, who were in the neighborhood. When help finally arrived, some of the soldiers had already been shot by the Redskins from the hills above, but the remainder of the company was saved from annihilation.

Encouraged by this little victory which had been virtually handed to them by an unqualified officer, they now moved upon that little town of Hutchinson. It was a small place then, but its inhabitants were well armed and aided by the farmers of the surrounding territory who had fled here with their families. They drove the savages off with bloody heads after a fierce struggle.

–22.–

RETREAT AND DEFEAT

From now on, after committing several more infamous acts, the Redskins retreated in haste, completely discouraged, before the advancing military forces from Fort Snelling commanded by General Sibley. At Wood Lake, about 60 miles from Fort Ridgely, they were overtaken and in the ensuing battle the Redskins met complete defeat. This finally convinced them that their uprising had been a total failure and that their cause was lost.

Thus they undertook their retreat toward the British territory. The Indians had with them many captive white women and children whose fate would no doubt have been terrible if they could not be freed. Thus, first of all one had to see to it that these unfortunate persons were released from their tormentors. Among the captives was 11 year-old Benedict Juni, at present a teacher in the New Ulm public schools. He had to help the Indians in driving stolen cattle. As Mr. Juni informed the author, he was treated fairly well. Most of the other white captives, however, were nothing more than slaves of their tormentors and thus were treated in the most cruel manner by the red scoundrels. The sad fate of the unfortunate white women, some of them with small children, who were at the mercy of these red devils, is beyond words.

The red scoundrels, too, knew full well what suffering from hunger, cold, etc., they were headed for. They knew that the time for hunting buffalo was now passed and that they could no longer expect any help from the great father, Uncle Sam. Hence, both sides soon agreed to enter into negotiations. One result then was that at least a number of the murderers were to receive their just punishment for their horrible actions.

One might assume that these rascals who within just barely five weeks had committed the most horrible cruelties and had slaughtered hundreds of innocent persons, destroyed over $1,000,000 worth of property and frightened and alarmed persons over the entire state of Minnesota, indeed, one might suppose that under such conditions these murderers would not enter into any negotiations whatsoever. Surely, they must have realized beforehand that the gallows were already erected for some, the penitentiaries for others. But these assumptions proved all wrong.

Whoever has had opportunity to study somewhat of the nature of the Indian will have observed that he is a predator of the bloodthirstiest and most cruel type. The only difference between him and his bestial colleague is that he possesses the body of a human being in which is hidden the brooding beast which is forever planning evil. Just as the predator has no qualms about destroying an enemy and stilling its hunger by feeding on the victim, just so the Indian is unconcerned after committing murderous acts whether or not he will have to answer for this.

The inborn slyness of this higher beast, should he ever be brought to courts for an accounting of his crimes, depends on lies and other trickery suitable to get him out of the snares. And often, very often, the Redskin succeeds in clearing himself before the law since, as a rule, the necessary witnesses for a conviction are missing. Thus, and in no other way, can we explain the unconditional surrender of the red murderers. All their captives had previously been delivered to General Sibley at Camp Release, with the exception of a very few who had been taken away earlier by the Indians. Where, too, should one find the witnesses against them? They were all painted with the same color and mostly clad with nature's costume. A white man could not have identified any of them with certainty, and those whites who could perhaps have identified one or the other had been murdered with their families. So the scoundrels could risk the chance of surrendering to the General with an air of complete innocence.

Only some of the slyest and thus also the most well-known among them, such as Little Crow himself, Shakopee, Little Six, and a number of others, took care not to risk their skin in the camp of the troops. They knew only too well that their only way out was to cross into British territory and that the only thing they could expect from the U.S. was a good rope of hemp. But we shall soon see that also those Indians who were held captive by the troops were somewhat mistaken if they figured on being released soon. For all the state of Minnesota it was clear that the entire group of male mass murderers of the captured Redskins should be sent to eternity at once because they had taken part in the terrible crimes during the past months of August and September.

—23.—

TRIAL IN MANKATO

In Washington, D.C., however, the influence of the Quakers and other fanatics was such that sentiments immediately turned to the Redskins; altogether different opinions prevailed, and it was decided to bring the entire affair before the proper courts. As a result, all captives, including women and children were transported to Mankato, under strong military escort, where they were placed in several large log houses erected for this purpose. Day and night they were strictly guarded by soldiers.

That the bloodthirsty arch-enemies of New Ulm were transported to Mankato in bright daylight directly through the terribly afflicted town was an unjustifiable act of tactlessness of the military officials of that time. The red scoundrels were transported in more than 50 wagons surrounded by soldiers, and to see them was an insult to the feelings of the citizens of this place. As was to be expected, the New Ulmers and others who had been greatly injured were irritated at the sight of their torturers and attacked them furiously with stones, axes, etc. Many of the latter could therefore take with them a good reminder to their temporary destination, the town of Mankato.

It is a fact that many of the attackers were women, who had loved ones murdered by the red beasts, who had their homes destroyed or had some other devilish injury meted out to them. Considering the circumstances, could one blame the poor people for laying violent hands on their torturers, the destroyers of their happiness? Certainly not! Later on, nativist and puritanical newspapers, which had always looked upon New Ulm with utter dislike and constantly attempted to arouse suspicion against the town, printed in their pages that here only the women had fought. These papers thereby attempted to confuse the attack upon the captive Indians with the attack of the Indians on the town. This is just as contemptible a falsehood as the story that blamed the citizens of New Ulm for having at one time burned Jesus Christ in effigy.

Let us now pay a visit to the captured Redskins in Mankato. They are quite comfortably housed in warm log cabins and for them at least their food leaves nothing to be desired. On the whole, they are well treated and certainly do not think that some day they will have to give an accounting for the "little bit" of murdering, plundering, and burning which they allowed themselves in the months of August and September. They also knew well enough that there was no member of the tribe who, in order to prevent having his own neck come into contact with the hemp collar, would turn state's witness against another member of his tribe. There was no danger from that angle, for they knew that each one of them would rather submit to the cruelest of torture than to betray one of their tribe.

All this the red cut-throats knew. What they did not know, however, was that among them there was one of the cruelest murderers, a devil in human form, a scoundrel 20 times deserving of death, who would appear as the state's witness against all of them. He was a Mulatto who was married to a woman of their tribe. Years ago he had been adopted by the latter and was thus considered as one of their very own. Beginning with the first day of the outbreak, this black-yellow Negro was the cruelest of the cruel red murder gang. Hair-raising stories of deeds of cruelty were reported of this monster. But now captured, the cowardly brute trembled at the thought of a twenty-fold deserved death. In order to save his miserable life he appeared as a state witness against his own accomplices, against men of the tribe to which he had belonged for years.

Very well, said Pascha Mustapha, during the Greek war for independence to a Greek who had given him splendid service as a spy and traitor against his own people and fellow believers. Very well, your services were most valuable to us and here you also have the reward which is due you. But now, since everything is in order and you have received and pocketed your sinful reward, I shall have you beheaded, for a fellow like you, who betrays his own people, will betray me and my own just the same and at the very first opportunity. And so it happened that the traitor was at once executed.

Too bad that President Lincoln was no Pascha Mustapha and did not deal with the bad Mulatto as the Turk had done with the shameful Greek. The Mulatto showed himself as a splendid witness, for he brought things to the point that 38 of his shameful accomplices were sentenced to death and a number of others sent to the penitentiary. Among those sentenced to be hanged were to be sure some of the bloodiest murderers, as Cut Nose, White Dog, and several others.

But the people of St. Peter, New Ulm, and Mankato as well as those of the surrounding area had long since agreed that all male captives had doubly earned the death sentence. And so it happened that in several secret meetings plans were made to move to Mankato during a designated night and from all sides to take the guards by surprise, overpower the captive Indians, and send them all to their eternal hunting grounds. But the military command in Mankato received a report of this conspiracy à la Sicilian Vespers and tripled the guards around the log houses in which the Redskins were held captive. When a party of those who were seeking revenge appeared in Mankato, patrols that had been sent out picked them up immediately. Of course, they were given their freedom the next day, after they had promised to leave the city and to give up their plans of a mass execution of the prisoners.

Among those who wished to place the execution of the captured Indians as a badge upon their banners were many soldiers, especially from the five companies of the Minnesota Mounted Rangers, who had largely been recruited from the Upper Minnesota Valley and who were stationed at that time at St. Peter and surrounding area. Most of these people had more or less suffered from the murdering and burning of these red beasts, and one cannot blame them that they did not wish to recognize the captive Indians as prisoners of war, but as a gang of robbers of the cruelest type, which they really were.

An investigation of these incidents would therefore have aroused a cry of indignation in the entire Minnesota Valley, and so the higher ups found it advisable to silence the entire affair. One must know that in taking the military oath, the Rangers were to serve Uncle Sam only "against all Indians at war with the government of the United States of America." But since one could not depend upon the Rangers to guard Indian prisoners, more infantry was ordered to Mankato to augment those already there in order to prevent a repetition of the above mentioned incident. There were then no further attempts to turn over the red devils to "Judge Lynch." From now on, in spite of the terrible hatred towards the captive Indians, the law was allowed to take its course.

—24.—

THE 38 MURDERERS AND RAPISTS

In the meantime, the appointed day for the execution of the 38 Indians who had been sentenced to death drew nearer and nearer. The condemned had been placed in a separate building. To prevent their escape they were all chained to the floor. It was not an easy matter for the Mulatto to serve time with those whom he had betrayed during the last days of their lives. The contempt which was shown him by his murderous accomplices at every suitable opportunity, as well as their furious glances directed toward him were not destined to sweeten life for him during this period.

The day before the execution, I was ordered to Mankato with my company of Minnesota Mounted Rangers to help keep order. There I had an opportunity to pay a visit to these 38 Indians condemned to death. Accompanied by an elderly officer, Col. Miller, who was at that time Military Commander of the town and later Governor of Minnesota, I started out and soon thereafter I faced the condemned criminals. They were human figures that sat there on the floor, huddled together in Indian fashion. But from all the pores of their human bodies there lurked the bloodthirsty beast, and a shiver went down my spine when I thought of the terrible misery which these 38 murderers had brought to so many peace-loving families. Only the thought that these assassins would meet their punishment on the gallows the next day restored my peace of mind.

Among the condemned there were several whom I had known in years gone by. It was in my house at Fort Ridgely and in the home of that fine interpreter named Quinn where I had met and often seen them. Particularly two of them I knew very well. White Dog, a young Indian of splendid physique, about 24 years of age, and an older Redskin of about 45. I had seen them a number of times. White Dog, by the way, was an Indian Don Juan, of whom they said at that time, that he did not merely "turn the heads" of young Indian maidens, but that he had succeeded with a number of white women as well. Furthermore, he was really a wild fellow. When he could secure fire-water by paying ten times its price to some white scoundrel, he became so awfully drunk, that he was placed in a dark hole of the main guard quarters of the Fort more often than he liked. He was then, as might be expected, one of the greatest scoundrels among all the other red scoundrels during the Indian uprising. That he, who was otherwise a sly Indian, should be caught in the trap at Camp Release and give himself up to General Sibley in the hope of receiving a pardon can only be attributed to the fact that he had a love affair with a white woman who had been taken captive by the Indians. She had assured him that her influence and her testimony would certainly free him. But the lady was mistaken. The shameful atrocities of the red scoundrel were so definitely proved to him that all the pleading, wringing of hands, and the tears of this white woman could not save him from the gallows.

The other old Indian whom I have mentioned was perhaps not quite as bad as White Dog, but nevertheless also a top scoundrel among the other red scoundrels. I became better acquainted with him on a cold winter day in 1860 at Fort Ridgely. At that time, through the intercession of interpreter Quinn he received for his starving family two sacks filled with provisions of various types, especially salted meat from the storehouse of the Fort and, of course, free of charge. Since the Redskin, in general, spares his pony more than his wives, he loaded one sack apiece, which must have weighed at least 50 pounds, upon each of the two squaws who were accompanying him. He himself mounted his strong pony and was about to ride away, paying no attention whatsoever to his two wives, and whether they could follow him with their heavy loads through the deep snow like work horses. But Major Morris, a good man, at that time Commandant at the Fort, did not agree with this manner of treating women and ordered the Redskin to get off his pony, put both sacks on the pony and lead the same through the snow. The Indian protested because this was an injury to his dignity. But he was dismounted more quickly than he liked by two soldiers who were just passing by and who were given a sign to do so by the Commandant. The sacks were tied together with ropes and placed on the pony's back and the Indian had to lead him home. He was further told that if he did not let his pony carry the load to his tent, which was about two miles away from the Fort, he should never set foot upon Fort Ridgely again.

As an eyewitness of this comical incident, I, as well as a number of others got a big laugh out of this. When I saw this Indian again on the evening before his execution and asked him whether he remembered me, he said he did. At the same time he assured me that it would have been his greatest satisfaction to overpower me, and thus be able to decorate his belt with my scalp. Of course, I thanked him in the name of my scalp for the great honor accorded to it, and assured him that in return, and to prove my friendship, I would be present tomorrow at the place of execution to see him hanged. A devilish look, a wild flash of the eyes, was the answer I received from the Redskin. To be hanged is the worst type of death for the Indian. He would rather, if he had a choice, burn a slow death at the stake than to end his life on the gallows.

—25.—

CRIME AND PUNISHMENT

The 26th of December 1862, the day of the execution of the 38 condemned Indians, was a beautiful winter day! The unusually mild weather for this season contributed to the fact that thousands of spectators came from far and near to witness the gruesome spectacle with their own eyes. It certainly was a very unusual thing that 38 of the worst criminals were to face eternity at the same time and on the gallows. To be sure, it was not curiosity alone which brought many of the spectators from great distances, but a certain feeling of satisfaction to see that here at least some of the red murderers met their fate and received their well deserved punishment.

The gallows were in a circular-shape scaffold. The platform, on which the condemned criminals stood fairly close to each other, was held in place by a strong rope. Now they were brought in under strong military guard and, singing weird dirges, took the places assigned to them on the platform. As I was on horseback and near to the gallows I had the opportunity of closely observing the 38 criminals before the fateful platform fell, upon which they stood with the rope placed professionally about their necks. And I must admit that they faced death courageously. Firmly and regularly resounded their weird song, then—a single blow from a sharp axe cut the rope that had held the platform, and the 38 murderers were hanging like puppets on the iron hooks. No, not all of them! The rope of one heavy fellow had broken and the Redskin lay twitching on the ground. But not for long, for some minutes later he was hanging properly beside his dead comrades.

During the execution, the other Indians who were housed in the log cabins were made conscious of the eventful moment by the weird songs of the condemned, and they fell to their knees and—prayed. Here one can really see what civilization, the converting to Christianity, does to riffraff of this type. For their prayers did not come from hearts that were rueful and tortured by the consciousness of having done evil, but were only the hypocritical cloak of powerless rage, because they could not come to the rescue of their condemned comrades-in-crime, because it was not possible for them to do what they had so often done during their four-week reign of terror—bathe in the blood of the palefaces!

It was especially the feminine personnel of those condemned who, at the critical moment, gave vent to their sorrows and wild anguish by prayers as well as loud cries of woe. As noted before, the gallows had been erected right near their place of confinement, and the singing of the condemned signaled the gruesome act. One old squaw whose son, a half-breed Indian by the name of Henry Milford, who was one of the arch-scoundrels and who was ending his earthly career on the gallows today, acted as if she were insane. She pulled her hair and cried continuously that the father of her offspring was an esteemed white gentleman of Minnesota, who could have saved her son—had he but put in a word in his favor. Whether the old woman spoke the truth I do not know, but it is certain that Henry Milford was one of those half-breeds who was the offspring of wild free-love, by the way, and because he was fatherless, was adopted and brought up by the tribe of his mother. One must not allow oneself to be swayed by the sentimental and desperate outbreaks of wild sorrow of Indian women; for those outbreaks, as a rule and as we shall find out, keep pace with the wild cruelty of these Megaera (Furies of mythology).

Permit me now to say a few words here about the Indian woman, the squaw, in order that one may better understand her character. One usually assumes that the Indian woman is oppressed by her husband, condemned to continuous work, but otherwise a good-natured being.

It is true, the squaw is the slave of her husband who, when he is ill-humored or has nothing else to do, thrashes her soundly, or if he possesses several wives, beats all of them in turn. The squaw has no rights at all. She must therefore accept the cruelest treatment from her husband without any protest. It is also true that the Indian woman must do all the work. The Indian busies himself only with hunting or with war. Any other work which he should do would lower his manly dignity—so he believes, and in certain cases he would rather be beaten to death than to perform any manual labor. Since he is a nomad, he shies away from work, as all nomads normally do.

The son of the wild does not care to know anything about any other occupation than to ride across the prairies with his fleeting pony, to hunt—or to get scalps. Then he is in his element. The hunting, the struggle with his enemy, or rather the cunning slaughter of the same, these things he likes above all others. Any other work he detests and considers to be disgraceful. His reason for this is that he leaves even the hardest labor to his squaws.

Many years ago, the author was an eyewitness to a scene at Fort Ridgely which he never will forget, and which convinced him at that time already that it is very difficult to get the Indian to do any kind of work, no matter how easy or simple it may be. For many years, and even today, there have been laws which forbid, under strict penalty, the sale of whiskey or any kind of "firewater" to the Indians. In spite of this, in the years gone by one would frequently meet drunken Indians in our region who had received the forbidden whiskey either from dishonest whites and for very high prices, or from half-breeds who, by the way, are sometimes worse than the full-blooded Indians. In regard to the laws concerning alcoholic beverages, the half-breed—because some white blood flows in his veins—was not put on the same level with the full-blooded Redskin. He was, therefore, entitled to buy as much firewater as he desired or had money for. The half-breeds made widespread use of their privileges; they bought and then sold whiskey to their red tribesmen at high prices. Because of this forbidden trade that was always carried on outside of the agencies, it was very difficult, in most cases, to turn these illegal whiskey dealers over to the courts.

It was a beautiful October afternoon in 1859 when a drunken Indian galloped into the Fort and exercised on the parade grounds. The officer in charge at once had the Redskin arrested and brought to the so-called black hole at the guard quarters. Here he could sleep off the effects of his drinking, and when he finally awoke he was sentenced for an entire day to carry, accompanied by a guard, two buckets of spring water from down the valley to the Fort. At this time there was always a number of Indians, and particularly squaws, who were roaming about the Fort, begging. Thus there could not have been a more severe punishment for the Indian than to perform what was considered degrading labor by Indian standards. And so it happened that this Indian could not be induced, either by kind words or by threats, to take the hated water pails and start moving. Since all efforts failed, the day's officer on duty had four men advance with bayonets affixed. The Indian was placed in their midst, so that one bayonet was at his back, one at his front, and one at either side. But still the Indian scoundrel with his total aversion toward work refused to work off his punishment.

When, however, the command "Forward, march!" set the procession in motion and the bayonet of the soldier walking behind the Indian touched his back, then only, did the rascal begin to work off his sentence amidst laughter of the bystanders. All day long he had to be forced in the same manner, obviously with several changes of guards. I present this as partial proof and to show how difficult it is to civilize the Indians, that is above all, to get them away from the vagabond life of the nomad and to train them to become dependable, calm, and industrious people. We have seen from the preceding that the Indian with his aversion to work will burden his wife even with the hardest chores and, in gratefulness for her services, beat her soundly from time to time. As a result of this, the squaw spends an oppressed and wretched life. But if someone wishes to insist that the Indian woman is a good natured creature, to him I shall simply reply that he is greatly mistaken, for nowhere on earth is there a more cruel being to be found than the wife of a Redskin. The suppressed anger brought on by the often inhuman treatment she gets from her husband erupts at the first opportunity, and woe to the unfortunate person on whom these terrible furies unload their suppressed anger.

The slow torture of captives is generally left to the women of the red beasts and these dehumanized creatures perform this with such virtuous cruelty that one is led to believe, when one hears of such accounts, that these terrible women are not human beings, but demons from Hell. So much for the poor, suppressed, good natured squaw of the Indian; the latter virtue is generally assigned to her by women writers who do not wish to admit that the bloodthirsty beast can be harbored in women just as well as in men.

–26.–

April 1863—A Second Reign of Terror?

After the execution of the 38 Indian murderers in Mankato, time passed quite peacefully, although reports were circulated now and then that the Indians who had been forced back towards the British border were preparing to make a second attack upon the settlements in the Upper Minnesota Valley. The longed-for spring arrived and the necessary preparations were undertaken for a strong military Indian expedition, the objective was to put the remaining hostile Sioux out of action by either taking them captive or, by what would have been best, completely annihilating them. Now, in early April 1863, the cries of terror resounded that a band of Indians had made their appearance at the Watonwan River, near Madelia, about 30 miles from Mankato, and that they had murdered several settlers there, mainly Norwegians, and wounded others, and had driven a small unit from a nearby fort back to the same. The author, at that time stationed in St. Peter with his company, the Mounted Rangers, received the order to go to the threatened area with 50 men, in order to provide the settlers with the necessary protection and, if possible, to punish the red beasts for renewing their horrible deeds.

The preparations were quickly made, and an hour after receiving the order we sat in the saddle, richly provided with ammunition for the carbines and revolvers. And on we went. Men and horses luckily made it across the Minnesota River in stormy weather, and we rode on to Mankato. The supply wagons were already waiting for us there. Evening had come as we left Mankato, and we still had to ride 30 miles to reach that little fort on the Watonwon River. As we rode across the Blue Earth County River several miles away from Mankato, it became dark and a half hour later it was pitch black. It was, as they say, a wild night. The storm raged on and got worse and it was so dark that you could not see a thing. But we went into the night and over hedge and ditch in rough terrain. We simply had to reach and help the poor threatened settlers as quickly as possible.

It was also our desire to meet the red villains head on and cut the beast out of them with our razor-sharp sabers. All this made us forget the stormy weather and the dark night. Our scout was a foot soldier. He was ordered at the Mankato headquarters to show us the way. But since he was no horseman, he was already so scraped after half the journey that he cried with pain and had to be quartered in one of the supply wagons. With the dark night this made things even more difficult, since the supply wagons drove behind us, and we were without a scout leading us on. Nevertheless, we went on through storm and darkness, as we had given headquarters our word to move as quickly as possible and without stopping.

Finally, at somewhat after 1 A.M., we reached the little fort. Riders and horses were dead tired from the wild journey, as we had traveled 45 miles non-stop in a dark and stormy night. Naturally, the garrison at the little fort, with a unit of only 20 men, was glad to see us. Of course, this handful of soldiers didn't know whether or not the Redskins, after they had been beaten back, would return with reinforcements and slaughter them. We then heard more about the appearance of the Indians and their intentions.

Now let me explain why the Indians, who had been pretty much out of any danger, were motivated to leave the safety of their asylum and risk being captured and sent to eternity, as their comrades-in-crime had been dealt with in Mankato. To be sure, the first and main reason was the thought of revenge for the death of the 38 criminals, and also to steal as many horses as possible. Then it was the longing, I might almost say homesickness, even for the most restless nomads, to again come to that little piece of land where they have spent most of their youth.

Back then, if you paid a summer visit to the region where the town of Madelia is located today, the county seat of Wantonwan County, and from there—be it for the pleasure of hunting or to take care of business matters—you moved on to the little settlement of Lake Shetek, and if you remained receptive to natural beauty and kept a feeling for it, unlike those in this country who obliterated it entirely by restlessly chasing after the Dollar, then you will understand that it was partially a certain longing which brought a band of Indians there in the spring of 1863, a longing that motivated them to leave the inhospitable region by the British border and pay a visit to their old home grounds.

It was a beautiful piece of land, this region between Madelia and Lake Shetek which had hardly been touched by civilization. A huge expanse of a flower garden, filled with clear fish-filled lakes, mostly surrounded by woodland, lay before the traveler with a sense for natural beauty. Today, it looks quite a bit different. Farm after farm, a great deal of the land is under cultivation; waving fields of grains, meadowland where cattle of the neighboring farms graze by the hundreds— all of this testifies to the well-being of the farmers of the region. But the waving sea of flowers has disappeared and so have most of the woodlands around the lakes. Also gone with them are the robbing and murderous Indians, which must reconcile us, so to speak, with the loss of natural beauty brought about by the progress of civilization. The earlier masters here, the robber Indians, have now pitched their teepees in an area distant from here; and the farmer now in the field, the hunter or the fisherman, none of them now have to fear being struck down by a murderous bullet of an Indian while carrying on with their tasks. However, in earlier times it was different, as we shall soon learn.

It was on a beautiful morning in early April 1863 when a Norwegian, a resident of the vicinity of Lake Crystal, set off with his 13 year-old son to go fishing at the aforementioned lake. Neither son nor father thought that there might be a treacherous Indian hiding behind the high grass and bushes awaiting the moment to fire them a murderous greeting. Suddenly, there were 10 to 12 shots. The old Norwegian, struck by several bullets, fell dead, while the son, in spite of having been wounded, escaped to alarm the small fort nearby. The brave soldiers, mostly Norwegians, did not hesitate for a moment and, in spite of their small number, courageously and dutifully went after the red murderers, leaving the fort under the guard of only two soldiers. However, they could not fend off the enemy who outnumbered them three to one, and so they repaired to the fort, which was the only place providing some safety for the settlers in the region, and here they awaited the attack of the Indians.

And it didn't take long for the attack to come. The Redskins, proud of their victory at having driven back the hated soldiers in Uncle Sam's uniforms, followed hot on the trail of the soldiers, and attacked the fort. But also here, as earlier in New Ulm and at Fort Ridgely, their repeated stormy attacks failed against the cool-headedness and courage of the small group of defenders. The Indians retreated, and as one could no longer spot them, the farmers, who had sought refuge at the fort, didn't worry anymore and returned to their homesteads. However, letting down their guards proved costly to some of them.

In the beginning of this historical account, I have pointed out that such a carefree attitude, I could even call it dumb carelessness, in the face of danger of an Indian attack, invited disaster for many settlers. Even after the outbreak of the Indians that carelessness continued. It was especially the unreflected risktaking of many farmers, who had sought refuge with their families from the murderous blows of the bloodthirsty enemy, and then returned individually or in small groups to their farms to look after their pigs or cattle. Many a man lost his life on account of that. And as a rule, these were people who in the usual routine of things were not exactly foolhardy. Much rather, among them were several who under other circumstances might not have faced death all too courageously.

Neither with kind nor harsh words could one prevent some of these recklessly headstrong persons from risking their lives for the sake of a cow or a pig. All well-meant words of warning might just as well have been cast to the winds. Some of them were felled by bullets of the red murderers hiding somewhere under cover, while on the road to their homes, others were struck down on their farms. Most of these unfortunate victims of boundless recklessness were heads of families. In vain did their wives and children wait in their safe places for the return of husband and father. Many did not know, or did not wish to know, that the Indian was a treacherous, sneaking enemy, with whom one has to be constantly on guard and exercise the most necessary precautions.

At the time of the outbreak of the Indians in the summer of 1862, there were neither railroads nor telegraphs in the Upper Minnesota Valley. In order to transmit urgent messages one had to depend upon a good horse and a good horseman. And so it happened that about 24 hours before that stormy night in which this author with his 50 men encountering the above mentioned difficulties rushed on in order to bring much needed help to the endangered settlers of the Watonwan River. The Indians, though, knowing full well that the revengers of their numerous bloody deeds would soon appear upon the scene, again committed as many acts of cruelty as could possibly be committed in so short a time.

Again, as in the preceding summer, they forced their way into the dwellings of the farmers and murdered all whom in their great haste they could get hold of. In a home which was located 2 miles from the fort, the young wife had just gone to bed when three of the red scoundrels crashed in the door and forced their way into the bedroom. The husband, a young Norwegian, was in Mankato at the time, attending to urgent business. Fortunately, however, before leaving home, he had asked the Commander of the small fort to station two of his soldiers in the home for protection of his family during his absence. His request had been granted and two stalwart sons of the Northland formed the little garrison at his home. All were already sound asleep. Suddenly there was a crash. The door was forced open, and the crash of the same as well as of several shots aimed at the bed of the woman showed the two soldiers that their help had been asked for good reasons. Like lightning they jumped from their beds, but their guns were in the woman's bedroom into which the Indians had already forced their way.

Luckily, because of the darkness of night the Redskins could not spot the loaded weapons of the two soldiers. When the latter appeared on the battle scene, the Indians confined themselves, because their own guns were now empty and with no time to reload, to attacking the two Norwegians with their arrows which they carried without bows. But this was a poor attempt. The first one of the valiant Norse warriors immediately felled one of the Indians, and the powerful blows which the second Indian received made him, as well as the third Indian, decide to leave the house as rapidly as possible and attempt to find safety in flight. The unconscious Indian, lying on the floor, was now completely in the power of the two soldiers. One can readily imagine what they did to the scoundrel when they found that the young woman had been severely wounded by one of the three shots that had been fired by the Indians. When he regained consciousness, he was sent to his happy hunting grounds by several well aimed shots.

Toward morning, just as we were preparing to leave, after men and horses had rested for several hours, 50 men of our regiment appeared unexpectedly from Fort Ridgely, in order to unite with us for a further and better pursuit of the Indians. The Commander of the fort at that time, Lt. Col. William Pfaender, certainly honorably known to most every Turner in the U.S., had, upon the first report of the appearance of the Indians on the Watonwan River, sent out these soldiers, in order to have them unite with the men who were sent out from the St. Peter Regiment. At that time one did not and could not know whether this relatively small Indian horde, which had so suddenly made its appearance at the Watonwan River, might not be an advance guard of a larger group of Redskins who could not forget the humiliating death of their 38 comrades on the gallows. But that the scattered Indians might have gathered a still respectable fighting force at one point, in order to appear among the palefaces once more and to devastate, this was a baseless fear. The horde of Redskins which appeared so suddenly at the Watonwan River had undertaken that expedition on their own.

Little Crow, the most cunning of the cunning red scoundrels, had admonished his warriors that from now on they should not go on the warpath against the paleface in larger numbers, but in small groups, which could more easily sneak through the defenses which now were established from the border of the state of Iowa to Fort Ridgely and from here towards Fort Ripley. "The white man has many soldiers in Minnesota," this chief had said to his subordinates, "who might easily cut off your return if you appeared in larger number. In fact, as you well know, your fate would be sealed."

And the old warrior was right, for the Indians who sometimes appeared at the border in groups of four or five were successful in nearly every instance, when they ambushed lone farmers who were working in the fields, and they stole horses, too. It was rare, indeed, that one of the red scoundrels was brought to justice for his cruel deeds. Usually, they would strike from a protective cover, and then disappear as quickly as they had come.

But with the beginning of the warmer season in 1863, when the military cordon at the border was augmented with more soldiers, particularly cavalry, the bloody activities of the red bandits were brought under control. Several were shot while they still tried to accomplish their crimes, and among them some were well known for their previous acts of cruelty.

On the morning of the 9th of April, 100 of us, all horsemen and well provisioned for a 5-day period, were in the saddle ready to pursue the red murderers. But since the Indians had a head start of nearly 30 hours we could not, under any circumstances, follow them directly towards the region of Lake Shetek. Should our attempt to overtake and punish them be crowned with success we would have to take a more lateral course through the prairie which, at this season, was entirely bare. Our objective there was to make their retreat through the prairie impossible.

—27.—

THE PRAIRIE

The kind reader who is unfamiliar with "prairies" or "steppes" will certainly permit a short explanation here. To tourists, who for the sake of curiosity or for the pleasure of hunting, visit these vast plains of the northwestern U.S. during the summer, the novelty value may not miss its effect; but even these, in most cases, will be blinded by the monotonous uniformity of nature, as well as by the apparently endless view. They also will often times be seized by an attack of the so-called prairie-fever, which is more an illness of the soul than of the body, and may be defined as a kind of homesickness. But he who is used to sojourn in these vast open spaces, across which one can roam for months without seeing a tree or shrub, finds it difficult to leave this monotonous territory which he has learned to love. In the summer of 1864, the author of this account met an old trapper in the northern part of the Dakota Territory, who had spent over 30 years living in a sod hut in this endless solitude. Only when he was in need of ammunition, tobacco, and salt, at most only once a year, did he go to some distant military outpost and traded pelts for these necessities. To the question whether he did not occasionally experience a longing for his former home in Illinois or for human companionship, the old man shook his head and stated that under no circumstances would he wish to leave this seemingly endless prairie, his present home, which he had learned to love.

It is certainly true that the waving sea of flowers in the prairie lands makes an unusual impression upon the feelings of a sensitive person. Imagine a plain as far as the eye can see, today it is red, in the course of two or three weeks it is yellow, then again shimmering in various shades of blue—there you have a picture of the prairie lands of the U.S. in summer. But how different is the appearance of these regions in winter, or even in the early spring. Terrible snows rage, at times with diabolical ferocity, across the immeasurable plains, and woe to the poor wanderer who has crossed the border of the prairie and is exposed to the raging elements. The entire, vast expanse is then nothing more than a huge shroud which buries all living things with its benumbing breath. In former times, when outposts of the U.S. Army sometimes were located several hundred miles apart, when it was necessary to move troops at the beginning of winter, or even in its midst, soldiers who were caught in such icy storms were doomed to perish.

In the winter of 1864, a company of cavalry on its way to Fort Wadsworth was exposed to a snow storm on the prairie and one-third of its men, as well as a number of horses, fell victim to the icy winds. If you have ever been surprised by a snow storm, even though this may have been in a civilized region, but far from a sheltering forest, and if you had the good fortune to escape with your life, you will never forget this terrible experience, this raging confusion of icy winds and whirling snows. To fight against the storm is an absolute impossibility, and if you are caught in this mess you may possibly save yourself by walking along the direction of the raging element and by this constant movement secure the necessary body heat; but woe to the unfortunate one who falls exhausted without having reached a sheltering forest or human habitation; he will, in a short time, be a rigid corpse. A peculiarity of this awesome phenomenon of nature is that, like with lightning during a thunderstorm, there is also a moment in which the heavy darkness is lifted and it is thus possible for the wanderer exposed to such a snow storm to get his bearings, even if for a second only. Fortunate is he who then sees a sheltering place which he will be able to reach. This, dear reader, is a rough draft of a description of a snow storm on the prairie in the winter or early spring. One does not have in one's power the ability to pen this phenomenon in its entirety. Only he who has made personal acquaintance with "Master Boreas" and was so fortunate as to wrench away in time from his icy grip knows the meaning of a snow storm out there on the prairie.

–28.–

THE WATONWON RIVER EXPEDITION

It was then, on the morning of the above mentioned April day, that we left the small fort on the Watonwon River to catch up with the fleeing Redskins in order to punish them for their past crimes and for those committed now. And forward we went as rapidly as the horses could carry us, for we had an approximate idea of the direction in which they had gone and we hoped to catch up with them on the next day at least. But the Indians also were well mounted and continuously lighted the dry grass of the prairie in our path, so that we had no other feed for our horses but the corn we had brought along, which was not sufficient in the long run. Nevertheless, the wild chase lasted five entire days, and in order to make the provisions last, the men as well as the horses had been put on half rations after the first two-and-a-half days. On the evening of the fifth day, tired to death from the day's race on horseback, we fortunately encamped in a sparsely wooded ravine.

Now a wild storm began to hit us with a fury only possible on the prairie, where there is no resistance to its raging course. We had built fires and had the necessary wood to keep them going, but had to keep at it in order to warm men and animals. The storm raged all night and there was no thought of sleep. We stretched out around the huge fires for which tree after tree fell as a victim, and hidden by the steep sides of the ravine our situation was, considering the circumstances, nevertheless still bearable. But a further pursuit of the Indians could not be considered any more. Not having been able to catch up with the red scoundrels made us angry. The next day, we undertook our return march through the snow drifts. There was no danger in terms of a possible attack, but it was a sad return.

The provision for men and animals had dwindled down to a two-and-a-half days supply at best, and yet the town of New Ulm, where we could stock up again, could not be reached before another 5 days. To make things worse, our spirits were downcast because we hadn't caught and punished the Indians for their recently committed crimes. But the survival instinct soon crowded out all other considerations. The hardships that were now to be faced cannot be easily told. But we were now approaching New Ulm and, fortunately, on the last evening of the expedition, about 30 miles from there, we found two abandoned log cabins, the half rotted straw roofs of which were welcome fodder for our horses.

Inside the houses was a small supply of frozen potatoes. We roasted them in the hot ashes. Even though this turned out to be a lousy meal, the men, who by now had developed ravenous appetites, ate it eagerly, for in the last 24 hours the last rations consisted of one cracker per person. Hunger is the best cook. Of course, we could have slaughtered one of our horses, but as long as the most urgent need did not call for this, we desisted. Among all the men there was not one who wished to give up the animal that had become dear to him. Of course, strange things are done in time of need. Had we not found the frozen potatoes on the evening of that cold and wet April day, disagreeably tasting as they were, but nevertheless satisfying an empty stomach, we would have had to decide by lot which one of the horses to kill in order to defeat our hunger.

Col. Marshall, later Governor of the state of Minnesota, who joined us with 50 men from Fort Ridgely at the Watonwon River was the superior officer who then took command of the expedition. He was a jovial gentleman. Because of his affability and particularly because of his good humor, he contributed not a little to keep the men in a constantly good mood in spite of all unpleasantness and hardship. Whichever member of this expedition were today to return to the region where we had pitched our camp for the last sad night, he would certainly not be able to get his bearings there. It is the same place on which now is located the progressive little town of Springfield in Brown County. In a saddened mood, because we had not succeeded in overtaking and punishing the red robbers, we left this wretched place, where we had spent the last night, hungry and sleepless. Nevertheless, we were conscious of the fact that we had fulfilled our duty and that we had merely been forced to abandon pursuit of the red murderers because of the disagreeable weather and the lack of provisions.

When we arrived at New Ulm, we found the people there quite worried. Rumors circulated that powerful bands of Indians had again appeared on the scene and with the intent to attack soon the now well-defended Turner town. It was the opinion of everyone that a renewed struggle with the red brutes would begin shortly. One can easily imagine, therefore, the rejoicing with which we were received. We brought assurance that the number of Indians who had committed the new atrocities along the Watonwon River was very small, and that another attack of the Redskins upon New Ulm was not to be expected. Our growling stomachs were satisfied, for which each of us was greatly indebted to the friendly host of the Dakota House, Mr. Adolph Seiter. Men and horses had a rest for a full 24-hour period. Then we returned to our camp at St. Peter, where the people also received us jubilantly and all the more so, since false news had circulated there that we had been completely annihilated by masses of attacking Indians.

–29.–

PEACE

Peaceful days followed. No new rumors of Indian attacks were circulated. But this calm did not last long. After about three weeks alarming news reached St. Peter. Indians had suddenly appeared at the farm of Lt. Col. William Pfaender in Milford, only three miles from New Ulm. They shot a farmhand named Bosche while he was busy plowing, and they stole two valuable horses. Immediately, the author received the order to head for New Ulm with the largest part of his company, to garrison the town and to pursue the Indians who were possibly hiding in the surrounding woods. When we arrived at New Ulm we were informed right away that a large number of people in the area surrounding the town had decided very definitely, after this renewed cruelty of the red scoundrels, to turn their backs on their homesteads which they had learned to love, and never to return. But appropriate arrangements were now made so that this reverse migration of people resulted in the departure of only a few. Two to four soldiers each were quartered in the homes of the farmers who lived at some distance. The rations of these soldiers were, of course, procured from the company. Nearer to town the people were calmed by the constant patrolling of the region by day and night.

Peace and confidence returned again, and even though occasionally alarming rumors were afloat regarding the appearance of Indians here and there, they were always rumors of the kind that could quickly be disproved and be declared falsehoods. Through the efforts of the Commander at Fort Ridgely, Lt. Col. William Pfaender, the main purpose of the Indians' appearance along the borders, that of stealing horses, was soon spoiled. Fairly good-sized military expeditions far out on the prairies kept the Redskins on the run, scattering their bands, so that they lost all desire to return to the edge of the frontier. Everyone breathed easily again and the star of hope and trust shone for all.

Before I end my history of the Indians' outbreak, I take the liberty to report what happened to the red ruffian, Chief Little Crow. Exactly a year after the terrible attack, kindled by the bloody arch-savage of the Dakota Sioux, which cost the lives of many people, two Indians, father and son, appeared in that vast Minnesota forest region known as the Big Woods. They had come to pick wild berries and, as a sideline to this peaceful pursuit, to steal horses when the opportunity arose. Two Norwegian hunters, also father and son, who happened to be in the region at this time, saw the two Indians without being noticed by them. Knowing full well that the scalp of an Indian was worth a fine price, they shot the old Indian at once, while the young one escaped, but was later captured and taken to Fort Snelling for safekeeping. Of course, the two Norwegians did not know at the time who the red villain was, whom they had just sent to the eternal hunting grounds. Later, upon close examination of the corpse, it was determined and also verified by the captured son that the one who was shot to death was none other than the bloodthirsty Chief of the Dakota Sioux, Little Crow. Identification was made by an old fracture of an arm and by the peculiar shape of the teeth.

We shall now close this history with the partially satisfying feeling that at least some of the red scoundrels, having met their fate, died on the gallows, which they deserved a hundredfold! And finally, their leader and arch-scoundrel, Little Crow, deserted by all who at one time were close to him, accompanied only by his son and not at the head of his one time proud band of warriors, wandered hungry through the deep woodland solitudes. Here his murderous course of life was brought to an appropriate and well-deserved end by the bullets of two white hunters!

–30.–

APPENDIX

For the orientation of the reader in regards to the most important places which played a role in the preceding account of the Indian Uprising, the following will provide further information.

New Ulm

New Ulm had to bear the brunt of the first attack of the Indians. Those who were murdered by the Indians at both agencies on the morning of the 18th of August, as well as the majority of people killed on their farms, had been treacherously attacked by the red devils and slaughtered without being able to resist.

The town of New Ulm, with very few exceptions inhabited by Germans, was and is still today the county seat of Brown County, Minnesota. The first settlers and the founders of the place came here in the year 1854. Since most of them hailed from the region of Ulm in Württemberg, Germany, and had treasured the memory of their earlier homeland, the newly founded community was given the name of New Ulm, in honor of the old and venerable city of the old Fatherland.

Most of these Württembergers and several other Germans were members of an organization formed in Chicago. They founded a settlement up here at the boundary of the Indian reservation. But even in those days they had to suffer much from the roving Redskins, even though they showed them every kindness. In 1856, an agreement was made between the group mentioned above and the settlement society of the Turners, and as a result of this, many Turners from the larger cities of the Union, but especially from Cincinnati, Ohio, came here to settle permanently. So it happened that this Turner settlement, as the place had from now on been frequently called, developed into a progressive little town. In the summer of the year 1862, it could call 200 buildings and over 900 citizens its own.

The location of New Ulm is charming, but the town is too widespread, which naturally made its defense difficult. Built upon three terraces, only the business section on the middle terrace, and a part of the upper terrace could be defended. At the very beginning of the struggle, the lowest part of the town had to be abandoned, because there were not enough defenders and many houses were scattered outside of the line of barricades. It was due to these circumstances that during the second attack only 40 centrally located buildings could be saved, while the large number went up in flames.

Fort Ridgely

Fort Ridgely is located 18 miles above New Ulm. During the time of the Indian outbreaks, it was a military post and a real fort, if you will. For many years now, it has been abandoned, and at the present time is in ruins. Before the Civil War, it regularly had a garrison of four companies of the U.S. Army. At the outbreak of the southern rebellion they were ordered to the theater of war and were replaced by a relatively weak force consisting of volunteers in the case of attack. The location of the fort is very unfavorable. During the two-day conflict with the Indians, it was saved only because of its cannons and the skilled gunners.

The Indian Agencies

The Indian agencies, civilization factories for the Redskins, were located beyond the above mentioned fort, the Lower Agency 12 miles, the Upper Agency about 40 miles from the fort. Here, a number of government buildings, dwellings for the officials, a blacksmith and wheelwright's shop, etc., had been erected. Furthermore, the authorized dealers, who had the exclusive right to sell the Indians their poor wares at a good price, had their dwellings and warehouses here. All of these buildings have disappeared long ago, and the ground upon which they once stood has since become private property, so did the farm region, of which a part had been plowed and planted by the government for the red lazy bones.

Between these agencies and Fort Ridgely on the one side, and in the direction towards New Ulm on the other side of the Minnesota River, most of the wild brutes' murderous deeds were committed. Especially the places on the left shore of the river were the scenes of many criminal acts. Here entire families fell victim to the bloodthirstiness of those red devils.

Mankato

The town of Mankato, where the 38 murderers received their hundredfold deserved reward at the gallows, is located 28 miles below New Ulm. Had the latter place been taken by the Indians, Mankato could not have been saved, because its location is extremely unfavorable for defense!

✻✻✻✻

These are the places which more or less must be called to mind in connection with the outbreak of the Sioux Uprising in August of 1862. The terrible drama unfolded partly within these places and partly between them.

PART THREE—ILLUSTRATIONS

The following illustrations were obtained from the Brown County Historical Society, New Ulm, Minnesota.

Captain Jacob Nix, Commandant of New Ulm, had previous military experience in the 1848 Revolution in Germany, and subsequent to the Uprising served in the U.S. Army in numerous western campaigns.

Charles Roos, Sheriff of Brown County at the time of the Uprising, appointed Jacob Nix as Commandant of New Ulm.

Lt. Col. Wilhelm Pfaender, like Nix a participant in the 1848 Revolution in Germany, was one of the original co-founders of the first Turner Society in America at Cincinnati, Ohio in 1848, which joined forces with a Chicago German Land Association in founding New Ulm, Minnesota.

John Other Day, age 42, had been a Christian and a farmer for six years prior to the Uprising, and was praised by Nix for his courageous actions on behalf of the settlers.

Little Crow, Chief of the Sioux, led the Uprising, which had tragic consequences for his own people, and would result in the deaths of over eight hundred settlers.

Fort Ridgely in 1862, located 18 miles from New Ulm, was saved, according to Capt. Nix, "only because of its cannons and the skilled gunners."

German plays were first presented in 1857 at the Turnhalle in New Ulm, which was the town's social, cultural, and political center; it was burned to the ground during the Uprising, but another building was constructed later.

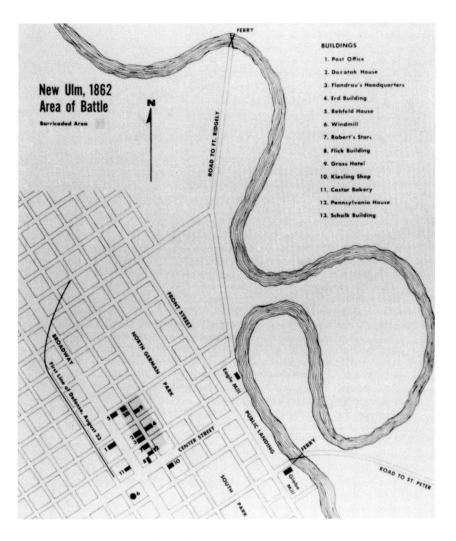

New Ulm, 1862, Area of Battle.

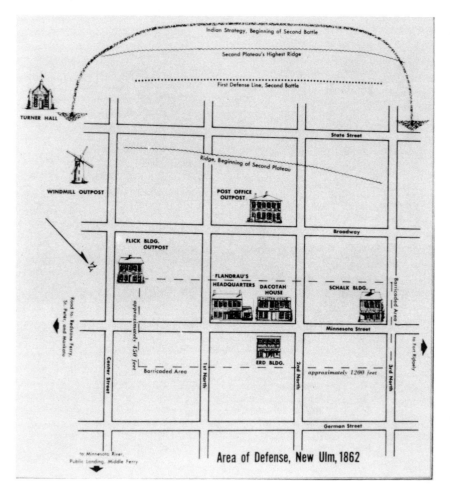

Areas of Defense, New Ulm, 1862.

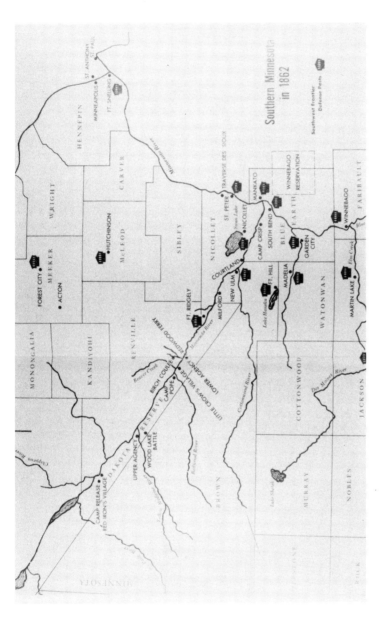

Southern Minnesota in 1862—Note the locations of the Upper and Lower Agencies, Fort Ridgely, and New Ulm along the Minnesota River. Mankato, further down the River would have been next, had the uprising not been brought to a halt at New Ulm.

OTHER PUBLICATIONS

Volume 1 (1989)

George Theodore Probst/Eberhard Reichmann
The Germans in Indianapolis, 1840-1918.
200 + xii pp., illustrated. Index by Elfrieda Lang.

Volume 2 (1991)

Theodore Stempfel's 1898 Festsschrift:
Fünfzig Jahre unermüdlichen deutschen Strebens in Indianapolis/Fifty Years of Unrelenting German Aspirations in Indianapolis, 1848-1898.
Trans. & ed. by Giles R. Hoyt, Claudia Grossmann, Elfrieda Lang and Eberhard Reichmann. 150 + vii pp., illustrated. Index.

Volume 3 (1991)

Eberhard Reichmann, Editor
Hoosier German Tales—Small and Tall.
333 German-American anecdotes, legends, memoirs and jokes from oral and written Indiana sources. English-language version with some bilingual entries. 258 + xx pp. ISBN 1-880788-00-4.

Volume 4 (1993)

Willi Paul Adams
The German-Americans. An Ethnic Experience.
Trans. & adapted from the German by LaVern J. Rippley and Eberhard Reichmann. 46 pp., illustrated. ISBN 1-880788-01-2

Also available

Witter's Deutsch-Englische Schreib- und Lese-Fibel/German-English Primer (1881).
Reprint Edition 1987. 95 + viii pp. Introduces old German script. No knowledge of German required.